NOTRE DAME
THE OFFICIAL CAMPUS GUIDE

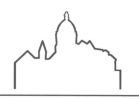

NOTRE DAME
THE OFFICIAL CAMPUS GUIDE

Damaine Vonada

Photographs and Drawings by
Robert F. Ringel

University of Notre Dame Press
Notre Dame, Indiana

Library of Congress Cataloging-in-Publication Data

Vonada, Damaine.
    Notre Dame, the official campus guide / Damaine Vonada
        p.   cm.
    Includes bibliographical references (p.   ) and index.
    ISBN 0-268-01486-8 (cloth : alk. paper)
    ISBN 0-268-01484-1 (pbk. : alk. paper)
    1. University of Notre Dame—Guidebooks. 2. University of
Notre Dame—History.   I. Title.
LD4114.V65   1998
378.772'89—dc21   98-18607

This is so classic. I'm sitting in my room. The wind is blowing outside, and the leaves are coming off the trees. There are L.L. Bean-clad students frolicking below my window, and in the distance the bells of Sacred Heart are chiming the "Alma Mater." To top it all off, somebody just started playing some excellent Bach on the new piano in the chapel. What a school!

—from a student's letter home, 1991

CONTENTS

INTRODUCTION

Visitors are seldom disappointed in Notre Dame. They invariably arrive with the expectation of seeing something special, and what they find is one of the loveliest and most well planned universities in the nation. The campus is landscaped to perfection with a preponderance of Collegiate Gothic architecture and splendid buildings that provide a gorgeous backdrop for the noble endeavors of education. Many observers say that Notre Dame has a sense of place. Perhaps that is because the university has such an abiding sense of purpose, which is neatly defined by an oft-quoted phrase: Notre Dame not only teaches students how to make a living, it also teaches them how to live.

The campus consists of an interwoven fabric of buildings whose coordinated architectural forms and materials provide a fairly artful meld between the old and the new. It has only a handful of landmarks—the most celebrated being Notre Dame's Golden Dome—and no "signature" buildings. There is, however, an incredible amount of religious iconography that not only lends a special flavor to the campus but also underscores Notre Dame's Catholic character. God, as they say, is in the details, and you would expect to see a certain amount of ecclesiastical art on a campus that has a Basilica and a statue of the Virgin Mary atop its trademark Dome. What is most impressive about Notre Dame's art, however, is that there is so much of it, that it takes so many forms, and that it is displayed in so many different locations. Symbolism abounds at Notre Dame, and that is why, as you stroll the campus, you should get in the habit of not just looking *ahead*, but also looking *up* and *around*. If you do, you'll discover some delightfully playful symbols and statues that pertain specifically to Notre Dame and its students—Knute Rockne in bas-relief, a schoolboy weeping over his poor grade, an Irish terrier mascot called Clashmore Mike, a baseball pitcher winding up.

You'll also quickly discover that Notre Dame is a very user-friendly place. The university is accustomed to hosting large crowds, and when folks come calling, it knows how to treat them very well. Notre Dame's level of hospitality is all the more remarkable because it seems effortless and does not interfere with the educational function of the university. There are directional signs everywhere, and handy campus maps are not only free but very freely distributed. You'll also find refreshing parks, wooded areas, lakes, fountains, and, perhaps most pleasurable of all, plenty of benches for rest and relaxation. The university is also an eminently civil place where people are polite and cordial to visitors. You'll find students holding doors open for you, and if you look too lost, they'll inquire if they can help you find something. Guided tours of the campus are available, and you really should take one, since they're conducted by students, who, after all, are the fundamental reason for Notre Dame's existence. The guides are well-informed, glib, and witty, and they never fail to charm with their anecdotes and stories. They also are a great way to get an understanding of the enthusiasm, energy, and pride that permeates the campus. As one university official astutely observed, "Adults can convey prose about Notre Dame, but only the students can convey its poetry."

THE HISTORY

The University of Notre Dame was founded by Rev. Edward Sorin, a 28-year-old French priest who was a member of the Congregation of Holy

Cross. In 1842, Father Sorin and a small group of religious brothers arrived at an old mission site in northern Indiana near the frontier settlement of South Bend. With little money but enormous ambition, Father Sorin established an educational colony that was dedicated to the Blessed Mother and grandly called the University of Notre Dame. It consisted of elementary and high schools, a trade school, religious novitiates, and a college curriculum based in the humanities. For years, Father Sorin struggled to find students and finance his dream of creating one of the world's great Catholic universities. He pragmatically accepted students of any religion, and any method of tuition payment was welcome. One man, for example, supposedly paid for his son's schooling by building the steeple on Notre Dame's church.

Through his wits and his will, Father Sorin managed to keep his infant university alive, but he also had great timing. By the mid-eighteenth century, not only were the first great waves of immigrants from Catholic Europe starting to reach America's shores, but the railroads had started a transportation revolution that quickly put Notre Dame within easy traveling distance of cities such as Cleveland, Detroit, and Chicago. The university no longer had to go begging for students, and as Catholics began to prosper in the United States, so did Notre Dame. The university's expectations —like those of the great American middle class that it has served so well —always seem to be rising. After World War I, Rev. James Burns, C.S.C., a Michigan City, Indiana, native who had once

Father Sorin

worked as a printer in Notre Dame's trade school, became the head of the university. Father Burns was a progressive educator and the first Notre Dame president to hold a Ph.D. He began to strengthen and modernize the university by reorganizing the curriculum into separate colleges, raising a $1 million endowment and creating a Lay Board of Trustees to manage it. Within a few years, the trade, grade, and high schools were abolished, and Notre Dame was poised to live up to its name as a true university. President Burns and his immediate successors also got a tremendous helping hand from Coach Knute Rockne, whose remarkably successful football teams proved an incomparable asset in publicizing and promoting Notre Dame's educational mission.

Following World War II, Notre Dame experienced rapid growth and set ambitious academic goals. In the administration of Rev. Theodore Hesburgh, C.S.C., the university admitted its first women undergraduates, built one of the largest library buildings in the land, garnered national and international respect, and began to fulfill Sorin's dream of its becoming "one of the most powerful means of doing good in this country." At more than $1.7 billion dollars, Notre Dame now has one of the largest university endowments in the nation. Recent campus expansion has included construction of research laboratories, four new dormitories, and one of the most technologically advanced classroom buildings in the world. While much of the university's growth has been spurred by the ongoing development of its research and graduate-level programs, Notre Dame's primary focus and forte is still undergraduate education. The Congregation of Holy Cross transferred control of the university to a lay-dominated Board of Trustees in 1967, but the Holy Cross priests and brothers continue to play a major educational, ethical, and religious role in maintaining Notre

Dame's Catholic character and shaping the values of its students.

THE CAMPUS

Notre Dame's 1,250-acre campus includes two lakes and is located near the city of South Bend in north central Indiana. It's about 90 miles east of Chicago and easily accessible from U.S. 31/33 and Interstate 80/90 (the Indiana Toll Road) via Exit 77. All public roads are on the perimeter of the campus, which has only two entrance gates: the Main Gate off of Notre Dame Avenue and the East Gate off of Juniper Road.

Historically, Notre Dame Avenue was the primary entryway to the university, but its function now is largely ceremonial because Notre Dame is a pedestrian campus. By not surrendering to the power of the automobile, the university has been able to preserve the natural beauty of its campus as well as maintain an academic ambiance and sense of community that is the envy of many other institutions of higher learning. As you can see from Notre Dame's multitude of pathways and bicycle racks, foot power is the dominant method of transportation, and because the campus is not dissected by roads, there are no street addresses. Building names and numbers are used instead. Since you cannot do a "driving tour" of Notre Dame, you're going to have to walk the campus if you want to see it. That may sound inconvenient, but it's really a blessing, because in order to fully appreciate Notre Dame you have to experience it. A quick drive-by in the sealed off space of a gaseous bus or air-conditioned car could not possibly do justice to the subtleties, the art, the spirit, or the mystique of Notre Dame.

The University of Notre Dame is a place that pays great attention to details, and the campus has a very deliberate organizational plan that dates back to its earliest days. The basic unit is a quadrangle or "quad" consisting of buildings that form "walls" around an open space. The buildings are arranged along a north-south or east-west axis, which typically terminates with a structure that serves as the quad's focal point. Because of their focal points and strong visual lines, quads are an inherently dramatic way to arrange buildings, and just as one instrument will "answer" another in a musical composition, the buildings along the opposite sides of a quad are supposed to relate or "talk" to each other. Notre Dame's campus consists of a network of quads that intersect each other at right angles. This system of axes and cross axes not only provides intimate individual spaces, but also integrates and interconnects different parts of the campus. The logic of the quads lends the campus a certain orderliness and seamless quality that is the foundation of much of its beauty and appeal.

The use of the quadrangle in American collegiate design originated with Thomas Jefferson when he planned the University of Virginia in the early 1800s. Rev. Edward Sorin, who was Notre Dame's founding father, rightly ascertained that the quadrangle was exceptionally well suited to the flat topography of northern Indiana, and in the university's Main Quadrangle, his concept of Notre Dame Avenue leading to the Main Building and its Golden Dome is considered one of the best uses of the axis and focal point in the United States. Notre Dame's quads were all developed during different eras, and you can get clues to their history just by looking at their buildings. The yellowish brick buildings in Main Quad and Sorin Court, for instance, date to the origins of the university, and their design elements—particularly the formal iron staircases ending at second-story entrances—reflect the French heritage of Father Sorin and his companions. Those Collegiate Gothic buildings on South Quad indicate the Rockne era; plain boxy buildings of the 1950s and 1960s are from President Hesburgh's tenure; and the contemporary structures on DeBartolo Quad were erected during the administration of Notre Dame's current president, Father Edward Malloy, C.S.C.

PLANET NOTRE DAME

Notre Dame is a world of its own making, a self-contained academic village that functions as an intellectual meritocracy. It's populated primarily by some 8,000 undergraduates who are very bright—their average SAT scores are more than 300 points above the national average—and the university endeavors not only to give them an excellent education but also to turn them into national leaders. Notre Dame is also a residential university with the majority of its undergraduates living on campus in residence halls. Since the university does not allow sororities or fraternities, students develop a deep sense of community and dorm affinity that foster the "Notre Dame family," whose ties often last a lifetime. "Although I left Notre Dame," observed one alumnus, "Notre Dame has never left me."

As a private and independent entity, the University of Notre Dame is not part of any other institution or any larger political entity. Its address is *not* South Bend, Indiana. It is *Notre Dame*, Indiana, and the university even boasts its own ZIP Code—46556—and postmark to prove its autonomy. The university also has its own police department, fire department, television and radio stations, power plant, railroad, laundry, medical facilities, art museum, and a "Mister Manners" who directs special events such as building dedications and oversees the fine points of protocol. Notre Dame's telephone exchange—631—conveniently corresponds to "N.D. 1" when you push the buttons on a phone, and if you're talking to someone on campus, you'll undoubtedly notice that there is a special Notre Dame language of slang and acronyms. Just to

The Grotto

help you translate the meaning of SYR and JPW, this guide includes a Glossary of some common Notre Dame words and phrases.

THE MYSTIQUE

The great paradox of Notre Dame is that it requires no explanation, yet constantly needs to be explained. It is one of the most visible and well-known universities in the nation, if not the world. Pope Paul VI said that Notre Dame was his favorite university, and yet it is also a place that captures the intense devotion of thousands of "subway alumni," who come from all walks of life and have never even set foot on the campus. Notre Dame lays claim to what are arguably the nation's most famous college coach (Knute Rockne), most often heard fight song (the "Victory March"), most recognizable nickname (Fighting Irish), and most legendary players (the Four Horsemen). One survey even discovered that more people wear clothing with the Notre Dame logo than that of any other college or university in the nation.

Quarterback Joe Theismann once remarked that if you could find a way to bottle the Notre Dame spirit, you could light up the world. The university is indeed a place of optimism and possibility, for its religious foundation encourages a concentration on the universal values of goodness, truth, and freedom. Norman Mailer says he likes Notre Dame because "you can say the word 'soul' there and no one snickers." Of course not, since 'soul' is what Notre Dame is essentially about. Religion may be muted elsewhere in our increasingly secularized society, but at Notre Dame it's ringing loud and clear—chapels in every dormitory, a Basilica, a Lourdes-like Grotto, and the Mother of God bestowing her blessings from the Dome. There is also a running—and revealing—campus joke that goes something like this: The President of the United States visited the Pope and noticed a gold telephone with a direct line to God. The

President phoned the Almighty for some advice, and the White House was billed $10,000 for the call. The next month, the President was visiting Notre Dame when he noticed that there was also a gold telephone on Father Malloy's desk. He again phoned the Almighty, but this time the charge was only twenty-five cents. The President contacted Father Malloy and asked how it could possibly be so much cheaper to telephone God from Notre Dame. "From Notre Dame," explained Father Malloy, "It's a *local* call."

Yes, everybody knows of Notre Dame and its reputation. The university occupies a singular place in American education and culture, and the paraphernalia, the football images, the jokes, and the stories are legion. But nobody seems to fully comprehend the university until they've actually shared in its rituals, witnessed its pervasive sense of spirit, and become part of the mystique themselves. Notre Dame has its own ethos, a unique combination of religious values, athletic tradition, academic achievement, and inspired loyalty and comradeship among undergraduates and alumni. Those elements are the essence of the mystique, and if any of them were to disappear, the university would not be the same. Like any vital culture, Notre Dame has its own defining legends and folklore, and its multitude of multi-layered traditions are the means by which it keeps its identity through the changing times and generations. The only thing that explains Notre Dame—and its mystique—is Notre Dame. Which is precisely why you should personally visit the campus instead of merely buying a sweatshirt; it's the difference between making a long-distance and a local call.

CREATURE COMFORTS
Sleeping and Eating

The campus has limited overnight accommodations, and on home football game weekends, hotel and motel rooms for miles around are booked months in advance. One bed and breakfast near downtown South Bend has been reserved for the next five years by a family of season ticket holders. The campus tours and visitors office in the Eck Center (219/631-5726) has general information about local hotels and motels, and you can also try the Inn at Saint Mary's (219/232-4000), which is located on the campus of nearby Saint Mary's College. For accommodations during football season, your best bet is to contact the South Bend/Mishawaka Convention and Visitors Bureau at 800/392-0051. Finding a place to eat, on the other hand, will not be a problem at Notre Dame. The campus offers a variety of choices ranging from casual concessions in the Stadium and other athletic facilities to formal dining at the Morris Inn.

The Morris Inn (21)—Notre Dame's on-campus hotel has the great advantage of being within walking distance of all university buildings, events, and recreational facilities. Each of the rooms boasts a view of the university, and the inn is also joined to Notre Dame's Center for Continuing Education by an underground concourse, which is very handy for guests who are attending meetings or conferences. This is a full-service hotel with a "white tablecloth" dining room, a cocktail lounge, and a small gift shop nicely stocked with Notre Dame memorabilia. During football weekends, graduation, and special campus events such as JPW, you probably won't find any room at the Morris Inn, because it's booked for trustees and other special guests of the university. You can, however, enjoy the inn's outdoor Irish Courtyard on football Fridays and Saturdays; it's held outdoors under a tent and features brats, burgers, and big-screen TVs tuned, of course, to the Fighting Irish.

The Morris Inn dining room is open daily, but unless they're breaking bread with parents or professors, you won't find many students eating here. This is the place where the *adults* on campus meet, greet, and eat, especially at lunch. The atmosphere is quiet and subdued; the background music classical; the buzz decidedly academic; and the menu—featuring items such as escargot, veal, and pheasant—clearly caters to grown-up tastes and wallets. The food is quite well prepared, and you'll find the service friendly and efficient. Do try to get a table near one of the large windows; they have wonderful views of the campus. Reservations are recommended, 219/631-2000.

Sacred Heart Parish Center a.k.a. St. Joseph's Hall (31)—Since this building was once used as a seminary, it's not surprising that its guest rooms are often small and their furnishings truly monastic. The lack of amenities, however, is more than compensated for by the center's extraordinary location on the north bank of St. Joseph's Lake. Notre Dame alumni have priority during football weekends and special events, but rooms are usually available at most other times. There is no dining room or room service. Please call ahead to make your reservation, 219/631-9436 or 219/631-7511.

North and South Dining Halls (60 and 17)—Although geared to student appetites, both of Notre Dame's dining halls offer a wide variety of well-prepared and reasonably priced, cafeteria-style meals. In fact, according to a recent survey by a preventative medicine group, Notre Dame has some of the most healthful campus cuisine in the nation. All the breads and pastries are made in the university's bakery, and other unexpected pleasures include a nice selection of gourmet coffees, a waffle bar for weekend brunch, and special theme dinners such as the popular candlelight buffets held after home football games. The dining halls are open daily, and even though they're strictly self-service, being in the good company of the undergraduates—energetic, exuberant, intelligent, well mannered, and, after all, the whole point of the university—is in itself a wonderful

experience. You'll find menus and hours posted in the lobbies of both dining halls as well as all the residence halls. Or, you can call the automated menu line, 219/631-0111.

The Huddle, Huddle Mart, and Allegro in LaFortune Student Center (43)—The Huddle and Huddle Mart are, respectively, a food court and a convenience store/deli; both of them open at 7:30 a.m. and close very late. The long hours not only accommodate erratic student schedules, but are also a real convenience at this residential university where the majority of undergraduates cannot easily drive to get snacks or sundries. The Huddle is a good place to get fast food, while the Huddle Mart has salads, hot sandwiches, and beverages. It's also a good place to pick up film, batteries, health and beauty items, and other sundries. Just outside the "Huddle" entry on the east side of LaFortune, you'll find tables and chairs, which, when the weather cooperates, provide a pleasant place to enjoy your food and the views of Evans Memorial park. The Huddle and Huddle Mart both provide campus delivery service. Their hours may vary during the summer and football weekends or special events, 219/631-6902 (Huddle); 219/631-6903 (Huddle Mart).

Allegro is a coffeehouse tucked next to the bottom of the stairs in LaFortune's basement. Most people come for the gourmet coffees, teas, and cocoa, but the menu also includes pastries, muffins, and sandwiches. Although it's open daily, hours vary with the season. Phone 219/631-6936.

Greenfields in the Hesburgh Center for International Studies (156)—Open Monday through Friday, Greenfields features gourmet breakfasts (French toast stuffed with peaches, and Irish soda bread) and has moderately priced lunch specials. The atmosphere is casual but subdued, with lots of folks reading while they sip at their cappuccino or café au lait, 216/631-8578.

Common Stock Sandwich Company in the College of Business Administration (152)—A good place for a quick breakfast (bagels and pastries) or lunch (hot dogs and deli-style sandwiches), it's open from early morning to midafternoon, Monday through Friday. You can also get a variety of bottled beverages and YOCREAM® here, 219/631-5912.

Poché in Bond Hall (14)—With both day and evening hours during the academic year, this cafe is definitely structured for Notre Dame's architecture students. Its day schedule is Monday through Friday from 9:00 a.m. to 2:00 p.m.; the evening schedule may vary. The menu includes pasta, pizza, and sandwiches, 219/631-8372.

The Irish Cafe in the Law School (37)—Open from early morning through midafternoon, it's a good place for a light breakfast, lunch, or snack. Fare includes bagels, soups, deli-style sandwiches, and gourmet coffees, 219/631-9481.

Waddick's, first floor of O'Shaughnessy Hall (56)—Its location in the liberal arts building makes this eatery ideal for some academic eavesdropping. It has soups, salads, sandwiches, and "the best coffee on campus." Open Monday through Friday, 7:00 a.m. to 5:00 p.m., during the school year. Special hours on football Saturdays, 219/631-8469.

"The Pit," basement of the Hesburgh Library (72)—For those who like their food really fast, this is manna, albeit not from heaven but from vending machines. It's nothing fancy, but there are tables and chairs for at least a semblance of civility with your shrink-wrapped sandwich. You can descend into The Pit whenever the Library is open.

FIVE TIPS FOR FIRST-TIME VISITORS

1. Keep in mind that Notre Dame is private property, and you will need permission from the officers at the entrance gates before driving on campus. Visitors should park at the Eck Center or in the parking lot south of the Hesburgh Center

for International Studies, both of which are near the Main Gate. Parking is also available in the lot at the corners of Bulla and Juniper roads near the East Gate.

2. Residence halls are *not* open to the public, but you can visit most of the other buildings on campus. However, you will need to get permission before entering any classrooms, laboratories, or offices.

3. Guided tours of the campus can be arranged through the visitors' center located in the Eck Center along Notre Dame Avenue. The tours are extremely interesting and typically last about an hour. Most tours provide a general overview of the university, but you can also arrange special interest tours tailored to topics such as history, sports, and religion. Call the Eck Center 219/631-5726 for more information.

4. Complimentary maps of Notre Dame can be found throughout the campus; prime locations include the Eck Center (520) and LaFortune Student Center (43). The Alphabetical Key and Numerical Key provided in this guidebook coordinate with the maps and are intended to make your using them more convenient.

5. Because of the popularity of Notre Dame football, many people plan to visit Notre Dame in the fall. The crisp and sparkling Indiana autumns do bring great color to the campus, and the football hoopla energizes the entire university. However, each season brings a distinctive look to Notre Dame, and you'll also find that accommodations are much easier to find when there are no football games. In fact, winter is a particularly good time to really see Notre Dame. With the leaves off of the trees, the many good views of the campus get even better, and the fine points of its architecture are all the more visible.

MAIN QUADRANGLE

Locating Main Quad is easy, for it's the home of the revered Main Building, whose glorious Golden Dome and likeness of Our Lady can be seen all over campus. Determining Main Quad's place in the Notre Dame universe, however, is quite another matter. The quad long ago ceased to be the true geographic center of the university, but it will forever remain the psychological center, a place that exists largely in the hearts and minds of the Notre Dame family. This is both the university's historic district and its most hallowed ground, the site of the two structures—the Main Building and the Basilica of the Sacred Heart—that summarize its beliefs, its mission, its purpose, its heritage, and its spirit.

Father Sorin deliberately made the Main Building the focal point of his young university, and he also planned Notre Dame Avenue to be a tree-lined boulevard that, like the grand entrance to Versailles, would visually as well as physically lead people to it. Then in the late 1800s, he crowned the Main Building with a gold-coated dome. Creating a Golden Dome at the height of the Gilded Age was a stroke of public relations genius, for it provided the university with an inspired symbol that has proved to be priceless. "Who but Notre Dame," architect Francis Kervick once asked in admiration, "would have dared to lay out a mile-long, grand boulevard culminating with a dome of gold?"

While the Dome dramatically marks the Main Building as the heart of Notre Dame, the adjacent Basilica of the Sacred Heart steadfastly maintains its soul. Not only does the Basilica give Main Quad the nickname of "God Quad," but

Main Building

the cross atop its spire is also the highest point—230 feet—on campus. Thus it provides very visible evidence of the lofty position that religion has always occupied at Notre Dame.

"God Quad" does indeed have a reverent quality. It is a sublime space: peaceful, serene, and well-ordered with symmetrically placed buildings hemming the east and west sides. At its center, a wonderful arboretum balances the works of man with the work of nature to make Main Quad seem like a sanctuary. You almost want to whisper here, but you don't, mostly because this quad is such a surprisingly *musical* place. Its sounds are many and filled with the joy of youth and the warmth of tradition—the noble bells of the Basilica tolling the hours; beloved hymns ascending from early Sunday mass; a clear, sweet soprano practicing in Crowley Hall; band members proudly trumpeting the "Victory March" beneath the Golden Dome; show tunes and tap shoes resounding in Washington Hall; restless rock songs blaring from open dormitory windows. The music echoes from and around the quad's aged buildings, whose worn bricks have forever captured the character of the early, aspiring Notre Dame. For the university's founding fathers—Sorin, Dillon, Corby, Lemonnier, Morrissey, Walsh—Main Quad *was* Notre Dame, and to this day, you can almost *feel* them listening to the rhythms of the campus.

It was on Main Quad that Notre Dame first took shape as a university. All of the rest of the campus—every classroom building, laboratory, residence hall, statue, library, stadium, discovery, theory, art, and tradition—emanates from its venerable buildings. English professor Frank O'Malley once said that there is blood in these bricks. He was absolutely right, for the men and women who wrested a great university from the Indiana prairie were single-minded and totally willing to commit their lives to realize the idea as well as the ideals of Notre Dame. Theirs is a classic American success story—poverty, hardship, against-all-odds perseverance, and ultimate success beyond any expectation. Father Sorin and his followers were immigrants who started Notre Dame on a prayer and a shoestring, and Main Quad stands as the first concrete testament to that accomplishment.

THE MAIN BUILDING AND GOLDEN DOME (36)

With its great glistening Dome and ambitious assortment of gables and spires, this resplendent building looks like Notre Dame's capitol, and it is. Nobody has made that status official, of course, but the Main Building is the substantive as well as symbolic crux of the university. Many metaphors have been used to describe it—cradle, hub, bedrock, anchor, beacon. The truth is, the Main Building functions as all of those things and more. This is the seat of the university's administration; the site of its early academics; the emblem

FLORA AND FAUNA

Because the sheer variety of the overall landscaping (which the university groundskeepers meticulously maintain) greatly enhances its buildings, Main Quad's splendid arboretum is the source of much of the enchantment that this part of the campus holds for people. It dates back to the 1870s, when Brother Philip Kunze, C.S.C., a Silesian-born calligrapher and penmanship teacher with a very green thumb, began landscaping the grounds in front of the Main Building. His great passion was trees, and if you look south-ward from Main Building, you can still ascertain the general pat-tern—deciduous trees in the middle of the quad and evergreens along the sides—that he developed for planting them. Some of the trees you see are horticultural landmarks; others have become sea-sonal attractions in their own right. Probably the most photo-graphed plants on campus are the magnificent saucer magnolias in front of the Main Building. In late April and early May their bril-liant pink blossoms provide a dazzling counterpoint to the gold of the Dome and bright blue of the sky. Also quite pretty in the spring are the white dogwoods alongside the entrances to Walsh Hall. You'll notice various kinds of pine trees planted on the lawn before the dormitory, while next door at Sorin Hall, American elms grow beside the front steps. Red maples and sugar maples dominate the center of the quad, and the paper birch (look for the white trunk) between LaFortune Student Center and the Sacred Heart statue is the largest of its kind in Indiana. Northwest of Crowley Hall stands a great bur oak, an ecological signpost marking the transition be-tween forest and prairie. In the fall, long after the other trees in the quad have shed their red and gold mantels, the bur oak holds on to its bronze-colored leaves.

The arboretum harbors all manner of birds and small animals such as rabbits, but the undisputed lords of this creation are the squirrels with the reddish brown fur that you see scampering every-where. If they look well fed, it's because they are. Students routinely give them handouts, and, in truth, the squirrels are rather spoiled. They've grown so accustomed to contact with humans that if you have a snack, they'll practically accost you to get their share. The squirrels, like the swans and ducks that hold sway on the lakes, have few, if any, natural enemies on campus, and its lushly landscaped grounds are such a haven for them that one alumna has observed, "All animals go to heaven, but the really lucky ones get to go to Notre Dame first."

of its coming of age, and the image that most people have of Notre Dame.

The Main Building and Golden Dome are without a doubt the university's foremost icons. They are the most photographed places on campus, and their likeness is proliferated so widely that it appears on everything from the august Laetare Medal to trinkets sold in the bookstore. In deference to the Dome, even Notre Dame's football players wear golden helmets. Alumni *adore* the Main Building. It's the very center of their affection, admiration, and affinity for the university. The Dome, in fact, serves as their universal identification card, transcending time and

*The Laetare Medal
display honors men and
women—among them
Dorothy Day, actress
Helen Hayes, novelist
Walker Percy, and Joseph
Cardinal Bernardin—
who have received Notre
Dame's Laetare Medal for
illustrating the ideals of
the Church and enriching
the heritage of humanity.
An American counterpart
of the papal "Golden
Rose," the medal dates
back to 1883 and is
considered the most
prestigious award given to
this nation's Catholics.
After the 1997-98 Main
Building restoration, the
Laetare display was moved
from the Bascilica.*

space to indicate their common kinship in the Notre Dame family. One and all, they are *Domers*, and for them, the merest glimpse of the Dome means they are home.

The Main Building is not just a Notre Dame landmark, but an American landmark as well. In 1978 it was placed on the National Register of Historic Places, and the U.S. Postal Service has included its image in the Historic Preservation Series of postcards. In addition, the Golden Dome has become one of the standard topographic features that airplane pilots enjoy pointing out to their passengers. Like the Grand Canyon or Mississippi River, people who are flying by will crane their necks to get a look at it. The Dome now even shines on the World Wide Web. A video camera is constantly directed at it, so the Notre Dame faithful can access color pictures of the Golden Dome 24 hours a day via the university's home page at www.nd.edu.

Some critics say it's fortunate that the Dome attracts so much attention, because the Main Building's busy architecture is so eccentric that it defies description. Willoughby Edbrooke, who designed the structure in 1879 and would later plan Georgia's domed capitol and federal buildings in Washington, D.C., called the architecture "modern Gothic." According to Professor Francis Kervick, the mastermind of Notre Dame's South Quad, the Main Building is "an eclectic and somewhat naive combination of pointed windows, medieval moldings, and classical columns." Others have simply shrugged it off as "modern Sorin." For the record, architect Michael Smith, Notre Dame's Director of Facilities Engineering, says that below the roof the Main Building is Gothic, that the mansard-like center roof is Second Empire, and that the Golden Dome is Classical. What all these opinions tell us about the sum and substance of the Main Building is really quite simple: it's an American original. But then, what else would you expect of a building designed by an Episcopalian from Chicago for a school on the Indiana prairie that was started by a French Catholic priest and whose earliest students included Potawatomi Indians and was attended by inordinate numbers of offspring from immigrant Irish families?

Actually, the structure you see today is Notre Dame's third Main Building. It had two predecessors, the first was completed in 1844 and replaced by the second in 1865. Main I was topped by a tower with a statue of the Blessed Virgin, while Main II had a tin dome and Blessed Virgin statue. Both were multi-purpose buildings that, from refectories to rhetoric classes, housed virtually the entire university operation. On a warm April day in 1879, a fire started in Main II, and within a few hours the entire building, much of its contents, and three neighboring structures were gone. That night students camping out in one of the surviving buildings wryly started to sing choruses of "The Old Home Ain't What It Used to Be." As it turned out, the aftermath of the fire would become Notre Dame's finest hour.

What is now known as the Great Fire of 1879 was the watershed event in Notre Dame's history, a calamity comparable to the Chicago Fire or San Francisco earthquake in impact and effect on the university. It was a tragedy that the university turned into a triumph, a true trial by fire that served as the rite of passage for Notre Dame's maturity into a great institution. Ultimately, the flames also forged an incomparable badge of courage, a Golden Dome that now stands as the consummate sign of the Notre Dame spirit. The fire was still smoldering when Notre Dame's president, Rev. William Corby, began making plans to rebuild. He hastily issued diplomas to the seniors and sent the rest of the students home with the assurance that they would have a new Main Building in time for fall classes. Father Sorin, who was on his way to Europe, rushed back to Notre Dame and blamed himself

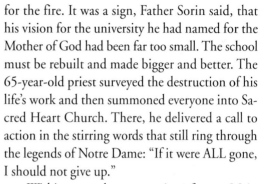

for the fire. It was a sign, Father Sorin said, that his vision for the university he had named for the Mother of God had been far too small. The school must be rebuilt and made bigger and better. The 65-year-old priest surveyed the destruction of his life's work and then summoned everyone into Sacred Heart Church. There, he delivered a call to action in the stirring words that still ring through the legends of Notre Dame: "If it were ALL gone, I should not give up."

Within a month, construction of a new Main Building was under way. More than 300 laborers worked nonstop throughout the summer, making and laying an incredible 4,350,000 bricks in order to fulfill Sorin's dream, Edbrooke's design, and Corby's promise. When the students returned, they found a grandiose structure consisting of four stories plus a basement. It included classrooms, dormitories, study halls, faculty quarters, offices, chapels, dining rooms, a library, and museum space. In addition, the building had been outfitted with every convenience—indoor plumbing, gas lights, and steam heat. The Main Building cost Notre Dame more than $1 million, and assistance came from far and wide. There were raffles, lotteries, and benefit concerts. Alexis Coquillard, the university's first day student and nephew and namesake of a South Bend founder, donated $500. General Sherman sent tents. A railroad waived shipping fees for building materials. Across the road at Saint Mary's Academy, the women of Notre Dame's sister school offered to buy a statue of Mary to replace the one lost in the Great Fire. Artist Giovanni Meli of Chicago was commissioned to execute *Our Lady of Notre Dame*, a statue modeled after a sculpture of the Virgin erected by Pope Pius IX in Rome's Piazza di Spagna.

Meanwhile, the Dome was being completed atop the Main Building. The staggering cost of constructing the building had put the university in debt, and many officials wanted to pinch pennies and simply paint the Dome. Father Sorin,

Football coach Frank Leahy used to admonish his players that "the Lady on the Dome is watching us," and one of Notre Dame's longest-held traditions is that any freshman whose room faces the Golden Dome will be sure to succeed academically.

however, was stubbornly insisting on having it gilded. "We will not cease," he had declared at the start of the Main Building's construction, "until we place a great golden dome atop it, and above that the statue of Our Lady, so that everyone who passes this way can look up and see why this place succeeds." When the committee holding the purse strings balked at his Golden Dome idea, Father Sorin used his position as Superior General of the Holy Cross order to become its chairman. Then he boycotted meetings to shut down the committee until the members agreed to give the Dome a Midas touch. Its first coat of gold leaf would, of course, prove to be a public relations gold mine.

Outside, the Main Building has changed very little over the years. East and west wings were added in 1884, and the Dome has been re-gilded several times. The building was 116 years old before its exterior was gingerly renovated with a new roof and windows, fresh paint, and a much-needed cleaning for those millions of bricks (one admiring contractor even painted his scaffolding in the Notre Dame colors of gold and blue). Inside, however, the changes were constant. As the university grew and new classroom buildings and dormitories appeared on campus, the Main Building gradually became the province primarily of administrators. Again and again, the wonderful old rooms were modified, re-modified, and "modernized" to meet Notre Dame's needs, and it became the most recycled building on campus. Finally, in 1997, the university embarked on a comprehensive renovation and restoration of the Main Building's interior. Plans included re-opening the top floor for the first time in a half century, returning public spaces to their original configuration, adding a ceremonial entrance on the north side, and, for the sake of authenticity, having classrooms in the building to preserve its historic teaching purpose.

When you have the opportunity to visit the Main Building and climb its tall front staircase,

Here are a few figures that will let you size up the lustrous Lady and the Dome that have had such a powerful impact on Notre Dame.

Our Lady Statue:
Material—cast iron covered in gold leaf
Height—19 feet
Weight—4,400 pounds

The Dome:
Circumference—139 feet
Height—225 feet, including the statue
Gold covering—8 ounces of 23-carat gold leaf applied in strips 3 microns thick

Year first gilded—1886
Year last re-gilded—1988
Cost of gilding in 1886—$860
Cost of re-gilding (including statue) in 1988—$286,000

you'll literally be retracing the footsteps of tens of thousands of students, professors, priests, brothers, and sisters whose collective efforts over the last 150 plus years have resulted in the center of learning that we now call Notre Dame. As so many have done before you, you might want to stop for a few minutes to have your picture taken on those well-worn stairs. Every fall, the entire faculty, dressed in full academic regalia, walks down them on their way to the school year's opening mass. There was a time when the Main Building steps were taboo for undergraduates; only those who had earned a Notre Dame degree had the right to use them. Now they are the site of one of the favorite rituals of football Saturdays, the band's pregame concert and "step-off," with fans marching behind the musicians all the way to the Stadium.

When you enter the Main Building, you'll notice that the entryway bears the coat of arms of the Congregation of Holy Cross. Just past the vestibule are the Christopher Columbus murals that Italian artist Luigi Gregori painted in the 1880s at the request of the patriotic Father Sorin. A hundred years ago, these impressive murals held an enormous fascination for the American people and were widely publicized. Long before football, they helped to promote the university's reputation, especially after the U.S. Post Office duplicated one of them—*Return of Columbus and Reception at Court*—on a postage stamp issued for Chicago's famed Columbian Exposition of 1893. Gregori was a colorist renowned for creating extraordinary effects with vivid hues, and during the Main Building's restoration, these and other works by the artist were meticulously refurbished by the Conrad Schmitt Studios of New Berlin, Wisconsin. These twelve historic murals now offer a telling look at Victorian perspectives as well as unique portraits of Notre Dame's nineteenth-century community, many of whose members Gregori used as his models.

Starting at the vestibule doors and walking

WHO WAS FATHER SORIN?

He was a young priest in a young order who had come to a young country, and that was an ideal combination. It is said that when Father Sorin arrived in the United States, the first thing he did was kiss the ground. Love at first sight, obviously, and why not? Behind him lay France, where the Church was just recovering from the anticlerical attacks of the French Revolution. His own Congregation of Holy Cross had been recently formed; it had neither an entrenched bureaucracy nor burdensome layers of established procedure to get in his way in the New World. Ahead lay only opportunity and possibility in a nation that—like Sorin himself—was bold, adventurous, enterprising, resourceful, determined, optimistic, and practical. The United States was the perfect place for a man with ideas and ambition, and Father Sorin had plenty of both. "America," he wrote, "clearly seems to be my path to heaven."

Edward Frederick Sorin was born near Laval, France, in 1814 and from an early age felt called to the priesthood. Ordained at 24, he joined the Congregation of Holy Cross two years later and in another two years was heading for America to work for the Bishop of Vincennes in the Indiana hinterlands. The bishop dispatched him to an outlying farm to start a primary school and novitiate. Instead, Sorin borrowed money without permission and set about starting a college. The frustrated bishop conveniently remembered an old mission site near South Bend, more than 200 miles away. Sorin said he'd love to have it. The bishop warned him of harsh winters and told him to wait until spring, but Sorin set out in November. On the day that he and a small group of Holy Cross brothers arrived—November 26, 1842—the ground was deeply covered with snow. Sorin looked enthusiastically around and declared that the white landscape with its frozen lake reminded him of the purity of the Virgin Mother. The only shelter was an old log cabin, yet Sorin grandly christened it *l'Université de Notre Dame du Lac*, the University of Our Lady of the Lake. The following spring, he found that was a misnomer, for the melting snows revealed not one but *two* lakes on his 524 acres of woods and prairie. Although he should have named the university "*des* Lacs," it was one of the few times the priest would ever be mistaken about anything regarding Notre Dame.

Young Father Sorin may have been a loose cannon, but it soon became obvious that he had a definite target. The pluck he displayed in starting Notre Dame would be his *modus operandi* for the remain-

continued

der of his life, a life dominated by pure devotion to the Blessed Mother and absolute dedication to turning that rude cabin into a university. Starting with only $300 and the invaluable assistance of the Holy Cross brothers, Sorin opened a grade school, a high school, a trade school, and a college. He became a master of creative financing. Sorin accepted pigs, potatoes, or plots of land in payment of tuition; sold the shoes, coffins, and bricks made by the trade school students; started farms; developed the South Bend neighborhood of "Sorinsville,"; and even sent a contingent of brothers to join the California Gold Rush. Sorin knew that the way to attract students was to keep Notre Dame in the public eye, and no matter how empty the college coffers might be, he managed to put on a good show. He staged band concerts and festive Fourth of

July parties for the citizens of South Bend; exhibited artifacts from Notre Dame's museum at the Chicago World's Fair; invited bishops to building dedications; bought a magnificent carillon; courted the press; and, with an idea worthy of Madison Avenue, put a Golden Dome on top of the Main Building.

Father Sorin was not only the founder of Notre Dame and its first president, but also an important figure in the Congregation of Holy Cross. In taking over the old mission, he served as a local superior, and by the time he was 40 was the regional provincial. In 1868 Sorin became the congregation's head man, and as Superior General moved its world headquarters from LeMans, France, to the Presbytery at Notre Dame. Father Sorin would hold that post for the next quarter century; his previous position as Notre Dame's president had lasted for 23 years. While several priests succeeded him as president, none of them could really rule Notre Dame while he was still alive. Everybody knew that Father Sorin was its first and foremost leader. He was the university's *Father* in the broadest sense of the word—yes a priest, but also its progenitor, protector, provider, and ultimately patriarch. Sorin could rub shoulders with Popes and politicians then come back to the campus and play marbles with his "little princes" in the grade school. He chaired the board of trustees, but the day after the Great Fire was pushing a wheelbarrow loaded with bricks. At the unveiling of the *Sorin* statue in 1906, Father John W. Cavanaugh astutely noted that Father Sorin's true monument was Notre Dame.

More than a century has passed since his death, but remarkably, Sorin is still very much a *presence* on the campus. His chalice is still used at mass, and people speak of him as if he is merely off on one of his endless fund-raising trips and will be back any day now. They describe him as a missionary, educator, visionary, showman, statesman, and, perhaps most accurate—and American—of all, *operator*. His story has evolved into the university's seminal epic, and Sorin, as its primary hero, is the parent of its folklore and the fabled Notre Dame mystique.

"If the edifice stands, we will never regret the price and the sweat that it has cost us."
—Father Edward Sorin

Although the only Native Americans that Christopher Columbus encountered were in the Caribbean region, Luigi Gregori portrayed the natives in his murals with clothing, spears, and shields from Plains Indian cultures. Someone had once donated a collection of North American Indian artifacts to Notre Dame, and the Italian artist mistakenly used them as props in his paintings.

down the hallway toward the Main Building's rotunda, you'll see the mural *Christopher Columbus, Discoverer* on the west wall. For the face of Columbus, Gregori used Rev. Thomas Walsh, C.S.C., who at the time was president of Notre Dame. Father Walsh appears as Columbus in all of the murals except for the one depicting the explorer's death. In *Discovery of Land, Friday, October 12, 1492* (east wall), the man with the magnificent beard is engineering professor Arthur Stace, and next to him is English professor Joseph Lyons, the future namesake of Lyons Hall. The fellow looking toward the New World is university librarian James Edwards. Gregori put himself in the largest mural, *Return of Columbus and Reception at Court* (west wall); look for him—and his mustache—just behind the painting's red drapery. Columbus died in poverty and obscurity in a Franciscan monastery, and *Death of Columbus, Valladolid, May 20, 1506* (east wall) depicts his unfortunate end. In this mural, Gregori used Father Sorin's likeness for Columbus. The model for the monk leaning on a cane was Rev. Louis Neyron, C.S.C., while Gregori used Brother Albeus Clarke, C.S.C., for the solemn monk standing beside him. It is said that Father Neyron refused to pose for Gregori, so the artist worked from a sketch that he made on the sly while they were having dinner.

The rotunda, with its beautiful balustrade and radiant murals, lies beneath the Golden Dome and is the most stunning part of the Main Building's interior. The ethereal figures in the murals represent the arts and sciences, and Gregori painted them on the rotunda's ceiling after he completed the Columbus series. Since they had to be painted on a curved surface, Gregori supposedly practiced the figures by first painting them on bowls he obtained from the university's kitchen. Notice that Gregori put *Religion* at the very center of the ceiling. She is symbolically stretched across the earth, and the white, green, and red colors in her robe signify, respectively, faith, hope, and charity. *Philosophy* wears a crown and is seated on a throne. *History*, the winged figure in a white robe, is about to write in a book held by Father Time. Clad in the gold of power and purple of royalty, *Science* holds a shining scepter that denotes the light of knowledge. *Fame* holds trumpets, while *Music* play a lute. And finally, *Poetry*, who glories in the laurels of her crown, has just written the words *Numine afflor* which, appropriately, indicate divine inspiration.

BASILICA OF THE SACRED HEART (29)

There are three things that you need to keep in mind about this Basilica: (1) it is a work of art; (2) it is a landmark that has become both a place of pilgrimage and a tourist attraction; and (3) it is first and foremost a house of God. This is Notre Dame's mother church, the campus's premier place of worship, and the greatest physical manifestation of the faith that underpins the university. The Basilica is used primarily to fulfill the spiritual needs of the Holy Cross community and Notre Dame's students, but it also serves as the home of a local congregation, Sacred Heart Parish.

Although the Basilica's name refers to the Sacred Heart of Jesus, which was an object of intense devotion in the nineteenth century, the Basilica's origins go back more than 300 years to a crude log chapel that missionary Claude Allouez built beside St. Mary's Lake in the 1680s. In the 1840s, Father Sorin arrived at the site to begin his pastoral mission and built a church that he dedicated to the

Tintinnabulum and Umbrellino (Bell and Umbrella): Displayed on the right and left sides of the Main Altar, these two ceremonial symbols indicate Sacred Heart's distinctive status as a basilica. The tintinnabulum, a bell carried as a sign of recognition in processions, bears the insignia of the Pope as well as Sacred Heart's coat of arms. The red and yellow striped umbrellino is considered a sign of honor for the church, and it is also used in processions. In days of old, the umbrellino was actually used as a protection from the elements, but now it is strictly symbolic. Sacred Heart's umbrellino has been extensively embroidered with coats of arms and other insignia associated with the Pope, the Church, and Notre Dame.

Sacred Heart. The university soon outgrew that "Old Church" and in 1868, Sorin ambitiously began the Gothic structure that you now see standing just west of the Main Building. The church took more than 20 years to complete, but when it was finished, Notre Dame had a lofty spire next to its new Golden Dome. Then as now, they form a powerful pair of symbols—the Dome signifying the university's academic mission and the spire proclaiming its faith.

Father Sorin designed the church in conjunction with Rev. Alexis Granger, C.S.C., an unassuming Frenchman who was then the parish pastor, and Irish-born Brother Charles Borromeo Harding, C.S.C., the hard-working, largely self-taught campus builder. Their Gothic Revival design definitely reflects the French taste of Notre Dame's founding father, and because the church was constructed with local materials—legend has it that the interior columns contain tree trunks—it was nicknamed the "Cathedral of the Prairie." Historically as well as religiously, Sacred Heart occupies an inimitable place, witnessing the funerals of Sorin, Rockne, and sculptor Ivan Mestrovic; the prayers of an Italian cardinal who would become Pope Pius XII; untold numbers of baptisms, weddings, communions, and ordinations; and the tens of thousands of visitors who come every year to experience the beauty and holiness of this place. The church underwent its most recent restoration and renovation in the 1980s, and in 1992, the Vatican recognized Sacred Heart's historical significance and importance as a center of worship by designating it a minor basilica. This is a rare honor, for only about 40 churches in the United States have been accorded basilica status.

You'll find the Basilica of the Sacred Heart anchoring the northwest corner of the quad. It was constructed from bricks in the shape of a Latin cross with complex but perfectly balanced Gothic features—spires and spirelets; stained glass, tripartite, and roundel windows; curved

Sacred Heart

apsidal chapels—that give it the inspired look of a medieval cathedral. Sacred Heart's main entrance is on the south facade at the base of the tower supporting its conspicuous central spire. The peak of that soaring spire is topped by a gold cross, which appears rather small from the ground but is actually 12 feet high. Above the doors, you'll notice the papal coat of arms (a triple crown tiara over the keys of St. Peter), which indicates the church's status as a basilica. Sacred Heart's coat of arms is displayed just left of the doors: a striped umbrellino (a papal symbol) over the cross and anchors (a Christian symbol of hope) that signify the Congregation of Holy Cross.

The louvered arches you see on the tower enclose 24 bells, 23 of which comprise the oldest carillon in the United States. Imported from France and originally installed in a tower in front of Old Church, the carillon was yet another of Father Sorin's projects. The carillon bells were blessed in 1856, and each of them was given a name—Mary of the Nativity, Mary of the Seven Dolors, etc.—pertaining to the life of the Mother of God. For years, the sound of the carillon playing the "Alma Mater" meant "lights out" in the dormitories. Although today's students can stay up all night if they wish, the "Alma Mater" is still played every evening. The final bell, which is one of the grandest in the United States, was blessed in 1888 during Father Sorin's Golden Jubilee. Named for St. Anthony of Padua, it is an immense bass bell, or bourdon, more than seven feet tall and weighing 15,400 pounds. In comparison, the nation's celebrated Liberty Bell is about one-third that height and weighs just over 2,000 pounds. The sonorous tones of the St. Anthony bell can be heard for miles, but it is rung only on great and solemn occasions. Many believe that if you pray to St. Anthony while the bell is sounding, your petition is sure to be granted.

On Sacred Heart's east facade, the Memorial Door has become famous for its motto, "God, Country, Notre Dame." It honors the men of Notre Dame who died in World War I and was the precursor of the Clarke Memorial Fountain on North Quad. The doorway's Gothic trappings also anticipated the South Quad, for it was designed by Francis Kervick and Vincent Fagan, the university architects whose mastery of the style produced many of the wonderful buildings erected there in the 1920s and 1930s. The armor-clad statues flanking the doorway were done by

The Collection Plate: Sacred Heart had to be built in stages because it took Notre Dame decades to raise the $375,000 that was ultimately spent to complete the church in the 1890s. A century later, $7 million was needed to refurbish the Basilica. That project, however, only took a couple of years, largely because of New York stockbroker and university trustee Thomas Coleman, a 1956 graduate who was the restoration's primary benefactor.

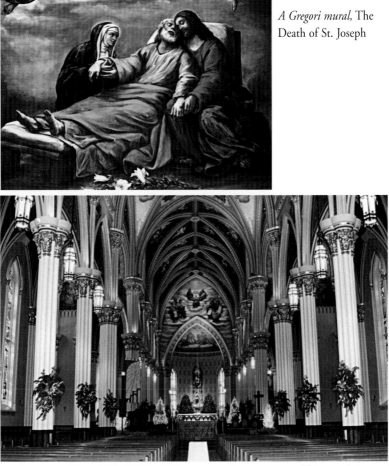

A Gregori mural, The Death of St. Joseph

The recently restored interior

art professor Rev. John Bednar, C.S.C. They represent two defenders of the faith: Joan of Arc, patron saint of France, and Michael the Archangel, patron saint of soldiers. Just inside the doorway, you'll notice a light fixture made from an army helmet that was worn by Rev. Charles O'Donnell, C.S.C., who served as a chaplain during World War I and later became president of Notre Dame.

Although the exterior of the Basilica of the Sacred Heart is certainly impressive, it does not even begin to prepare you for the majesty and opulence of the interior. The size of the church—275 feet long and 114 feet wide—is really rather modest, but it has high, vaulted ceilings—they

East door of Sacred Heart

reach to 60 feet—complemented by pointed lancet arches and towering columns that constantly lead the eye upward to give the illusion of great space. Blue and gold, which are traditionally associated with Mary, are the predominant colors, and given the profusion of stars and angels that adorn the ceiling, the effect is, frankly, heavenly. Sacred Heart is absolutely chock-a-block with paintings, sculptures, stained-glass windows, and other works of art that were intended not only to beautify the church but also to instruct worshippers. Scholars have intensely studied these treasures, and numerous books and papers have been written about their religious scenes and symbolism. It would probably take you days to adequately see, let alone fully experience, the Basilica's artistry. Informative guided tours are available, and you can arrange for one by calling 219/631-7329. However, if you'd like to visit Sacred Heart on your own, there are certain "must-sees" that you'll find enjoyable as well as enlightening.

The marvelous stained-glass windows were designed and produced in the studios of the Carmelite nuns in Le Mans, France, and they were installed over a period of 15 years, beginning in 1873. These windows are now considered priceless because comparable stained-glass windows in

European churches were all destroyed during World Wars I and II. Altogether there are 116 windows consisting of more than 1,200 individual panels, and in the late 1980s, they were all repaired and reconditioned by the Conrad Schmitt Studios as part of Sacred Heart's restoration. Dozens of saints, apostles, theologians, and biblical scenes are portrayed in the windows. Many of the figures are life-sized, and you'll notice they were so carefully crafted that the faces are always whole and never marred by the leading. Two of the windows in the west transept are particularly noteworthy: one on the north side depicting the Sacred Heart of Jesus that inspired the Basilica's name and another on the south side showing Father Sorin presenting the building to God.

Both the murals on the walls and ceilings and the Stations of the Cross are the work of Luigi Gregori, Notre Dame's first artist-in-residence. Father Sorin recruited Gregori from the Vatican, and the artist was supposed to work at Notre Dame only a few years. However, he succumbed to Sorin's power of persuasion as well as the lure of Notre Dame's building boom and stayed for 17 years. Gregori's luminous *Exaltation of the Holy Cross* graces the ceiling of the Lady Chapel, while the imposing murals of the east and west transepts celebrate events in the life of Mary. In the sanctuary, the ceiling above the altar portrays the Hebrew leaders Isaiah (scroll), David (harp), Jeremiah (scroll) and Moses (tablet) from the Old Testament, plus the evangelists Matthew (angel), John (eagle), Luke (ox), and Mark (lion) from the New Testament.

The Basilica has three altars. Walking north from the main entrance, the first one you'll come to is the Altar of Sacrifice, followed by the Main Altar, and finally the Bernini Altar in the Lady Chapel in the rear of the Basilica. The contemporary-style Altar of Sacrifice was installed after Vatican II called for increasing lay participation in the liturgy. It faces the congregation and was

The Ties That Bind: Although students have dubbed Sacred Heart the "weekend wedding factory," there is probably no better reflection of how profoundly the university affects undergraduates and remains a part of their lives than the Basilica's phenomenal popularity as a site for their marriage ceremonies. No nuptials are allowed there during football Saturdays, Advent, or Lent, but throughout the rest of the year, the Basilica averages four weddings—two in the morning and two in the afternoon—every Saturday. The demand is so high that most couples have to book their dates more than a year in advance, and Sacred Heart even has on-staff wedding coordinators to handle the reservations. The only people eligible to be married in the Basilica are members of Sacred Heart parish and Notre Dame students, alumni, faculty, and administrators.

Ivan Mestrovic

constructed from old pews and choir stalls. Father Sorin had the French Gothic Main Altar made in Paris. A piece of architecture as well as art, this exquisite golden altar represents the New Jerusalem with turrets, battlements, gates, walls, and doors. It is topped by a beautiful spire and the Lamb of God. The third altar is believed to have been made by students of Rome's famed master of the Baroque, Giovanni Bernini. Also covered in gold, this elaborate altar is known for its flowing, dynamic lines. The "pelican at her piety" displayed on its base is an image commonly used to represent Christ in religious art.

Seven side chapels are located north of the Basilica's transepts, and the Lady Chapel is probably the most renowned, primarily because of the eye-catching Bernini Altar and the handsome Madonna and Child statue prominently displayed above it. A Lady Chapel dedicated to Mary was a common feature in Europe's Gothic cathedrals, and it was also copied in this country at St. Patrick's Cathedral in New York City. Because of Father Sorin's great devotion to the Virgin, the Lady Chapel was completed in 1888 for the fiftieth anniversary of his ordination. This chapel is now often used for small weddings and funerals and is especially lovely at Christmastime, when it is elegantly decorated with trees and lights to celebrate the Nativity.

Just west of the Lady Chapel is the Chapel of Holy Angels with the celestial spirits shown in its stained-glass windows.

Mestrovic's The Descent from the Cross

Next on the Basilica's west side is the Baptismal Chapel. Dedicated to Our Lady of Victories, the chapel contains Sacred Heart's original, custom-made baptismal font, which was installed in 1871. It's followed by the Holy Cross Chapel, where John Cardinal O'Hara, C.S.C., is entombed. The university's president from 1934 to 1940, he imported noted scholars as visiting professors and recruited European intellectuals fleeing the Nazis to come to Notre Dame. Father O'Hara was the first member of the Congregation of Holy Cross to be named a cardinal, and in tribute, the class of 1928 has traditionally placed red roses in this chapel. The sculpture near the front of the chapel is *Return of the Prodigal Son* by Ivan Mestrovic.

Sacred Heart organ

On the east side of the Basilica, the Reliquary Chapel is located to the right of the Lady Chapel. It holds relics of the Twelve Apostles, a piece of the True Cross, and numerous other objects of veneration. When Sacred Heart was built, it was customary for churches to have a figure representing a saint, and here it is St. Severa. A young martyr

---

THE HOLTKAMP ORGAN

Visitors often remark that one of the unexpected pleasures of visiting the Basilica is the sound of its pipe organ. Actually, the organ is played every day. It can be heard not only at mass, but also, much to the delight of visitors, whenever students and faculty members from the music department are using it for practice or recitals. The organ, which has nearly 3,000 individual pipes, was custom-built for the Basilica in the mid-1970s by the Holtkamp Organ Company of Cleveland, Ohio. At 20 tons and 38-feet high, it was too tall to fit in the Holtkamp factory and had to be assembled piece-by-piece in the Basilica. The organ was a gift from Charles and Marjorie O'Malley of Woodside, California. Mrs. O'Malley was both a member of the Fisher family that helped start General Motors and an expert horticulturist. Her family had so many ties to the university that when she developed two new varieties of camellias, she named them "Notre Dame" and "Golden Dome."

Artistic License:
Luigi Gregori made many
friends while he was at
Notre Dame, and
although he delighted in
putting them in his
paintings, his work in the
Basilica also provides a
look at his own life. In the
east transept mural
Presentation of the
Blessed Virgin in the
Temple*, he included his*
wife, his daughter, and
himself (the man in gray).
The fellow who is rather
unkindly depicted
breaking a rod (a symbol
for St. Joseph, Mary's
husband) is one of his
wife's old boyfriends. For
the entire time that
Gregori worked in Sacred
Heart, he was plagued by
one of its sacristans, who
complained constantly
about the messes caused by
the artist's paints and
scaffolding. But Gregori
got the last laugh by
putting the unpleasant
sacristan in the Stations of
the Cross. Look for him in
Station No. 10; he's the
surly-looking fellow
stripping Jesus of his
garments.

from the third century, her bones are contained in lead boxes beneath the head and feet. Next comes the Brother André Chapel, which is also called the Immaculate Conception Chapel. In addition to windows depicting the life of Mary, it contains a statue of Blessed Brother André Bessette, C.S.C., who was beatified in 1982 for his work among the sick and needy in Montreal. The statue was done by Rev. Anthony Lauck, C.S.C., professor emeritus of art at Notre Dame. Finally, the Holy Family Chapel honors the life of St. Joseph and is the site of Ivan Mestrovic's masterpiece, *The Descent from the Cross.* The sculptor did the sketches for this magnificent pietà while he was a political prisoner of the Nazis and completed the sculpture in 1946. Made from white Carrara marble, it is a compelling, compassionate work; Joseph of Arimathea supports the body of the dead Savior, while the Blessed Mother and Mary Magdalene grieve. Mestrovic used his own face for Joseph of Arimathea, and his wife Olga was the model for the women. The pietà was exhibited at New York's Metropolitan Museum of Art before going on display at Sacred Heart in 1955. This massive—12 feet tall and weighing seven tons—sculpture was transported by a flatbed trailer truck across the highways and byways of several states, and when it arrived, part of the Basilica's wall had to be removed in order to get it inside.

Before you leave Sacred Heart, do take a few minutes to visit its museum, which is in the Sacristy where sacred vessels and clerical vestments are kept. The museum is one of those proverbial "best-kept secrets," and it holds artifacts pertaining to the history of Notre Dame as well as the Catholic Church in America. Among the many rare and fascinating items are the mortar and pestle that Gregori used to mix his paints, a tiara and chalices from Pope Pius IX, a cassock that belonged to Pope Paul VI, and a six-foot-high processional cross presented to Notre Dame by Napoleon III and Empress Eugénie.

Liturgically and administratively, Sacred Heart is actually two churches. Under the direction of the Campus Ministry, the university has the primary use of the main church, while the members of Sacred Heart Parish worship in the historic Crypt in the Basilica's basement. The parish offices are housed behind the Basilica in the Presbytery (35); built in 1869, this historic structure was Father Sorin's base of operations when he headed the Holy Cross order, and he died there in 1893. Masses are said daily in both the Crypt and the Basilica, and when the university is in session, there is Exposition of the Blessed Sacrament in the Lady Chapel on Friday afternoons. Schedules are published in the *Observer*, *This Week*, and the Sacred Heart bulletin, which you can obtain in the Basilica's vestibule. For more information, call Campus Ministry, 219/631-7800; the Basilica, 219/631-8463; or Sacred Heart Parish, 219/631-6861. Visitors are welcome at the Basilica of the Sacred Heart, but you will not be able to tour it during masses and other ceremonies.

CORBY HALL (27)

Once the students who lived in Corby Hall carved their initials in the bricks alongside its trademark front porch. Now that porch is renowned for its rocking chairs, because Corby Hall is home to many Holy Cross priests and brothers. This building does not actually face Main Quad, but it has stood just west of Sacred Heart Basilica since 1893 as yet another testament to Brother Charles Harding's fortuitous talent for construction. Its name, however, is a tribute to Rev. William Corby, C.S.C., a New Yorker who was the initiator of the law school, proud owner of a Studebaker carriage given him by the student body, a Civil War veteran, Father Sorin's constant comrade, and the only president of Notre Dame to serve two separate terms (1866-72 and 1877-81).

Father Corby statue

Corby Hall

Father Corby's service as an Army chaplain made him one of the most fascinating footnotes in the annals of the nation's history. He was one of the eight Holy Cross priests that Father Sorin—partly out of patriotism, partly because he saw an opportunity to defuse anti-Catholic sentiments—sent to minister to Union soldiers. Father Corby went to the Army of the Potomac, and in July 1863, fate took him to Gettysburg with General Meade's Irish Brigade. By the second day at Gettysburg, the fierce fighting made it obvious that many of the men would be killed, but there was no time for the priest to hear their confessions. Father Corby climbed on top of a rock and gave the entire brigade an absolution just before they went into battle, telling them not to desert their flag or turn their backs on the foe. His action deeply affected both the men and their officers, and in 1910, a statue of Corby blessing the Irish Brigade was erected on the battlefield at Gettysburg. The following year, a copy of that statue by Samuel Murray was dedicated at Notre Dame, and it now stands before Corby Hall on top of a rock that was brought from Gettysburg. Notre Dame's students, who have a genius for finding football metaphors, have christened the statue *Fair Catch Corby*, because the priest's raised arm looks like the game signal.

In memory of Father Corby, Notre Dame's Alumni Association presents its annual Corby Award to a graduate who has exemplified the university's values and spirit while serving in the U.S. armed forces.

SORIN HALL, A.K.A. SORIN COLLEGE (26)

The beehive-shaped turrets that architect Willoughby Edbrooke placed at the corners of Sorin Hall not only give this residence hall the gracious look of a French chateau but also distinguish it from all the other dormitories at Notre Dame. Its appearance, however, is just one of the things that makes this hall unique. Sorin occupies a singular place in the university's history and as a result has developed an

Sorin Hall

unrivaled identity and sense of tradition. Aside from being the most storied dorm on campus, this is arguably also the proudest.

The opening of Sorin Hall in 1889 was a milestone for both Notre Dame and Catholic higher education. It marked the first time that the university had a separate dormitory building, and even more significant, it offered private rooms, which heretofore had been unheard of at a Catholic college or university. In fact, the concept of private rooms was very much a novelty in those late Victorian times, and there was considerable concern about what all that privacy might lead to once young men were liberated from the communal living conditions that were then the norm of dormitory life. The university's primary motive for building Sorin Hall had really been quite simple: the Main Building, where students from grade school to college all lived en masse, was getting too crowded. In addition, the times were changing, and one of Notre Dame's most valuable assets has always been its ability to constantly adapt and improve to meet the shifting needs of the larger society. Progressives such as Rev. John Zahm saw private rooms for college men as one of the swells on the wave of the future. Fortunately, Father Sorin did too, and with the patriarch's approval, Notre Dame built its first residence hall.

In the planning stages, the new dormitory was called "Collegiate Hall," an obvious reference to the older students who were to have the privilege of living there. Its cornerstone was laid on May 27, 1888, the year that Father Sorin was celebrating his fiftieth anniversary as a priest. Although the students and faculty had already given him a carriage and two horses for his Golden Jubilee, they had an even better present in store for the 74-year-old priest when he turned out to bless the cornerstone. They started calling the promising new structure "Sorin Hall." This salute to Father Sorin remained unchanged until 1969, when a group of Sorin residents decided to protest the

Father Sorin

Vietnam war by seceding from the university. The Sorinites' declaration of independence was a small wooden sign on the dorm's front porch that announced the creation of "Sorin College." The rebellion fizzled, but the sign is still there. No longer a symbol of dissent, it has instead become a small vanity signifying Sorin's status as Notre Dame's oldest dorm. The university's maps may say Sorin Hall, but you will almost never hear a resident call it anything but Sorin *College*.

At the time of its dedication, Sorin Hall's singular architecture was described as "mixed Gothic and Roman," and it contained a chapel, the law school, quarters for rectors and bachelor professors, and some 50, quite revolutionary single rooms. Perhaps to ease the minds of skeptical parents and alumni, the rooms were reassuringly described as "large enough to encourage study, and at the same time small enough to discourage visiting." These private rooms were definitely not for everybody. In point of fact, they had to be earned, since Sorin Hall was reserved for the cream of the academic crop, and students got to select their rooms based on their academic standing. The very first student to choose a room was senior J. E. Cusack, who not only was academically at the top of his class, but also happened to be a halfback on the football team.

As it turned out, Cusack was the first of an amazing number of varsity athletes who would live in Sorin Hall. Knute Rockne and Gus Dorais, the duo who transformed football with the forward pass, lived in the dorm's underground basement, which early on was dubbed "the subway." In the 1920s, the hall housed two of the famous "Four Horsemen": quarterback Harry Stuhldreher in the "subway" and halfback Don Miller on the third floor. Three of Notre Dame's Heisman Trophy winners—Johnny Lujack, John Lattner, and Paul Hornung—roomed here. So did All-Americans Pete Demmerle, Ken MacAfee, and Dave

Casper, as well as future coach Heartley "Hunk" Anderson and future athletic director Edward "Moose" Krause.

At present, Sorin Hall is occupied by a former Notre Dame basketball player from Washington, D.C., whose name now appears on the front pages far more often than it did on the sports pages during his varsity days. He is Notre Dome's president, Rev. Edward "Monk" Malloy, C.S.C., a member of the class of 1963 who holds advanced degrees in both English and theology. Since becoming head of the university in 1987, Father Malloy has overseen the development of DeBartolo Quad and West Quad as well as the renovation of many of Notre Dame's most venerable old buildings. His initiatives have also increased the number of women and minority students, bolstered Notre Dame's ties to South Bend, and produced the *Colloquy for the Year 2000,* a blueprint for the university's future. A professor of theology, he has a strong interest in ethics and is nationally known for his work to encourage volunteerism and community service. "Monk," as he is often called, also conducts a seminar every semester as part of Notre Dame's First Year of Studies program. He is probably the only university president in the United States who not only teaches an undergraduate class but also lives in a dorm with his students.

Father Malloy is just the latest in the long line of noteworthy teachers, priests, and mentors who have inhabited Sorin Hall. He, in fact, lives in the very room—number 141 in the northeast turret—that once belonged to the beloved Paul Fenlon, who was perhaps Notre Dame's quintessential bachelor don. The bachelor dons were unmarried professors who resided in the dormitories and, although they were laymen, had an almost religious devotion to not merely instructing but also guiding, advising, civilizing, and ultimately

The Four Horsemen

THE "NOTRE DAME VICTORY MARCH"

Even if it had contributed nothing else to the history and traditions of Notre Dame, Sorin Hall would be revered for being the birthplace of the "Notre Dame Victory March." As students and alumni will assuredly tell you, the "Victory March" is the greatest college fight song ever written. Certainly it's recognized around the world and, in addition to the stirring renditions heard at Fighting Irish football games, has been played at weddings, funerals, prisoner of war camps, and even military invasions. The song was conceived in 1908 by John and Michael Shea, two brothers from Holyoke, Massachusetts, who lived in Sorin Hall. Michael, a Notre Dame music instructor, composed the melody and practiced it on a piano in the dorm's first-floor reading room. John was a glib senior class president who edited both the *Dome* and *Scholastic*; obviously, he had a way with words, so he wrote the lyrics in his room. When the brothers were ready to wed the words to the music, the reading room was occupied. They went into Sacred Heart church and, in what was truly a blessed event for Notre Dame, used its organ to play their composition for the first time. The following spring, the "Notre Dame Victory March" made its public debut in the rotunda of the Main Building, and the rest, you might say, is musical history. After graduation, John returned to Massachusetts, where he began a career in state politics. Michael was ordained a Jesuit priest, studied music in Rome, and spent many years as a professor and music director at a seminary in New York state. After he died in 1956, Father Shea was brought back to Notre Dame to be buried in its Community Cemetery. Here are John Shea's much-loved lyrics:

Rally sons of Notre Dame,
Sing her glory and sound her fame,
Raise her Gold and Blue,
And cheer with voices true,
Rah! Rah! For Notre Dame.
We will fight in every game,
Strong of heart and true to her name.
We will ne'er forget her,
And will cheer her ever,
Loyal to Notre Dame.
    Chorus:
Cheer, cheer for Old Notre Dame,
Wake up the echoes cheering her name,
Send a volley cheer on high,
Shake down the thunder from the sky,
What though the odds be great or small,
Old Notre Dame will win over all,
While her loyal sons are marching
Onward to Victory.

enlightening their students. A courtly professor of English from Blairsville, Pennsylvania, Fenlon first moved into Sorin Hall as a student during World War I, and he also lived there throughout his teaching career and on into his retirement. When Fenlon died in 1980, he had spent more than 60 years in the dormitory. Fenlon was the last of Notre Dame's dons, and the St. Thomas Aquinas chapel in Sorin Hall now contains a plaque that honors his memory.

The first of Sorin Hall's dons, Colonel William Hoynes, also lived there for decades and left his mark on the dorm. Although he had spent some time in the Union Army, his rank was strictly honorary, the result of his taking charge of a group of student cadets that came to be known as the Hoynes Light Guards. The mustachioed Hoynes was dean of the law school and a bit of a dandy, given to flowery language and fancy clothes. One morning, just as he was emerging from Sorin Hall in his full sartorial splendor, some students opened an upper-story window and dumped a bucket of water on him. The prank so outraged Hoynes that the university added a porch to the front of the hall to protect their valued professor from any future deluge. Years later, the dormitory's colorful rector, Rev. John "Pop" Farley liked to distribute the students' mail from that porch, and now it serves as an outdoor stage for the Sorinites' rollicking Talent Show, an infamous autumn evening of skits, songs, and dance that is usually held on Parents' Weekend.

Although Sorin Hall is one of Notre Dame's smallest men's dormitories, it can nonetheless claim two past university presidents: Rev. Andrew Morrissey, who was the hall's first rector and blessed the addition of its north and south wings in 1897, and Rev. John O'Hara, a future cardinal who lived there while serving as Notre Dame's prefect of religion. With the dorm's prestigious heritage and very Victorian-looking rooms, it's not surprising that Sorinites display a strong camaraderie and sense of tradition. In a nod to the movie *Animal House*, they call themselves the "Screamin' Otters," and one of their favorite places to howl is the high-ceilinged turret room on the southwest corner of the first floor. On weekends, it's famous for late parties and loud music. Also on the first floor is a bronze statue of Father Sorin, and custom dictates that if Sorinites want to have good luck, they have to touch its right foot whenever they pass by. The statue has disappeared several times, presumably kidnapped by residents of rival dorms. When it vanished in the 1950s, postcards and telegrams began arriving at Notre Dame from all over the world. They were signed "Sorin" and had mischievous messages such as "Visited the Louvre today. Paris swings at night . . . " Other times, the statue was spotted in a rowboat on St. Mary's Lake or descending onto the campus in a helicopter. These adventures finally ended in 1983, when the statue's base was weighted with concrete and fastened to the hall's floor with iron rods. Since then, Father Sorin has stayed firmly in place, assuring the proud Soronites that they will continue to enjoy the luck of the Irish.

WALSH HALL (25)

Walsh Hall

The completion of Walsh Hall in 1909 was quite an achievement for Notre Dame, because this dormitory was Main Quad's final building. Its construction not only brought the core of the university to fruition, but also established the boundaries of the quad as you see them today. Moreover, the building itself was something of a triumph, for it was considered much more luxurious than its older neighbor, Sorin Hall. Like Sorin, Walsh Hall offered undergraduates individual rooms, but a raft of other amenities—built-in closets, suites with private baths, and a basement recreation area with billiards and a bowling alley—fostered the consensus on campus that it was "the best college dormitory in America." This was Notre Dame's original "Gold Coast," and since students had to pay a premium to live there, Walsh residents were soon stereotyped as coming from wealthy families.

Quite fittingly, the hall was named in honor of the university's sixth president, Rev. Thomas Walsh, C.S.C., who had taken charge of Main Quad's development during the 1880s. Raised in Montreal, Canada, Father Walsh had been educated in Paris and ordained in the United States. He was an erudite, energetic scholar who had modern ideas, and with the cooperation of sitting President William Corby, the aging Father Sorin groomed Walsh to be the university's future leader. When Walsh took office in 1881, he was only 28, the very age that Sorin had been when he founded Notre Dame. As president, Walsh both significantly expanded Main Quad's physical plant and steadily bettered Notre Dame's curriculum. He put Colonel Hoynes in charge of law, supported the Zahms in science and engineering, and imported editor Maurice Francis Egan from New York to bolster the liberal arts. Walsh also stretched the university's athletic horizons by allowing Notre Dame's first intercollegiate football game in 1887 (it was played against the University of Michigan, which won the contest, 8-0). His great promise, however, was destroyed by Bright's disease. Father Walsh died in 1893 at age 40, and Notre Dame's presidency passed to the kindly but conservative Rev. Andrew Morrissey. Only a few months later, Father Sorin was also dead. Today, the proximity of Sorin and Walsh halls provides a subtle but very concrete reminder of the historic tie between the patriarch and his protégé.

Walsh Hall was architect William Brinkman's only effort on Notre Dame's campus, and while many people are fond of its sunny yellow bricks and trademark bay windows, others scoff at its "convent architecture." One bachelor don even claimed he resided in Walsh Hall precisely because it is so unattractive; he much preferred to be

When Luigi Gregori chronicled the discovery of America by painting his famous murals in the Main Building, he used President Thomas Walsh as his model for Christopher Columbus. Walsh's gentle visage appears as the face of Columbus in all the murals except the final one, where Gregori substituted Father Sorin for the mariner's deathbed scene.

inside the dormitory looking out rather than outside looking at it. During World War II, Walsh
Hall was used by the Navy, and it remained a
men's dormitory until the early 1970s, when it
was extensively remodeled because of one of the
long-range cultural effects of that war: co-educa-
tion. The first women undergraduates arrived at
Notre Dame in the fall of 1972, a group of 325
trailblazers who were housed in the campus's first
"female residence halls," Walsh and Badin. Walsh
Hall's residents are now nicknamed the "Wild
Women" and known for fielding some very re-
spectable interhall sports teams, especially in flag
football. Every winter, they also host Walsh Week,
a lively celebration of games, contests, and films
that culminates in an SYR.

Washington Hall

WASHINGTON HALL (44)

The first play ever performed on the stage of Washington Hall was *Oedipus Rex* by Sophocles, and the actors did it entirely in Greek. But then, that was back in 1882. Attend a play here today, and chances are the dialog will *not* be Greek to you.

Washington Hall is center stage for theatre at Notre Dame, providing a splendid and historic backdrop for performances that run the gamut from independent student and residence hall players to quasi-professional productions by the Department of Film, Television, and Theatre. In recent years, live theatre has flourished at Notre Dame, and the department's marvelous Mainstage series is known for offering a wide variety of plays. Whether your tastes run to Shakespeare or Broadway musicals, you'll enjoy these stylishly staged productions, and the intimacy of the hall's auditorium—it seats only about 600 people— practically makes the audience part of the performance. You can obtain performance and ticket information by calling 219/631-5956.

One of the things you're sure to notice about Washington Hall is that the building's design is eminently suited to what goes on inside it. The architecture is, well, dramatic. Washington Hall was erected in 1881 to replace the Music Hall, which had been incinerated during the catastrophic Main Building fire, and architect Willoughby Edbrooke embellished this new structure with an ambitious mishmash of gables, moldings, and windows in his favored "modern Gothic" style. Topped by a spire, Washington Hall was supposed to echo the architecture of both the neighboring Main Building and nearby Sacred Heart Church. Father Sorin himself named the building in honor of his great hero, George Washington.

During the last hundred plus years of its existence, Washington Hall has served as the center of much of the university's cultural life. A steady stream of noted speakers—William Jennings

*"Someday, Rock," he said,
"when the team's up
against it, when things
are going wrong and the
breaks are beating the
boys, tell them to go in
there with all they've got
and win just one for the
Gipper. I don't know
where I'll be then, Rock,
but I'll know about it and
I'll be happy."
—Knute Rockne*

Bryan, Joyce Kilmer, Will Rogers, Henry James, William Buckley, Art Buchwald—has crossed its venerable stage, and the hall was the also the scene of countless concerts, commencements, shows, band practices, and, of course, Washington's Birthday celebrations. On Saturdays it was even a movie house. Notre Dame started showing films there in 1916, and students could attend for free. The intent was to keep them from seeing films of questionable content in South Bend, but going to the movies at Washington Hall became a campus custom that continued until the mid-1960s.

No self-respecting theatre, of course, would be without a ghost, and you will be pleased to know that Washington Hall is said to be the haunt of not one but three different apparitions. In fact, you can take your pick. They are (1) an unfortunate musician who swallowed his trumpet, died on stage, and has been moaning about it ever since; (2) a steeplejack who fell to his death in 1886 and goes angrily about slamming doors; and (3) George Gipp, the all-American football player whose spirit can now be heard running across the roof. The story, by the way, is that Gipp, who loved a good time, partied past curfew one night and was locked out of his room in Washington Hall. He ended up spending the night on the fire escape. There he caught a cold, which led to severe strep throat that caused his death and prompted Knute Rockne's fabled "Win one for the Gipper" speech. The Hollywood movie starring Ronald Reagan as Gipp made the actor very popular, and you might say it helped him enter politics, which resulted in his running for President, which . . . well, you get the idea.

LAFORTUNE STUDENT CENTER (43)

This building started as Notre Dame's Science Hall and was the brainchild of Rev. John Zahm, the foresighted priest who relentlessly

Washington Hall

pushed the university toward scientific and technological advancement. Designed by Zahm and
Willoughby Edbrooke in a vaguely classical style,
it was Notre Dame's first separate facility for science classrooms and laboratories, and after opening in 1883, the hall quickly became a hotbed of
experimentation. A dynamo installed in its basement provided Notre Dame with one of Edison's
latest wonders, electric lighting. Jerome Green, a
brilliant young electrical engineering professor
fascinated by Marconi's inventions, built his own
wireless telegraphy instruments. In the 1890s, he
became one of the first Americans to transmit a
wireless communication when he sent a message
from Science Hall to what is now Crowley Hall.
Albert Zahm, who was Father Zahm's kid brother
as well as a budding aeronaut, used the hall to test
his flying machines, launching his homemade
gliders from the roof and trying out propellers in
the building's two-story museum. One night
Zahm's assistant was trying to fly a foot-powered
model in the museum, when he lost control and
had to brace his feet against the walls and ceiling
to keep from falling. The next morning a Holy
Cross brother spotted footprints high on the walls
and, thinking they had surely been made by the
devil, promptly doused himself and the entire hall
with holy water. Science Hall became the
LaFortune Student Center back in 1953, but
Albert Zahm's aeronautical adventures there have
not been forgotten. If you look in the lobby,
you'll see a painting that portrays one of his early
biplane experiments and the startled onlookers
scattered in front of the building.

LaFortune, by the way, is still sustaining
campus movers and shakers. Its upper floors
house the headquarters of many important student clubs and organizations, ranging from government to a student-run alternative music
station, WVFI. Although the basement has the
Allegro coffee house and retail shops (you can
tell when there's an SYR by the line in front of

*The Huddle may look
like a totally modern food
court, but its origins
actually go back to the
late 1800s, when Brother
Leopold Kaul ran a sweet
shop in the Old
Fieldhouse. "Brother
Leep" served up lemonade
and chocolate-
marshmallow cookies to
several generations of
students before retiring
during World War I.
After the war, the
university opened a new
snack bar, and it was
briefly operated by two
South Bend businessmen.
They christened it "The
Huddle" because they
wanted students to gather
there. Gather they did,
and as a result, the
Huddle survived both the
Depression and another
World War before finally
finding a permanent
home in LaFortune
Student Center.*

LaFortune

the florist), LaFortune's main floor is where most students go to relax, socialize, and even study. With lots of chairs, sofas, and bigscreen TVs, it's very much like a huge family room, and the hospitable atmosphere there encourages informal concerts or impromptu performances by students (if you're lucky, you might catch an event such as the Glee Club's serenade of Christmas carols with a cookies-and-eggnog encore). But what good would a family room be without a kitchen nearby? And in the case of LaFortune, the kitchen is the Huddle, a large and much-used food court that features standbys such as pizza and hamburgers. The Huddle's considerable larder is supplemented by the deli counter at the Huddle Mart, a combination convenience store and eatery. Both of these establishments stay open well past midnight and will deliver any menu or store item to anyone at anyplace on campus (you might spot their tug-like vehicles transporting a cheese-and-pepperoni along the quad's pathways).

Nobody would have appreciated that kind of flexibility more than Joseph LaFortune, who graduated in 1916. A native of South Bend, he was allowed to attend Notre Dame even though he had no high school diploma, and because he had to work full-time, the university even arranged his classes in commerce around his schedule. Mr.

LaFortune moved to Tulsa, Oklahoma, after graduation and did very well there in the oil business. He chose to "repay a kindness to Notre Dame" by using some of his wealth to transform the university's science building into a student center. Three decades later, when LaFortune hall needed to be enlarged and updated, his family continued the payback by funding much of the project.

CROWLEY HALL OF MUSIC (42)

Until 1916, this two-story building was a three-story building. That's when a chemistry experiment gone awry caused an explosive phosphorus fire. The sparks not only cost the hall its top floor, but also prompted the construction of a dedicated chemistry building (now Riley Hall). Probably no classroom building on campus has been recycled as many times as Crowley Hall. It was originally used for engineering, then pressed into service for chemistry, pharmacy, architecture, law, psychology, and music, and at one point it even became a military recreation center. As the hall's identity shifted, so did its name. The aliases began with Institute of Technology, then changed to Hoynes College of Law, and finally ended with Crowley Hall of Music in 1976.

One of Notre Dame's oldest structures, this neat, rather dainty-looking brick building is located near the southeast corner of Main Quad and was built in 1893. It was another one of Father Zahm's pet projects, and he worked with Brother Charles Harding to design a proper facility for educating engineering students. The engineers quickly outgrew this hall, and after they vacated it in the early 1900s, the succession of diverse tenants began. In the mid-1970s, the hall was adapted for the last time when it was outfitted with studios and rehearsal rooms to become the newest home of Notre Dame's expanding Department of Music. This fine tuning occurred courtesy

Joseph W. Evans Memorial Crossroads Park (305)
Located directly behind Crowley Hall, this small, but very pretty plaza was named for a legendary philosophy professor at Notre Dame, and it serves as a shortcut between Main and South quads. It also makes a fine place for a respite, offering inviting benches, delightful landscaping, and as a charming bonus, the uplifting sound of young singers rehearsing in Crowley Hall.

of John B. Caron, class of 1945, a New York industrialist and university trustee. His gift was made in memory of his brother-in-law, Patrick F. Crowley, a Chicago attorney who was graduated from Notre Dame in 1933. Mr. Crowley and his wife Patricia played a principal role in founding the international Christian Family Movement, and in 1966, they were the first *couple* ever to receive the university's Laetare Medal.

The Department of Music has a 150-year history that can be traced to the beginnings of the university. Music, in fact, was so important to

NOTRE DAME'S BRICKS

One of the factors that contributes immeasurably to the beauty of Notre Dame's campus is the uniformity of the materials used on the exterior of its buildings. The predominating pattern consists of slate roofs, copper for spouting and other functional elements, Gothic accents done in neutral-colored limestone, and, most significant of all, "buff" bricks that allow new buildings to visually blend with the old. The bricks for Notre Dame's early buildings—including monumental structures such as the Main Building and the Basilica of the Sacred Heart—were produced on campus from rich marl deposits at St. Mary's Lake. The marl yielded ochre-colored bricks, which naturally established the color scheme for the entire campus. When the university was constructing North Quad in the 1930s, it needed a supply of color-compatible bricks to put on its new buildings. Paul Belden, who was a recent Notre Dame graduate, provided the solution. His family owned a brick company based in Canton, Ohio, and they were able to produce the blend of tan-toned bricks that Notre Dame wanted. The blend was named Santa Barbara, and it was used on virtually every new Notre Dame building constructed before 1980. That year, the Belden company developed a new, but similar blend for Notre Dame—Burbank—that has been lending harmony to the university's latest buildings ever since. By the way, the value of Notre Dame's bricks has risen considerably since Father Sorin began selling the university's homemade bricks. In the 1840s, the price was $3 per thousand. But in 1996 when Notre Dame's Stadium was getting its new addition, whole bricks that were original to the structure were sold as souvenirs for $125 *each.*

Notre Dame's founders that a music hall was one of the first major buildings they constructed on campus. That 1846 hall, like so many of Notre Dame's early buildings, was lost to fire, but music instruction at the university would both survive and continue to thrive, particularly in the area of sacred and liturgical music. With the university's introducing a fine arts requirement and going co-ed in the 1970s, the music department grew rapidly and is now renowned for its many first-rate performing groups. The two oldest of those groups, incidentally, also happen to be the most famous: the Glee Club, founded in 1915, and the Marching Band, which started circa 1846.

RECOMMENDED READING

Visitors desiring detailed information about the Main Building and the Basilica of the Sacred Heart should consult *A Spire of Faith: The University of Notre Dame's Sacred Heart Church*, and *A Dome of Learning: The University of Notre Dame's Main Building*. Both of these very scholarly books were written by Thomas J. Schlereth, Professor of American Studies at Notre Dame.

MAIN QUAD'S GREAT VIEWS AND SPLENDID SIGHTS

From the front steps of the Main Building looking south toward the Sacred Heart statue: Stand here in warm weather and you'll get a panoramic view of the splendid foliage and flowers in Main Quad's arboretum. Try it when the leaves have fallen from the trees and you'll be able to see the remarkable line of landmark statues—Sacred Heart, Sorin, Our Lady of the University—*that leads* from the heart of the campus toward Notre Dame Avenue. Speaking of hearts, if you look closely you can tell that the walkways leading south from the base of the steps to the Sorin statue form an elongated heart indicative of the Sacred Heart of Jesus. The "heart" was once used as a carriage-way to the Main Building, and at its center

Continued

stands one of Notre Dame's most notable representations of Christ: the Sacred Heart *statue with the simple Latin phrase* Venite Ad Me Omnes *("Come Everyone to Me") carved in its base. Sculpted by Robert Cassiani, the statue was dedicated during the 1893 commencement exercises, and its unveiling was one of the last public acts that President Thomas Walsh ever performed. Since the statue's Christ figure faces* Our Lady *on the Golden Dome and has his arms outstretched, Notre Dame students say that he is telling Mary, "Don't be afraid to jump, Mom. I'll catch you!" A few years ago, a severe storm knocked the statue onto the ground, and days passed before Jesus was back in his rightful place. An unknowing tour guide was walking backwards and explaining to his group how they wouldn't be seeing the statue. Suddenly he turned around, and there was Jesus. "My goodness," exclaimed the guide. "He has risen!"*

From the Sorin *statue facing north: This is the flip side of the view from the Main Building. The statue is positioned at the tip of the elongated heart, affording an absolutely splendid look toward the Main Building and Golden Dome. Sculpted by Ernesto Biondi, this memorial to Father Sorin was placed here in 1906, and a major east-west*

road then ran in front of it. Since the statue marked the university's main entrance, Father Sorin's likeness was purposely placed facing outward so that "the majestic form and features of the venerable founder" would be the first to welcome everyone coming to Notre Dame. With his proper priestly garb and flowing beard, Father Sorin does appear every bit the elder statesman ready to receive company. His hands hold a crucifix and a book, symbols of the faith and learning that were the focus of his life. And on the base of the statue, a Latin inscription provides a brief biography. This is what it says:

> To God, the Greatest, the Best
> In Memory of Father Sorin,
> Superior General of the
>   Congregation of Holy Cross,
> Founder of the University
>   of Notre Dame,
> Who was Renowned for his
>   Apostolic Virtue
> And Devoted to American
>   Catholic Education.
> Born February 6, 1814,
> He Lived for 78 Most
>   Fruitful Years.
> As a Token of Their Respect
>   and Gratitude,
> Students, Alumni, and Friends
> Erect this Testimonial.
> In the Year of Salvation, 1905.

SORIN COURT

Located immediately north of the Main Building, this small quad has long been considered the university's "backyard." Sorin Court enjoys landmark views of the Golden Dome as well as St. Joseph's Lake, and its historic buildings enclose a landscaped corridor that opens toward the water and is graced by a ceremonial drive. Constructed during the Main Building's renovation, the drive leads to a tasteful period entry on the building's north facade. Although this is now a rather quiet corner of the campus, the backyard was once crowded with support facilities. Walking here a hundred years ago, you would have come upon the Holy Cross sisters' convent plus the university's kitchen, printing press, power plant, stockyards, and privy. There was also a train station serving the Notre Dame & Western Railroad, a private branch of the Michigan Central line. The Zahm Special transported students to and from campus, and during football season, the station teemed with alumni arriving for the games. Most of the backyard structures disappeared years ago, but those that remain are among the oldest edifices on campus. Although they now have new uses, these time-honored brick buildings not only bring considerable charm to Sorin Court, but also make it a memorable place to visit.

EARTH SCIENCES BUILDING (77), FIRST YEAR OF STUDIES (34), AND BROWNSON HALL (94)

North of the Main Building on the west side of Sorin Court, the first three academic structures that you'll encounter were all built in 1855 as part of the convent of the Sisters of the Holy Cross. The first Holy Cross women came to Notre Dame from France in 1843, and for the next 115 years, their intense loyalty and labors on Notre Dame's behalf contributed immeasurably to its success. The convent, which remained open until 1958, was designed by Father Sorin and Brother Francis Xavier Patois, C.S.C., a young French carpenter who served as the university's earliest architect. Although the convent was a rather plain and functional building, its south side had a lovely circular chapel that is now the domain of earth sciences. The porch that you see marks the entry to the headquarters of First Year of Studies, the college into which all of Notre Dame's first-year students are admitted. First Year of Studies allows students to experience a broad curriculum of basic college studies before they commit to a

"OLD IRASCIBLE"

The structure called Brownson Hall is actually the second place at Notre Dame to have that name. The *original* Brownson Hall was the wing of the Main Building that housed the collegians. Both Brownson halls, however, memorialize Orestes Augustus Brownson, a philosopher, social reformer, and leading Catholic layman of the nineteenth century. Born in Vermont, Brownson was a convert and vigorous defender of Catholicism who not only knew the great literati of his time—Emerson, Hawthorne, Thoreau—but also published a successful quarterly dealing with political and social issues. Although intellectually gifted, Brownson was also ill-tempered, stubborn, and argumentative. He alienated many people, including Martin Van Buren, who blamed his 1840 defeat on Brownson's opposition. For years Father Sorin tried to persuade "Old Irascible" to teach at Notre Dame, but until his dying day in 1876, Brownson refused. Ten years later, however, Father Sorin finally got him to Notre Dame, albeit against his will. Brownson's family moved his remains to the Crypt of Sacred Heart Church, and his grave site can still be seen there today.

specific major. It also offers academic workshops, tutoring, and other advisory services through the First Year Learning Resources Center, which is located across the old convent courtyard in Brownson Hall. Notre Dame initiated the First Year of Studies in 1962, and it is now credited with playing a major part in the university's excellent 96 percent retention rate for freshmen, which is one of the highest in the nation.

Brownson Hall

LEWIS HALL (80)

Located just north of the old convent, Lewis Hall was built in 1965 as a residence for sisters pursuing advanced degrees, and it now is one of the university's largest women's dormitories. Julia Deal Lewis provided much of the hall's funding in memory of her husband, Frank J. Lewis, a Chicago philanthropist who liked to "drop in" on Notre Dame in a helicopter. Although the architect, Minnesota's Ellerbe Associates, gave Lewis Hall very modern, straightforward styling, its courtyard contains a superb bronze sculpture—Ivan Mestrovic's *Madonna and Child*—that is well worth taking the time to see.

Nicknamed the "Chicks," Lewis Hall's residents have a reputation for being fearsome competitors in interhall football, and they raise money for charity by hosting Camp Lewis, an outdoorsy event featuring crafts, bonfires, and singing. Between June and August, Lewis Hall also becomes a summer camp of sorts for Notre Dame graduates who participate in Alumni Family Hall, a popular program offering on-campus vacations. Alumni and their families not only room in Lewis Hall but also get to enjoy special liturgies, programs, and the university's cultural and recreational facilities.

MAIL DISTRIBUTION CENTER/ LAUNDRY DISTRIBUTION CENTER (96)

Once this building near Holy Cross Drive was a circa 1900 maintenance shed. But in 1991, after a fire destroyed the old St. Michael's Laundry near Lewis Hall, that humble shed was enlarged and transformed into a place that disperses two of the most essential items of undergraduate life—mail and laundry. The mail center here handles all of the university's in-house items, while the campus post offices processes first class mail. The laundry center serves solely as a drop-off and pick-up point for students; the actual washing and dry cleaning is done at the *new* St. Michael's Laundry (401) north of Douglas Road.

UNIVERSITY HEALTH SERVICES (46)

Built in 1934 on what is now the east side of Sorin Court, this fine structure has an entire wing that overlooks St. Joseph's Lake. Architects Maginnis and Walsh of Boston designed it with several gables and a tall copper fleche so that it would blend with their other campus buildings, and on the west facade, Notre Dame artist Eugene Kormendi executed a statue of Christ as *The Good Shepherd* and also of *St. Raphael*, the patron of nurses and physicians. The building was originally called the Student Infirmary, and, as its updated name implies, it continues to be used for health care. The facility includes inpatient as well as outpatient clinics, a laboratory, and a pharmacy.

ST. EDWARD'S HALL (45)

Whenever you see old pictures of Father Sorin with Notre Dame's grade school students, you can't help but notice the hint of fun in his face. Especially in his later years, when Father Sorin acquired a wintry beard, he looks very much like a Victorian Santa Claus surrounded by youngsters in bow ties and high button shoes. To those boarding school boys, he really was something of a Santa, treating them to peaches and sending a wonderful new toy—the velocipede—from Paris. Almost everyone at Notre Dame called them the "minims." But to the benevolent Sorin, the boys were "little princes," and in 1882, he had Brother Charles Harding, C.S.C., build them a proper "palace" on a site just northeast of

Brownson courtyard

Gate to Brownson courtyard

*Stained-glass
window of
Father Sorin
in St. Edward's
Hall chapel*

University Health Services

On November 21, 1925, Knute Rockne made his first communion in the chapel at St. Edward's Hall. A convert to Catholicism, Coach Rockne had been baptized the day before in the Log Chapel but kept it a secret from his son, Knute, Jr., who was one of the hall's minims. Knute Jr. was scheduled to make his own first communion on the 21st and as he approached the altar to receive the sacrament, Rockne surprised the boy by getting in line beside him.

the Main Building. It was a French-style, man-sard-roofed structure that Father Sorin named St. Edward's Hall after his own patron.

St. Edward's was a complete boarding school for boys between the ages of six and thirteen. It had classrooms, study halls, dormitories, a chapel, a recreational annex, playing fields, and a beautifully landscaped park outside the front door. In 1929, Notre Dame discontinued its grade school programs, and under the direction of architecture professor Vincent Fagan, St. Edward's was remodeled into a residence hall for undergraduate men. The annex was demolished in the 1930s to make room for Zahm Hall on the new North Quad, but when the Navy invaded Notre Dame during World War II and turned it into a virtual training base, St. Edward's—along with Sorin Hall—remained a dormitory for the relatively few men on campus who were actually university students. In 1980, a serious fire on the fourth floor badly damaged the building. Instead of summoning the wrecking ball, Notre Dame hired Cole Associates in South Bend to rebuild St. Edward's, restore its original architectural features, and construct a look-alike addition to provide more space for students.

Much of the character of St. Edward's Hall comes from the treasured stained-glass windows in its second-floor chapel. These eight brilliantly colored windows each contain between 200 and 300 pieces of glass, and they were all made in France: four by Hucher and Sons in 1888, and four by the Echivard studio in 1912. Three of the windows depict Saints Edward, Anthony, and Andrew, while the other five show scenes from the life of Christ. In the second floor stairwell, another Hucher and Sons window portrays Father Sorin, the Log Chapel, and the Main Building in rainbow-like shades of yellow, green, and purple. Fortunately, the windows escaped the worst of the flames in 1980, and they were fully restored by the DeVac company of Plymouth, Minnesota. Even the frames surrounding the windows designed in a complementary custom color called "Notre Dame gold."

Now on the National Register of Historic Places, St. Edward's is the oldest existing student dormitory on campus. It is also the only one whose residents don't have a nickname. They do, however, have a strong identity. The men of St. Edward's not only act in their own theatrical productions but also stage an annual charity carnival that, say some, makes them the "kings" of An Tostal. The dorm no doubt assumes its regal status from the landmark statue located in the pretty garden just a few feet from its front door. Made in Paris by the Froc-Robert studio, the statue represents Edward the Confessor, the English king who started Westminster Abbey and was later canonized. It shows Edward wearing a crown of crosses, and the building he holds is not the abbey but a replica of Notre Dame's Basilica of the Sacred Heart.

St. Edward the Confessor

LAND OF THE LAKES

Even when he first saw it in the starkness of early winter, the landscape around St. Mary's and St. Joseph's lakes immediately enchanted Father Sorin. A century and a half later, it is still the most pristine part of Notre Dame, a naturally scenic place where vestiges of the fringe of forest that he encountered can still be seen and enjoyed. The spring-fed lakes—St. Mary's to the west and St. Joseph's to the east—serve as a combination park and nature preserve, and although they are quite peaceful, the lakes have never been isolated. In the university's early days, the lakes provided food, ice, recreation, a bathtub, marl for bricks, and water for steam.

Today, people love to walk or jog on the interconnected trails and footpaths around the lakes; students swim and sail across the waters; couples stroll by the shoreline after SYRs; and there always seems to be somebody reading or relaxing on a bench along the banks. On any given day, you're likely to see roller bladers in spandex, nuns in veils, toddlers on tricycles, parents pushing strollers, and, of course, young lovers walking hand-in-hand.

The lights of the campus romantically reflect off the lakes at night, but most of the land surrounding them is actually a place apart from the university. Historically as well as legally, it belongs to the Holy Cross religious. Soon after Notre Dame started, the university began concentrating its academic buildings to the south and east of what is now Holy Cross Drive. The more secluded lake grounds became the retreat of the priests and brothers, and they built seminaries and other religious facilities there. When control of the university's operation was transferred to lay trustees in 1967, the Holy Cross congregation retained custody of the lake property.

You can get a good perspective on the lakes and their history from Old College and the Log Chapel, which are perched on the gentle hillside just south of St. Mary's Lake. Since those two structures represent the infant Notre Dame, they are a perfect place to start touring the lakes. Next, walk east to the beautiful outdoor shrine at the Grotto and then go across Holy Cross Drive to the pleasant finger of land between the lakes. Christened "the Island" in Notre Dame's early days, this land is now crossed by St. Mary's Road, and it provides a wonderful introduction to the serenity as well as the beauty of the lakes.

LOG CHAPEL (12)

In 1842, when Father Sorin and his band of Holy Cross brothers first arrived at the mission site that they would transform into a university, they found a small log cabin near St. Mary's Lake. It had been built a decade before and used as a chapel by Rev. Stephen Badin, an indefatigable frontier priest who resumed the missionary work that Father Claude Allouez, the Potawatomi's first "Black Robe," began near South Bend in the late 1600s. Father Sorin and his companions lived on the first floor of the cabin, and they put their chapel in its small attic. Until they could build more adequate structures, that rude cabin was the University of Notre Dame.

Log Chapel

The Log Chapel that you see today is *not* the cabin Badin built, but a replica. The original cabin burned down in 1856, and this copy was constructed 50 years later. Erected very close to the original's site, it serves as a rustic, but meaningful reminder of both Notre Dame's humble roots and the hardships faced by the missionaries who labored there. The plans for the Log Chapel were based on the memories of elderly Holy Cross brothers who had actually lived or worshipped in the Badin cabin, and it was constructed by William Arnett of Kentucky, a former slave who knew how to hand hew logs with a broadax. Father Badin is now entombed under the floor of the Log Chapel. Although he died and was originally buried in Cincinnati, he had often told Father Sorin that he wanted to be laid to rest at Notre Dame. After his cabin was reconstructed, Badin's remains were moved in order to finally grant his wish. Three other missionary priests are also interred beneath the Log Chapel: François Cointet, a classmate of Father Sorin's who died during the cholera epidemic that ravaged Notre Dame in the 1850s; Benjamin Petit, who passed away after accompanying the Potawatomis when they were forced to move to a reservation in Kansas; and the overworked Louis DeSeille, who died in Badin's original cabin. The young priest's final hours are depicted in *The Last Communion of Fr. Louis DeSeille*, a painting by Notre Dame artist John Worden that hangs near the Log Chapel's tabernacle.

Log Chapel altar

The simple interior of the Log Chapel is also enhanced by a painting of the Madonna and Child by Notre Dame's first artist-in-residence, Luigi Gregori. Its altar, which is made of cherry planks fastened by wooden pegs, came from a mission that Father Sorin started in nearby Bertrand, Michigan, for the Sisters of Holy Cross. Displayed in the sacristy are numerous items that belonged to several early priests and missionaries, including the vestments of Father Jacques Marquette, who accompanied the seventeenth-century explorer Louis Joliet. Although the Log Chapel is quite small, its enormous symbolic significance in Notre Dame's development makes it a popular site for weddings and baptisms, and you'll often see beaming parents and godparents bringing infants there. Also used for mass, prayer meetings, saying the rosary, and special events, the Log Chapel is usually open to the public on graduation and home football game weekends.

OLD COLLEGE (13)

Old College is often called the "Cradle of the University." It is the oldest structure on campus and has been in continuous use since it was constructed of bricks made from lake marl in 1843. You might say that this very modest and unpretentious structure was Notre Dame's first Main Building. Father Sorin had it erected as soon as possible in order to give his "university" some semblance of credibility, and Old College was initially a square, multi-purpose building that housed classrooms, the refectory, and sleeping quarters. He planned the building with Brother Francis Xavier Patois, C.S.C., a carpenter from Clermont, France, whose on-the-job training would render him the unofficial architect of several of Notre Dame's earliest buildings.

Old College was Notre Dame's first landmark structure, and it's known for the time-worn wooden sign that not only spells out its name in clumsy letters, but also signifies the building's long history. Over the years, Old College has been enlarged and modified countless times for a variety of uses—convent, band headquarters, bakery, farmhouse, guest house, and retreat house. During a campus housing shortage in the early 1970s, Old College housed a group of Notre Dame freshmen, and because a priest named

"The edifice is of brick, four and a half stories and not inferior in point of style or architecture to any of the Colleges of the United States, and is situated upon a commanding eminence on the verge of two picturesque and commodious Lakes, which with the river St. Joseph and the surrounding country, present a most magnificent prospect. The rooms are spacious, well ventilated and furnished with everything conducive to regularity and comfort."
—*early Notre Dame advertisement touting Old College*

Old College

Flanigan was their rector, the building was dubbed "Boys' Town." Old College is now used by the Congregation of Holy Cross as a residence for undergraduates who are considering joining the order as priests or brothers. Here, these university students experience the lifestyle of a religious community while still attending classes, participating in extracurricular activities, and working toward their academic degrees.

THE GROTTO OF
OUR LADY OF LOURDES (300)

Notre Dame's former president, Rev. Theodore Hesburgh, C.S.C., once observed that all universities have libraries, sports fields, and places to socialize. "But," he asked, "how many have a place to pray?" The Grotto is Notre Dame's praying place.

It was built in 1896 and is a replica of the internationally known cave near Lourdes, France, where the Virgin Mary appeared several times to 14-year-old Bernadette Soubirous, a peasant girl who was later canonized. Father Sorin had visited the French shrine several times and was very impressed with it. He reportedly even brought back bottles of the miraculous Lourdes water, and they were distributed nationally to anyone contributing to the construction of Sacred Heart Church. A few years after Sorin's death, a former Notre Dame student, Rev. Thomas Carroll of Oil City, Pennsylvania, donated much of the money needed to build the Grotto. Holy Cross provincial superior Rev. William Corby quickly approved its construction, and Notre Dame's Grotto—a one-seventh scale model of its French prototype—was built in only three months from boulders dug out of farm fields near the university. Its primary elements, like faith itself, are simple and direct: statues of the Virgin Mary and

LAND OF THE LAKES' GREAT VIEWS AND SPLENDID SIGHTS:
From the Grotto toward "the Island" and vice versa: What you have here comes under the category of double visions. "The Island" looks great from the grounds of the Grotto, and the Grotto, particularly at night when its candle lights dance in the darkness, looks really good from "the Island."

St. Bernadette, devotional candles, and a wrought iron railing for kneeling in prayer.

The wonder of the Grotto is not that people come to pray here, but that they come *constantly.* From the very day it was dedicated—August 5, the same providential date that Father Sorin left France for America—the Grotto has been the site of prayers, pilgrimages, and petitions to Mary. Its special solitude and sheer spirituality have made the Grotto a major American shrine, attracting not only the university's students, faculty, staff, and alumni, but also visitors from around the world. Day or night, no matter how late or early the hour, you can go to the Grotto and find folks young and old lighting candles and saying prayers. And every evening, come rain, shine, or one of South Bend's fearsome blizzards, the rosary is recited here, religiously, at 6:45.

Like all Notre Dame landmarks, the Grotto has its own set of customs and traditions. Before big games and final exams, the Grotto glows with candles lit by students, and in 1985, they lit so many prior to the Notre Dame-Michigan game that the shrine actually caught fire when the candles ignited their plastic holders. The Grotto is a favorite place for marriage proposals, and flowers are frequently left here—bridal bouquets, corsages worn by mothers at JPW, sprays freshly cut from backyard gardens. Every year, members of the senior class gather at the Grotto for a "Last Visit" of songs and prayers, and for many alumni, it's the first place they go when they arrive at Notre Dame and the last place they visit before they leave.

The power of the Grotto was poignantly expressed by Dr. Tom Dooley, a member of the class of 1948 who posthumously received the Congressional Medal of Honor for his medical work among the people of Southeast Asia. From his deathbed in 1960, the St. Louis native wrote a now-famous letter to Father Theodore Hesburgh expressing his feelings about the Grotto, where today a sculpture by Rudolph

Torrini, class of 1959, memorializes him. The statue depicts Dr. Dooley caring for two Laotian children, and a copy of his letter is displayed nearby. This is a bit of what he had to say: "But just now, and just so many times, how I long for the Grotto. Away from the Grotto, Dooley just prays. But at the Grotto, especially now, when there must be snow everywhere, and the lake is ice glass, and that triangular fountain on the left is frozen solid and all the priests are bundled in their too large, too long old black coats, and the students wear snow boots . . . if I could go to the Grotto now, then I think I could sing inside. I could be full of faith and poetry and loveliness

The Grotto in spring

The triangular fountain to which Dr. Dooley's letter refers is still at the Grotto. Titled "Living Water," the fountain was sculpted especially for the shrine in the 1940s by Connecticut-born artist William Schickel (class of 1944). Its figures of Jesus represent three images of water from the New Testament—Christ at the well, preaching from a boat, and washing his disciples' feet. The fountain stands over a spring that was uncovered during the Grotto's construction and is supposedly in the same relative position as the water that flows at Lourdes.

and know more beauty, tenderness and compassion. This is soggy sentimentalism, I know. Cold prayers from the hospital bed are just as pleasing to God as more youthful prayers from a Grotto on the lid of night."

The largest tree on campus—and in surrounding St. Joseph County—is the almost 100-foot-high sycamore growing on the Grotto lawn. It's also believed to be Notre Dame's oldest tree, for the sycamore probably sprouted even before the university was started in 1842. Legend has it that the tree's low, wide-spread limbs represent the outstretched hand of a Potawatomi Indian who died on the very spot where it now flourishes.

"THE ISLAND"

This area between the lakes is a positively splendid place to walk. The traffic is minimal and the atmosphere almost sacred, a wonderfully tranquil medley of broad lawns, shady sycamores, and pretty lake views in the truly pastoral setting of Holy Cross land. St. Mary's Road runs through the middle of "the Island," and if you follow it northwest toward Douglas Road, you'll find the woods increasing and the thicket growing denser. There are two Holy Cross buildings along the way—the utilitarian Holy Cross Annex (11) and Columba Hall (30), a brothers' residence. Built at the turn of the century, Columba Hall was named for one of its long-time residents, Brother Columba O'Neill, C.S.C., and it is also the site of the Solitude of St. Joseph, a retreat center. St. Joseph is the Holy Cross brothers' patron, and the statue just southeast of Columba Hall shows the saint tenderly holding the Christ Child.

If you walk far enough, you'll come to one of the most respected, yet least known places on campus. Few maps, in fact, even show it, but you will know when you have arrived there by the wrought iron entry arch on the southwest side of the road that says "Holy Cross." This is the Community Cemetery, burial ground of the priests and brothers and a place deserving of great consideration. Assuming Father Sorin was right and Notre Dame is the handiwork of Our Lady, then those interred here were definitely her agents. Make no mistake: they built Notre Dame. Beneath hundreds of small crosses lie the university's founding fathers and those who came after them: those who had the vision and those whose work made it a reality. Their names are the ones you see on Notre Dame's buildings, the ones you hear attached to its legends, and the ones that have faded into obscurity. Since death is the ultimate democracy and does not distinguish

Ancient Grotto guardian

Columba Hall

between a president and a plumber, their crosses are all identical and have been neatly arranged in soldier-straight rows reminiscent of Arlington National Cemetery. Here, however, there are no hordes of tourists, for the Community Cemetery is a very private place.

As you walk through the cemetery, you'll notice that the priests and brothers have generally been buried in the order in which they died. As a result, Community Cemetery provides a unique —and quite permanent—chronology of Notre Dame. Father Sorin lies at the foot of the large crucifix at the south edge of the cemetery. Next to him is Father Gilbert Français, a superior general who wanted his priests to also be scholars; not far away are presidents Morrissey and Burns, as well as Father Michael Shea, who co-wrote the "Victory March." Here also are the dedicated brothers such as Francis Xavier Patois who followed Sorin to America, as well as priests whose impact would extend far beyond the campus: the scientist Julius Nieuwland, the intellectual John Zahm, and the inimitable rector John "Pop" Farley.

Only a handful of non-religious have been given the honor of being buried in the Community Cemetery, and they all, of course, had some connection with the university. The first was professor Joseph Lyons, after whom the South Quad dorm is named, and he was followed by two of Notre Dame's foremost "bachelor dons," professors Paul Fenlon and Francis "Frank" O'Malley, who are buried in the same row. The pioneer aeronaut and Laetare Medalist Albert Zahm is here and so is Edward Lee Greene, one of the world's foremost botanists and nature writers at the turn of the century. Greene was held in such esteem that after he died in 1915, Father James Burns, C.S.C., the Holy Cross provincial, had a monument placed on his grave with the epitaph, "A man whom nature in all her phases attracted and engaged and for whom she opened a door leading unto the house of God." Finally, you'll definitely want to seek out the grave of John Mangan, the feisty Irish immigrant who spent 40 years as the university chauffeur. "Johnny," as everyone called him, knew that Holy Cross seminarians pray every day for those buried in the Community Cemetery. He always said that he wanted to be buried there so that a lot of people would be praying for him. He was, and they do.

ST. MARY'S LAKE

Of Notre Dame's two lakes, St. Mary's is the more park-like. It has fewer buildings, less trees, and more benches. In spring, this lake is the site of Fisher Hall's spirited regatta; in summer, people picnic on its banks; in winter, snowmen appear; and in the fall, the water turns a deep blue that brilliantly reflects the Golden Dome and Sacred Heart spire as well as the magic autumn hues. You can circumnavigate St. Mary's Lake via its footpaths all year long. When you do, you'll be treated to the sight of elegant swans gliding along the water, graceful old willows hugging the shoreline, the lovely statue of St. Thérèse "the Little Flower" on the bank above the north shore, and,

LAND OF THE LAKES' GREAT VIEWS AND SPLENDID SIGHTS
From the west side of St. Mary's Lake: Almost any locale along here yields exceptional views of the main campus, but the one from the extreme western tip of the lake really shows off the Basilica and Golden Dome.

St. Joseph's Lake

if you're very lucky, a heron or two coming in for a landing. If you're not so lucky, you'll find the poison ivy.

FATIMA RETREAT CENTER
AND SHRINE (3)

Built in the 1950s, the Fatima Retreat Center is not part of the campus but a separate ministry

operated by the Congregation of Holy Cross. Notre Dame students do come here routinely to participate in weekend religious encounters, and the grounds have some good views of the university. Although you can see the outdoor Stations of the Cross from the lake path, the center's best-known feature is a shrine representing Mary's apparitions before three children at Fatima, Portugal, in 1917. The lawn near the lake is dotted with bird feeders and is frequently invaded by a flotilla of friendly ducks, who look right at home as they leisurely preen themselves on the sunlit grass.

The old St. Mary's marl pits that proved so advantageous in building nineteenth-century Notre Dame were located only a few hundred feet from present-day Carroll Hall. Bricks made from the marl were not only used for campus structures but also became a cottage industry that put some much-needed cash in the university's coffers. By 1858, in fact, Notre Dame's kilns were producing about a half million bricks every year.

CARROLL HALL (1)

This men's dormitory is so far from the rest of the campus that students call it Notre Dame's "Siberia," and in winter, when snow blankets St. Mary's Lake for weeks on end, it can seem an especially remote and frozen place. That's the bad news. The good news is that Carroll Hall is the only undergraduate dormitory actually on a lake, and its idyllic location overlooking St. Mary's western shoreline ranks as one of the most scenic spots on campus. Yet another example of Brother Charles Borromeo Harding's building skills, the dorm was constructed in 1906 as a residence for the Holy Cross brothers and was christened Dujarie Institute in honor of their founder. Decades later it was converted to an undergraduate dormitory, and the name "Carroll Hall" was borrowed from the old high school wing of the Main Building.

Although Archbishop John Carroll was one of the nation's earliest and most esteemed Catholic leaders, the hall's residents have opted for a lowly nickname—the Vermin—in deference to the rodents that once ruled their basement. Carroll Hall has one of the smallest populations as well as some of the largest dorm rooms on campus, a pair of distinctions that, along with its isolation, help make the Vermin a real rat pack. Because of the Vermins' long-distance relationship with the rest of the university, they ride a lot of bicycles and are prone to be late for class (one Carroll resident who spent too much time in the shower explained his wet hair to his professor by saying he had fallen in the lake). The Vermin are most famous for their Halloween celebration. Carroll Hall's old-fashioned architecture and lonesome setting make it a perfect Haunted House, and there is always a long line of students waiting at the door to see what horrors—ominous chain saws, scary slides down the staircase, maybe even a few rats—wait inside.

ST. JOSEPH'S LAKE

There is a definite duality about St. Joseph's Lake, which manages to be reverent and recreational at the same time. Not only are the majority of Holy Cross buildings located here, but the lake is also the site of a much-used swimming beach and Boathouse. Actually, this presents some rather rare opportunities. At how many other places, for example, could you make the Stations of the Cross (they're posted in the woods just beyond the lake's southwest shore) while catching a glimpse of a crisp white sail?

The trails around St. Joseph's Lake are covered with a thick canopy of trees, and their shade cools the air and makes hiking or jogging there quite pleasant even on the warmest days. Although there are steps leading to the lake trails from the edge of Holy Cross Drive, most people begin their walks on the paths near Columba Hall. The Stations of the Cross, which were done in bronze by Ernest Thorne Thompson, are close by, and to the northwest across the water, the same sculptor's huge cross—*Crucifixion*—stands silhouetted against the trees. As you head counterclockwise around the lake, you're sure to notice the wide variety of wild plants—myrtle, honeysuckle, raspberries, goldenrod, roses—and if you stand near the water's edge, schools of small fish are likely to appear and wait for you to feed them. At the east end of the lake, you'll come to the picturesque Boathouse (92) and sands of St. Joe Beach, where Notre Dame students, faculty, and staff members go swimming when lifeguards are on duty. A short distance beyond them are Holy

LAND OF THE LAKES' GREAT VIEWS AND SPLENDID SIGHTS
From the north side of St. Joseph's Lake: The area between Moreau Seminary and St. Joseph's Hall presents a panoramic perspective of Notre Dame that includes three Notre Dame landmarks— the Golden Dome, Basilica, and the Hesburgh Library.

Cross House (47), a modern retirement and medical facility for retired priests and brothers, and the Province Archives Center (99), where the Holy Cross community's history and documents are preserved. The trail then passes two final buildings—Moreau Seminary and St. Joseph Hall—before veering south toward "the Island" and Columba Hall.

MOREAU SEMINARY (32)

The ground for this seminary was broken on May 13, 1957, one hundred years to the day after the Congregation of Holy Cross received the Vatican's official stamp of approval. The man who started the congregation by merging two groups of French priests and brothers was Rev. Basil Moreau, C.S.C. This modern training facility for future Holy Cross members is named in his honor, and a bust of Father Moreau by Ivan Mestrovic was commissioned for its opening.

Moreau Seminary Chapel

Moreau Seminary faces St. Joseph's Lake, and when you're traveling the lake trails, the building is impossible to miss. Architects Belli and Belli of Chicago gave it a distinctive curved shape, and the chapel juts toward the water with a huge wall of stained glass. Designed by Notre Dame art professor Rev. Anthony Lauck, C.S.C., the marvelous figures in the wall represent angels attending their Divine Master and are made from slabs of "jewel glass" bonded in concrete. The flame-shaped sculpture you see on the bricks of the seminary's south facade is called *Descent of the Holy Spirit* and was executed by David Hayes, class of 1953. Also on the Moreau grounds are Father Lauck's prayer monolith and an expressionist pietà by Waldemar Otto.

Monk Hoops:
Twice every week, the gymnasium at Moreau Seminary is the site of "Monk Hoops," the late-night pickup basketball games led by Notre Dame's president, Father Edward "Monk" Malloy.

ST. JOSEPH HALL A.K.A.
SACRED HEART PARISH CENTER (31)

This yellow brick building dates back to 1920, and before Moreau Seminary was constructed, it was the Holy Cross seminary as well as a residence hall for graduate students. Since 1994, St. Joseph's Hall has been used as an activity and education center by the members of Sacred Heart Parish, who worship in the Crypt of Notre Dame's Basilica. Architecture professor Jaime Bellalta provided the plans needed for its renovation, and the parishioners raised the money needed to create classrooms, offices, recreation, and meeting facilities. The bedrooms on the upper floors were even "adopted" by parish families, who personally took on the task of painting and decorating them.

Although the center is a well-proportioned building with elegant arched windows that look out on the lake, its best single feature has to be its lakeside setting. The steps on the south facade lead directly to the trails around the lake, making all of the natural beauty of the woods as well as many parts of the campus easily accessible by foot. Since the center sits on a slight rise above the water, the views are delightful. Luckily, you can have the opportunity to experience the views for yourself, because Sacred Heart Parish now makes those adopted bedrooms available to overnight guests. Even though the furnishings are minimal, the rooms are clean and reasonably priced. The Ritz it ain't, but you can't beat the center's location. And as a bonus, you'll get a unique wake-up call every morning, because the ducks that live on the lake usually commence their quacking with the sunrise. For more information about reserving a room, contact Sacred Heart Parish Center at 219/631-9436 or 219/631-7511.

THE CONGREGATION OF HOLY CROSS

The French Revolution wreaked havoc on the Catholic Church, and in its aftermath, Father Basil Anthony Moreau hoped to help repair the damage. On March 1, 1837, he formed an association of priests and brothers whose services as auxiliary clergymen, teachers, and missionaries would be available wherever they were needed. Moreau called this new apostolic community the Congregation of Holy Cross after Sante-Croix, the small town near LeMans where it was founded. After a few years, a society of sisters was also allied with the congregation, and the Holy Cross ministry quickly spread from France to other nations. Its members were especially successful in the United States, where they founded numerous parishes, schools, and colleges, including the University of Notre Dame, Saint Mary's College (Indiana), Holy Cross College (Indiana), St. Edward's University (Texas), the University of Portland (Oregon), King's College (Pennsylvania), and Stonehill College (Massachusetts). In addition, Holy Cross priests, brothers, and sisters currently serve in Bangladesh, India, Brazil, Chile, Peru, Haiti, Uganda, and Kenya.

Holy Cross members identify themselves with the letters "C.S.C.," and their emblem is a cross superimposed on two anchors. Anchors are an age-old symbol for hope, and the cross represents Christ. Thus, the emblem signifies that all hope comes from Christ.

RECOMMENDED READING

If you would like to know more about Notre Dame's early history, you should seek out *Notre Dame: One Hundred Years* by Rev. Arthur J. Hope, C.S.C. First published in 1943 by Notre Dame Press, this very readable centennial history remains a highly informative and entertaining volume. Although it is now out of print, it may be found in some libraries.

SOUTH QUADRANGLE

The South Quad is Notre Dame's grand mall, a long and almost luxurious expanse of dormitories and classroom buildings that covers the distance of nearly six football fields from the Rockne Memorial building to O'Shaughnessy Hall. Along the way, it not only intersects with Main Quad to the north and Notre Dame Avenue to the south, but also serves as a very well-traveled bridge between the east and west sides of the university

Sheer size, however, is only one aspect of South Quad's greatness. Thanks to a remarkable trove of Gothic architecture, it possesses the added—and far more significant—dimension of being the most classically collegiate quad on campus. Indeed, with its splendid assemblage of soaring arches, vaults, angles, and spires, there is something of a movie set quality about South Quad. Cast your eye on virtually any of its buildings, and you can easily envision a picture-perfect backdrop for pennant-waving students in raccoon coats who drive Stutz Bearcats and dance the Varsity Drag.

South Quad's character, in fact, was formed during the Roaring Twenties, an era when events both on and off campus resulted in the extraordinary structures that now constitute a veritable case study in collegiate Gothic architecture. Early in the twentieth century, there was a resurgence of interest in using Gothic architecture for public buildings, and the idiom was commonly translated to college and university buildings across the country. The end of World War I had also dramatically increased the nation's college enrollments. Accordingly, Notre Dame faced a housing crunch so severe that a sizable number of its

Alumni Hall gargoyle

students had to find quarters off campus. The administration viewed this situation with great concern, for it considered the students living in South Bend particularly susceptible to the relaxed social standards that were making the twenties roar. If the university hoped to hold its undergraduates to at least a lusty purr, it needed to build more dormitories.

President Matthew Walsh, C.S.C., turned to Professor Francis W. Kervick for help. The head of Notre Dame's architecture department, Kervick created a plan for a major new quadrangle in 1920. Running perpendicular to the Main Quad, it was designed to shift Notre Dame's future development to an east-west axis by displacing the cows and hogs from what was then university farmland. Kervick, who detested modern architecture, recommended Gothic buildings for his proposed South Quadrangle. It proved to be the ideal architecture for a university coming into its own during the 1920s. Notre Dame was no longer an obscure Midwest school, but enjoyed a national reputation because of its growing success academically and athletically. The majestic details of collegiate Gothic—steeply pitched gable roofs, finials, parapets, and lancet arches—were the perfect vehicle to proclaim the university's new-found prestige. Moreover, its skyward lines reflected both the spirituality that Gothic architecture symbolized during medieval times and the postwar optimism that was infecting the university as well as the nation.

Since Kervick's concepts would influence Notre Dame's physical form for decades, it was extremely fortunate that the university had the means to bestow the trappings of the Gothic tradition on his freshly hatched quad. Shrewd investments and fund-raising by the lay board of trustees were nicely augmenting the university's endowment, and the lessons of frugality learned during Notre Dame's early years of hardship were also paying off. In addition, the dollars generated

by Knute Rockne's electrifying football teams became available to enhance the entire campus as
well as help sustain it during the dreary 1930s.

Kervick teamed up with a colleague, Notre
Dame architecture professor Vincent Fagan, to
design South Quad's initial halls—the delightful
trio of Howard, Lyons, and Morrissey—in collegiate Gothic, and architects of subsequent buildings reveled in continuing the style. Father Walsh's
successor, Rev. Charles O'Donnell, C.S.C., over-
saw most of the quad's development in the late
1920s and early 1930s. However, because of the
launching of North Quad and a construction
slowdown during World War II, much of the
quad was not completed until the 1950s. Consequently, the style of South Quad's later buildings— Fisher, Pangborn, and the old bookstore,
for example—manifested the postwar period's pre-
vailing taste, with tried-and-true collegiate Gothic
forsaken for the far simpler and more massive
forms of modern architecture.

*Weeping student on
Howard Hall arch*

According to Kervick, the South Quad was
supposed to simulate "that sequestered peace one
feels on the common of an early American village." His intention has been admirably achieved,
for the quad's broad mall is today very much like
a village square, constantly crisscrossed by students emerging from dorms, walking to class, and
heading for the South Dining Hall. Many of the
elms planted when the Quad was new are now
grown tall enough to lend their shade to the stunning interplay of towers and turrets with gables
and gargoyles, and even the arrangement of
buildings borrows the private side / public side
pattern traditionally found in town squares. If
you stand at the flagpole near the center of South
Quad, you'll notice that it divides the "private"
cluster of residence halls on the west side from the
"public" academic buildings on the east.

One of the beauties of Gothic architecture is
its human scale. Since the style consists of many
individual elements that require considerable

craftsmanship, it has a level of detail that relates extremely well to people. As a result, South Quad's architecture lends it a certain personality—energetic, open, and outgoing—that presents an excellent contrast to the contemplative, somewhat subdued mood in Main Quad. Perhaps the most telling measure of collegiate Gothic's success at Notre Dame is that the quad has become the place people naturally gather on football weekends. In many ways, South Quad is at its dynamic best on those mellow autumn days, when its unique atmosphere—part street fair, part family reunion, part pilgrimage—synthesizes all the pre-game excitement and anticipation. Would-be quarterbacks scrimmage on the grass. Students manning concession stands hawk steaks, sandwiches, and sodas. Grown men show up dressed like leprechauns. Old friends meet with handshakes, hugs, and a tear or two. The names of Hornung, Holtz, Parseghian, and Powlus hang conspicuously in the air. A solitary bagpiper strolls through the crowd, and the "Cheer-cheer-for-old-Notre Dame" refrain echoes incessantly from the dorms. And all the while, the old grads clad in gold and blue plaid look appreciatively at the glorious quad that surrounds them and wax sentimental about the time-honored buildings that so handsomely graced their youth.

Howard Hall arch

THE WEST SIDE OF SOUTH QUAD

HOWARD HALL (15)

Howard Hall was South Quad's inaugural building, the first shot in the revolution of campus design and reorientation so effectively marshaled by Kervick and Fagan. Built in 1924, this dormitory not only debuted collegiate Gothic architecture at Notre Dame, but also was the first university building purposely created in direct relationship to other buildings. Its companion residence halls—Morrissey and Lyons—were completed the following year, and the masterful positioning of these three brick buildings formed a gracious courtyard that time has turned into a private mini-quad adjoining the larger South Quad mall. Architecturally, this venerable trinity is considered by many to be the crème de la crème of Notre Dame dormitories. When they opened, the halls were so impressive that students called them the "Gold Coast," and taken together, they still put on a great front, especially when their show of Gothic detail is viewed from inside the courtyard.

Howard Hall arch

Howard Hall's distinguishing feature is an open, double-barreled arch that both bisects the building and acts as a passageway between the courtyard to the west and Badin Hall to the east. The arch displays wonderful bas-reliefs that are especially charming on its east face. Above one side are two unmistakable symbols of autumn at Notre Dame—a football player and a squirrel. Above the other, an owl casts a sharp eye upon a tearful student bemoaning his exam book. The owl, of course, stands for wisdom, while the weeping youth recalls the "whining schoolboy" who represents the second age of man in Shakespeare's *As You Like It*.

The owl and the student are particularly appropriate for Howard Hall, since it was the first Notre Dame building named for a lay professor, Timothy E. Howard. Born on a farm outside Ann Arbor, Michigan, Howard entered Notre Dame in 1859 and earned his undergraduate degree by tutoring the minims. His first university post was as a professor of English literature, but he soon took on astronomy, scanning the heavens with a fine telescope that Emperor Napoleon III had donated to the university. The good professor, however, had his own sights set far beyond South Bend. After earning a Notre Dame law degree in 1873, Howard entered local politics, got elected to the Indiana Senate, and eventually became

*Howard Hall's chapel
holds a limestone
sculpture of the
Pietà by Jean de Marco.
It was anonymously
commissioned for the hall
and dedicated in the
Marian Year of 1954.*

chief justice of Indiana's Supreme Court. In addition, he somehow found time to write poetry and short stories, publish histories (including one of the university), become an expert on tax codes, lecture on law at his beloved alma mater, marry, and father ten children. When Notre Dame honored Howard with its Laetare Medal in 1898, he also became the first South Bend resident to receive that coveted award. A statue of his patron saint—St. Timothy—was done by art student James Kress and is now installed in the niche above the west face of the Howard Hall arch.

Howard Hall stayed a strictly male domain for 63 years until being converted to a women's dormitory in 1987. The new distaff residents were promptly dubbed "Ducks," presumably because of *Howard the Duck*, a less-than-stellar movie that was released shortly before they moved in. Since then, it's become a tradition for Howard women to roast —no, not ducks!— *marshmallows* on the night of the school year's first snowfall.

LYONS HALL (8)

Located directly across the courtyard from Howard Hall, Lyons Hall is justifiably famous for its lovely entrance arch, one of the most elegant and attractive architectural features found at Notre Dame. The arch frames what is arguably the prettiest view of St. Mary's Lake on campus, but Kervick had more than that single striking vista in mind when he designed Lyons Hall. Prior to South Quad, Notre Dame's development had focused primarily on the Main Building, largely ignoring the natural beauty of St. Mary's and St. Joseph's lakes. Kervick intended for the South Quad in general and Lyons Hall in particular to correct that oversight by directing the campus toward the lakes. In addition, he purposely positioned the Lyons arch opening so that its lake view could also be enjoyed from a variety of places in the quad.

Lyons Hall arch

Like the Howard Hall arch, the Lyons arch was also embellished with bas-reliefs and a patron saint statue. In the niche on the courtyard (east) side of its arch stands a likeness of St. Joseph. It was placed there because the hall is named after Joseph Lyons, who arrived at Notre Dame as an orphan and eventually became one of its most dedicated professors. Trained at first as a shoemaker in the Manual Labor School, Lyons began to take classes and managed not only to earn a degree but also graduate with honors in 1862. He joined Notre Dame's faculty as an English instructor and moved into a modest room in the Main Building. There he joined the ranks of Notre Dame's bachelor dons, an avuncular cadre of professors who devoted themselves to mentoring their students. In 1869 Lyons wrote the university's silver anniversary history, and ten years later, when the Main Building burned, it was Lyons who went to Canada to give Father Sorin the heart-breaking details of the disaster. Lyons died in 1888 and was laid to rest in the Community Cemetery, the first layman ever accorded the honor of being buried among the Holy Cross priests and brothers whose life work had also been Notre Dame.

SOUTH QUADRANGLE'S GREAT VIEWS AND SPLENDID SIGHTS Of St. Mary's Lake: Although the view at Lyons arch is unequaled, the lake also looks very good looking through the arch from the north entrance steps of the South Dining Hall. For a closer (and definitely quieter) vantage point, go to the Founders' Monument.

Lyons Hall

Perhaps Kervick had Joseph Lyons's story in mind when Lyons Hall was on the drawing board, for he incorporated quarters for lay professors into the dormitory's design. Most were in the wing east of the arch, but he did locate a few of the faculty rooms over the arch itself. Kervick was obviously satisfied with the fruits of his labor, since he himself moved into Lyons Hall and lived there for many years. A pious man, Kervick was also responsible for the beautiful Lyons chapel, a subterranean, medieval-like sanctum reached by a winding staircase.

Lyons was once an honors hall for Notre Dame's most scholarly students, but it got a totally new identity in 1974, when it became one of the first halls changed from a men's to a women's dormitory. The ladies of Lyons, a.k.a. Lyonites, have established themselves as some of the best athletes on campus by winning interhall championships in football and soccer. Every year, they also sponsor a charity volleyball tournament and fun run. In the spring, Lyonites can be spotted sunbathing on "Lyons Beach," the land that descends from the rear of the dorm to St. Mary's

Lake. They use that same slope for sledding during long winter nights. As for the Lyons arch, even after dark, its lights-shimmering-on-the lake view is enchanting. This makes the arch a favorite place for residents to say goodnight to their dates, thus serving a romantic purpose that even Kervick with his painstaking plan could never have anticipated.

MORRISSEY HALL (10)

Morrissey Hall was Kervick's and Fagan's baby, both the centerpiece and the pièce de résistance of their pet courtyard. It was the largest, costliest (a considerable $725,000 in 1925), and most lavishly detailed of their collegiate Gothic trio. Morrissey has come to be known as "the Manor," an appropriate sobriquet obviously inspired by its tall, castle-like entrance tower. With its carved lintels and decorative ogees, the dormitory lords over the heart of the courtyard with an authoritative air worthy of the abode of some feudal chatelain. Some call the dormitory's architecture inspiring. Others find it forbidding.

Just above and to the left of the hall's main entrance, you'll notice a statue mounted in a masonry niche. The X-shaped cross on the front of the niche tells that the statue represents the crucified apostle St. Andrew, the patron saint of the hall's namesake, Rev. Andrew Morrissey, C.S.C. Born in Ireland, Morrissey came to the United States as a youth and received his education at Notre Dame. He was serving as the university's Director of Studies when he was unexpectedly propelled into the presidency by the deathbed request of his young predecessor, Rev. Thomas Walsh. Shortly after Morrissey took office in 1893, Father Sorin also died, making him the first Notre Dame president completely free of its founder's formidable presence. Morrissey's twelve years in office, however, proved to be a holding pattern rather than the launching pad for a new

About the time that the insignia of Oxford and Cambridge were installed in Morrissey Hall, the University of Notre Dame proudly acquired its own newly created shield: a blue field with a gold cross, a silver star, two wavy lines, and an open book with the Latin words Vita, Dulcedo, Spes. Blue and gold, of course, are the traditional colors of Mary, while the motto, which translates as "Life, Sweetness, and Hope," comes from an age-old prayer to the Blessed Mother. The cross indicates the Congregation of Holy Cross; the star, Mary's status as the Star of the Sea; the wave-like lines, Notre Dame's lakes; and the book, learning.

era at the university. Although the world at large was progressing into the twentieth century, he was determined to keep Notre Dame both debt free and tied to its past. A kind and genial man, the portly Morrissey clucked over the minims like a mother hen, busying himself checking their ears and tracking down packages sent by their mothers. He wanted Notre Dame to remain a "compact, tidy little boarding school" and waged an ongoing tug-of-war with Rev. John Zahm, the Holy Cross provincial who believed that the university had a far more important destiny. After Morrissey's presidential term ended and he took over as provincial in 1905, Zahm departed Notre Dame for good.

Ironically, the hall that bears Morrissey's name was one of the first buildings to herald Notre Dame's growth into the "intellectual center" that Zahm had always advocated. On the site where the university had once had a rude barn, this aspiring Gothic edifice was erected in 1925. Its west wing displayed an outdoor pulpit reminiscent of European cathedrals, and the richly appointed entrance hall had the look of a gentleman's club with fine wood paneling and a fireplace. For academic inspiration, the dorm was also outfitted with a painting of a student pouring over a book and the shields of the world's great universities.

Morrissey Hall is now in its eighth decade as a dormitory, and the men of the manor no longer spend their evenings lingering by the fire in neckties and suit coats. Instead, they have turned Morrissey into one of the most active—and charitable—dorms on campus. Combining fun and philanthropy, the "Manorites" annually sponsor both a Polar Run (in their underwear) to raise scholarship money and a student film festival that benefits an outreach center. They always have breakfast outdoors on the morning of the first football game, and following their traditional Christmas SYR, treat their dates to pancakes in the South Dining Hall.

The dorm's exceptional camaraderie may stem in part from its historically close quarters, where generations of Manorites dwelled in some of the most cramped rooms on campus. Particularly notorious were the Dirty Thirty, the basement habitats whose occupants had access to only two showers. Recent renovations and updates, however, have dispatched the Dirty Thirty, enlarged the residents' rooms, and added lounge, laundry, and study areas. On the outside, Morrissey got a new roof and some other repairs, but its famous facade was kept timelessly intact.

KERVICK AND FAGAN

They were New Englanders and they were architects, but otherwise, the two men whose happy collaboration established South Quad and made collegiate Gothic Notre Dame's signature architecture could not have been more different. The Massachusetts-born Kervick was quiet, introspective, and a bachelor. An Ivy Leaguer schooled at the University of Pennsylvania, he had studied in Europe and traveled widely. Kervick was the master planner who could conceive great schemes such as South Quad. Fagan, on the other hand, was a family man. A Connecticut native, he graduated from Notre Dame in 1920 and had a reputation as a wit and storyteller who enjoyed an audience. It was Fagan who gave South Quad its special personality, for he focused on nuance and details, devising the playful masonry carvings and ornamentation that lend a uniquely Notre Dame touch to the timeless Gothic styling of its buildings.

The contrasts between them, by the way, even extended to the written word. While the loner Kervick authored a serious tome titled *Architecture at Notre Dame*, the gregarious Fagan formed *another* partnership with his brother-in-law, band director Joseph Casasanta. Together they produced two popular Notre Dame fight songs, "Hike, Notre Dame" and "On Down the Line." Casasanta composed the melodies, while Fagan penned their peppy lyrics.

Bond Hall

BOND HALL (14)

From the steps of Bond Hall: With its 19 stately steps and pretty plaza, the front entrance of Bond Hall is not only a pleasant place to linger, but also provides a fine, eastward view of Main Quad's arboretum.

Now serving as Notre Dame's School of Architecture, this beautiful building just north of Howard Hall was originally the university library. It was built in 1917 and named the Lemonnier Library in honor of Rev. Auguste Lemonnier, C.S.C., a native of France and the nephew of Father Sorin. The accomplished Lemonnier was a lawyer who possessed a flair for languages and a talent for art. When he became president of Notre Dame in 1872, Lemonnier had the laudable intention of bettering its academic status by improving facilities and setting standards suitable to higher education. Sadly, he never realized his ambitious plans for a "well equipped college." After only two years in office, Lemonnier died from nephritis at the age of 35. He did, however, manage to leave Notre Dame one very important legacy—a general, centralized library where all students could use and borrow books.

After Lemonnier initiated the university library in 1873, miscellaneous faculty and club collections were gathered and organized at one location in the Main Building. Its holdings were modest—at first only about 1,200 volumes—but Lemonnier's brainchild is believed to have been the first circulating library established at any Catholic college or university in America. Virtually the entire library was lost in the infamous 1879 fire, but it grew Phoenix-like out of the ashes and by 1895 had expanded into a collection of more than 50,000 volumes housed in the new Main Building. The library's tireless director, James Edwards, so diligently amassed books, artifacts, and manuscripts that some materials even had to be stored between the beams of the Dome.

Clearly, the burgeoning collections needed a home of their own, and just in time for Notre Dame's Diamond Jubilee celebrations, the new Lemonnier Library building was completed. Curiously, it was constructed almost due west of Walsh Hall on farmland that was some distance from the Main Quad. According to campus lore, the location was chosen to separate the library from Main Quad's older, fire-prone buildings. Another explanation is that the site anticipated a new east-west quad that never materialized behind Walsh and Sorin halls. Whatever the reason for its placement, the Lemonnier Library made a magnificent birthday present for Notre Dame. It was the first structure at any American Catholic college or university specifically built as a library, and architect Edward Tilton of New York dressed the building up in true Classic style with a low-hipped roof, a symmetrical facade, and Ionic columns defining

The Notre Dame Shield on Howard Hall

Morrissey Hall

Bond Hall

The Founders' Monument

Since the School of Architecture's demanding curriculum emphasizes design experience, Notre Dame's architecture majors have tackled projects ranging from reproducing a Palladian arch to creating houses for the local chapter of Habitat for Humanity. The long, often grueling hours they devote to their designs have become legendary. If you notice empty coffee cups and soda cans stacked inside the windows of Bond Hall, it's a sure sign that the "Arkies" have been working all night . . . again.

the round-arch entryway. Sheathed in Indiana limestone, the Lemonnier Library remained the only stone building on campus until, coincidentally enough, the modern Hesburgh Library was constructed in 1963.

After the Hesburgh Library opened, this building became the province of Notre Dame's architecture department, which for many years was part of the College of Engineering. Architecture enjoys a special place in the university's curriculum. The earliest classes were taught just after the Civil War, and in 1898, Notre Dame introduced a bachelor of science degree program that was a first for the state of Indiana as well as the nation's Catholic universities. As the department grew in size and stature, it evolved into a full-fledged School of Architecture renowned for its requirement that students spend a year living and studying in Rome. In addition to a five-year bachelor's degree program in architecture, the school currently offers a master's program with concentrations in both classical studies and urban design.

As it turns out, the Classic elements that Tilton bestowed on Bond Hall so long ago have now made it the perfect setting for the university's architects, who are pioneering an educational movement back to the time-honored design traditions of ancient Greece and Rome. Led by chairman Thomas Gordon Smith in the early 1990s, Notre Dame's School of Architecture was the nation's first program in decades to embrace the discipline of a Classical curriculum. The school has since been hailed as "the Athens" of the new Classical movement, and it boasts the only fully accredited Classical architecture curriculum in the United States.

The three principles of Classical architecture are beauty, utility, and strength, and all three were well utilized when this building was completely renovated and enlarged in the mid-1990s. Starting with a multi-million dollar gift from Memphis architect William Bond, Jr., class of 1950, Professor

Smith worked with the Ellerbe Becket company to design an American Renaissance style addition that harmonizes perfectly with Tilton's original, well proportioned exterior. Inside the building, a stunning architecture library now balances computer terminals with soaring columns, and a new café (appropriately called Poché, a term for the shaded "pockets" of space that appear on blueprints) caters to the students' late hours and tall appetites. Most impressive of all, Bond Hall's exquisite two-story foyer was given a colorful facelift. That wonderfully detailed oval space now dazzles visitors with bright and sunny hues, which are yet another of the enduring elements of Classic design.

BADIN HALL (18)

An elevated front porch complete with an inviting swing easily identifies Badin Hall, which, instead of facing the South Quad mall, is situated

Father Badin

perpendicular to it. Located due east of Howard Hall, this historic dormitory has stood its ground since 1897, when it was originally christened St. Joseph's Industrial School and served as the headquarters for the manual labor program where poor boys learned carpentry, tailoring, and other trades. The building's no-nonsense purpose was matched by its architecture, for Brother Columkille Fitzgerald, C.S.C., designed a rather plain, vernacular facade with only a single central gable and buff brick walls to coordinate it with the grander buildings on Main Quad. After Notre Dame phased out its trade school in 1917, the building became a dormitory. Sizable wings were added on the north and south sides, and it was renamed Badin Hall.

Over the years, the hall not only housed the campus bookstore, a cafeteria, a barbershop, and a travel bureau, but also was home to the two latest presidents of the university. Father Theodore Hesburgh resided in Badin in the late 1940s, when he served as chaplain to World War II veterans attending Notre Dame; Father "Monk" Malloy lived there as an undergraduate during the early 1960s. Since Badin's residents have a long tradition of community service, the hall now also makes a fitting location for some offices of Campus Ministry, which fosters spiritual growth and supports programs of Notre Dame's Center for Social Concerns.

When Notre Dame became coeducational in 1972, the first two residence halls converted to women's dormitories were Badin Hall and nearby Walsh Hall (on Main Quad). Badin's male inhabitants had dubbed it the "dungeon," but with the arrival of the ladies, Badin's austere image was transformed. Decorative curtains appeared on the windows, and, wonder of wonders, a convenient laundry room was actually installed in the basement. Today, Badin is Notre Dame's smallest women's dormitory, and its residents are nicknamed the "Attitude," a sobriquet that, considering their few numbers, probably comes in quite handy. In addition to sponsoring various charity events, they maintain a strong alliance with the men of Carroll Hall, which has the distinction of being the smallest dormitory on campus.

Chances are the present residents of the two halls aren't even aware of it, but there is a remarkable historic precedent for the Badin-Carroll connection. Badin Hall memorializes Rev. Stephen Theodore Badin, the first Catholic priest ordained in the United States, and the bishop who conferred Holy Orders upon him was none other than John Carroll, the future namesake of Carroll Hall. It was, in fact, Bishop Carroll who dispatched Father Badin to minister in the wilderness territory beyond the Alleghenies. There he would not only become a veritable Johnny Appleseed of American Catholicism but also procured the land upon which the University of Notre Dame was founded.

A native of Orleans, France, Badin came to the United States in 1792 to escape the vicissitudes of the French Revolution. He was ordained the next year and promptly sent west to sow the seeds of faith. His first assignment was Kentucky, a difficult and lonely mission for a 25-year-old urbanite who barely spoke English. Badin was the sole priest serving the new state's few and far-flung Catholics. He traveled constantly, spending weeks at a time on horseback and arriving at settlements before dawn in order to hear confessions before morning mass. A man of rigid and resolute faith, Badin handed out harsh penances, opposed dancing and liquor, denounced camp meetings, and crustily sparred with the local Protestant clergy. He also steadily acquired the real estate necessary for building the Church's foundations in an often hostile land. By the late 1820s, his mission had shifted north of the Ohio River and would spread into the old Northwest Territory states of Michigan, Illinois, Ohio, and

Indiana. Near South Bend, he began ministering to the Potawatomi people and purchased 524 acres of land that included two small lakes. Badin later deeded that land to the Bishop of Vincennes, who then turned it over to Rev. Edward Sorin, another French immigrant of great zeal and determination. Father Sorin promptly named the property *Notre Dame du Lac* and proceeded with the Herculean task of creating a university upon it. The aging Badin, having been the instrument of Notre Dame's first and greatest gift, continued his itinerant ministry. He died in 1853, and his body is now entombed on campus in the Log Chapel near the Founders' Monument.

BOOKSTORE BUILDING (19)

Designed by Notre Dame architecture chairman Frank Montana and his colleague Robert Schultz, this buff brick, slate-roofed building first opened its doors in 1955 as the Hammes Bookstore. It was the gift of Mr. and Mrs. Romy Hammes of Kankakee, Illinois, whose enterprises included automobile dealerships and housing developments. As generous supporters of many Catholic causes, the Hammes family, like the university, had a great devotion to the Virgin Mary.

At that time, the Hammes Bookstore was one of the nation's largest and most up-to-date college bookstores, and its arrangement of merchandise—logo clothing, souvenirs, school supplies, jewelry and religious items on the first floor; textbooks and trade books on the second floor— remained virtually unchanged until the enterprise moved to the new Eck Center in 1998. The bookstore stocked a mind-boggling selection of Notre Dame memorabilia, and it quickly became a campus bestseller. Students jammed the aisles to buy textbooks and sundries at the start of every semester, and on football weekends, notoriously long lines formed at the door, as Irish fans eagerly waited their turn to buy the latest batch of sweatshirts, trinkets, and mugs.

Much of the store's success was because of the efforts of Conan Moran, an Irish-born Holy Cross brother whose dedication was exceeded only by his business savvy. Affectionately known as "Brother Bookstore," he spent 40 years managing the store, nurturing it from an afterthought

BOOKSTORE BASKETBALL

The basketball courts behind the old bookstore building weren't fancy (regular players knew to avoid the manhole cover), but they had the unbeatable distinction of being the birthplace of one of Notre Dame's favorite traditions, the intense, campuswide tournament known as Bookstore Basketball. The games began in the early 1970s as part of An Tostal, the campus's annual springtime festival. Students formed a handful of impromptu teams and staged their own playoff on the bookstore courts. Since then, the backyard event has mushroomed into the world's largest basketball tournament with some 700 teams competing for the highly coveted championship. In showers, sunshine, sleet, and snow, the games are always played outdoors, and the players come from practically every segment of the university—women as well as men students, varsity and non-varsity athletes, faculty, clergy, staff, and administration. Its democratic premise underpins Bookstore Basketball's wide appeal, for it allows computer nerds to play alongside All-Americans and the All-Americans to compete against the university's "top" player, President "Monk" Malloy. A former Fighting Irish basketball letterman, Malloy remains an enthusiastic player. He has been part of several Bookstore Basketball teams, which, predictably, have been named "All the President's Men." Coming up with an unusual or humorous team name has actually become a competition in and of itself among Bookstore Basketball's participants. Over the years, they've easily scored with offbeat monikers such as "Dolly Parton and the Bosom Buddies," "Five Seniors Without a Job," "Ignorance Is Bliss," "Pontius Pilate and the Four Nail Drivers," "We Got the Tools but Not the Talent," and "Dr. Quasimodo to Proctology, STAT."

Dillon Hall detail

Alumni Hall

Knights of Columbus Hall

Dillon Hall sundial   *Alumni Hall sundial*

Badin Hall

Bookstore Basketball

stuck in the basement of Badin Hall to a full-grown retail establishment with one of the largest collegiate catalog operations anywhere. According to Brother Conan, the catalog started by accident in the late 1940s, when he mistakenly ordered too many tee-shirts. He mailed an advertisement to the alumni and sold out of the shirts so quickly that he had to reorder. *Voilà!* The bookstore's popular sales catalog was born. Brother Conan died in 1992, and five years later, the university turned over the bookstore's operation to Follett College Stores, a national retail chain while retaining the Hammes name.

When the bookstore has moved to the new Eck Center, this building is scheduled to be demolished and replaced by a new structure housing Campus Ministry and academic activities such as the First Year of Studies.

KNIGHTS OF COLUMBUS
COUNCIL HALL (85)

Although this small but beautifully crafted building nicely dresses up the northwest corner where South Quad and Main Quad intersect, you probably won't take much notice of the architecture if you see it on a football Saturday. That's because you'll be totally distracted by the young men who are out front on the lawn riding unicycles, juggling Indian clubs, and furiously grilling a couple of thousand steak sandwiches. They're the proud members of Notre Dame's Knights of Columbus, and every so often one of them will try to drum up some customers by putting on a plaid kilt, mounting a stepladder, and shouting exhortations to the pre-game crowd. "All right, you people," he'll yell. "Steak and soda pop. Only $5. And it's for the retarded children. Only $5. Go Irish! Eat Steak!"

Those savory steak sandwiches have not only become the staple of many a hungry fan's personal game plan, but are also the primary fund-raiser for several charities supported by Notre Dame's Knights. Their chapter, Knights of Columbus Council 1477, occupies a unique place within the national K. of C. fraternity. Started in 1910, it was the first collegiate council established by the Knights of Columbus. Among its 41 charter members were university president John W. Cavanaugh and young John O'Hara, a gifted undergraduate who would later become both the head of Notre Dame and a cardinal of the Catholic Church.

Council 1477 grew rapidly after World War I, and its members eventually became involved in service and religious projects that ranged from forming an orchestra (called the "Knightingales") to selling war bonds to sponsoring the Bengal Bouts to serving as ushers at mass. By the time the Notre Dame's Knights celebrated their fiftieth anniversary, a survey revealed that 90 percent of the nation's K. of C. councils had at least one former member of the Irish group on their rosters. Today, more than 800 student, faculty, and alumni members give Council 1477 the distinction of being the K. of C.'s largest college chapter.

The Knights are also the only Notre Dame student group with a building all their own. The K. of C. "clubhouse" is a splendid collegiate Gothic structure with distinctive, double lancet arches facing the South Quad. Built in the early 1930s, this brick and limestone building was designed by the Boston firm of Maginnis and Walsh. It served as Notre Dame's third post office until 1967, when the university acquired a larger, more modern facility to move its mail. Stamps ultimately gave way to steak sandwiches through the efforts of Eli Shaheen, class of 1934 and loyal member of Council 1477. The Sturgis, Michigan, industrialist made such shrewd investments on behalf of the Knights that they were able to negotiate a horse trade with the university: a $500,000 scholarship fund in exchange for use of the vacant post office building.

Although the building's exterior has changed little since the 1930s, the interior has been modified into a comfortable Council Hall with offices, study areas, a meeting room, and amenities such as a big-screen TV and pool table. It is, of course, a private, members-only facility, where the Knights socialize, conduct their rituals, and foster activities that promote the principles of charity, unity, fraternity, and patriotism. The doors, however, are always open to visitors on the morning before a home football game. Then you can go inside to participate in one of the Notre Dame Knights' most nostalgic traditions: nonstop showings of the irresistible 1940 movie, *Knute Rockne—All American*, starring Pat O'Brien as the beloved Irish coach and a very young Ronald Reagan as George Gipp.

ALUMNI HALL (23)

When people approach the university from Notre Dame Avenue, Alumni Hall is the first dormitory they encounter. It occupies a highly visible and strategic position, marking the boundary between the residential and academic sides of South Quad as well as the picturesque expanse where South and Main quads meet. Notre Dame could not have picked a better spot to put Alumni Hall, for it is one of the most impressive collegiate Gothic buildings on campus. Built in 1931, the hall displays some of Maginnis and Walsh's finest handiwork: decorative battlements, oriel windows, and a corner tower complete with gruesome gargoyles that are said to be modeled after those at the Cathedral of Notre Dame in Paris. Perhaps even more importantly, the exterior of Alumni Hall abounds with captivating stone carvings that are not only marvelous to see but also summarize various aspects of student life at

Clashmore Mike on Alumni Hall

Notre Dame. You'll have to look closely to locate some of them, however, because vines cover many of the hall's bricks and evergreens obscure parts of the walls. But this uniquely Notre Dame ornamentation is well worth the effort, for it puts the university in a fascinating pictorial context.

Starting on the east side of Alumni Hall, you'll find a bas-relief of a rotund man clutching a football. That's none other than Knute Rockne, and the nearby profiles of a dog depict Clashmore Mike, the terrier who was an early football mascot. Near the center of the east side's battlements, there is a young man holding a book and an hourglass, a gentle reminder that study time is precious. Go to the south side of the corner tower and look toward the top. You'll notice a sculpture of a young man in a cap and gown holding a diploma. He's "Joe College," a Notre Dame graduate confidently facing South Bend, and presumably, the world at large. The west side of Alumni Hall and the east side of neighboring Dillon Hall form a quiet, verdant courtyard that offers a pleasing northerly view of the quad. Inside the courtyard, the gable below Alumni Hall's chimney holds a sundial marking the afternoon and evening hours, while Dillon Hall has a corresponding one for the morning hours. The robed figures on Alumni Hall represent two great, but very different, Catholic philosophers from the thirteenth century: St. Thomas Aquinas, the "Angelic Doctor," and St. Bonaventure, the "Seraphic Doctor." On the north facade, the dormitory's main entrance is enhanced by bas-reliefs of two students (one reading, the other writing), while the chapel doors have a Madonna and Child sculpture. After Alumni Hall opened, the chapel—with its altars from Italy and Stations of the Cross handmade in Oberammergau, site of the centuries-old Passion Play—was dedicated to St. Charles Borromeo, patron of Notre Dame's then president, Rev. Charles O'Donnell, C.S.C.

Knute Rockne on Alumni Hall

The name Alumni Hall was chosen to recognize both the loyalty of Notre Dame's graduates and their deep pockets when contributing to the university. In the 1930s, the dormitory was considered quite palatial. Its rich appointments—fireplaces and wood paneling—were complemented by modern amenities such as private showers, slots for used razor blades, and the only electric elevator on campus. Since the cost of boarding here was also higher than at any other Notre Dame dorm, Alumni quickly became the most prestigious address on campus and, along with its companion, Dillon Hall, was dubbed the "Platinum Coast." When Navy trainees took over the campus during the 1940s, Alumni's undergraduates did their part for the war effort by doubling up. Things got so crowded, in fact, that residents claimed the only way somebody could come in the front door was if someone else went out the back.

With Clashmore Mike exhibited on the hall's exterior, it's no surprise that the men of Alumni call themselves the "Dawgs." Also not surprising is their long-standing rivalry with Dillon Hall. Alumni's "preps" and Dillon's "jocks" have often staged a battle of insults on the grounds of their mutual courtyard, and before the annual Dillon Pep Rally, the Dawgs typically attempt to swipe all of Dillon's shower curtains. Known for their fierce dorm loyalty and pride, the Dawgs consider their hall the "Center of the Universe" and even have their own "Dawghouse" newsletter. Through the decades, Alumni's residents developed many traditions, but the most famous now seems to be their annual Wake. This week of black comedy burlesques the rituals of a funeral and ends with an SYR.

DILLON HALL (20)

Held every autumn on the Thursday evening before the first home football game, Dillon's popular Pep Rally is a warm-up for the next

Dillon Hall detail

night's first all-school pep rally. Although smaller than the main event, it is by no means less spirited. The "Big Red," as Dillon's residents fancy themselves, use the opportunity to put on togas, bring in a band, do their best to defame the Alumni Dawgs, and just plain party on the dorm's front lawn. With many zany skits, songs, chants, and cheers, the Big Red entertains hundreds of people, and even the head football coach and some of his players stop by to help whip up the crowd.

The hall's namesake, Rev. Patrick Dillon, C.S.C., might well have approved of the pep rally's high jinks. The Irish-born priest became Notre Dame's second president in 1865, at age 33. Dillon was not only young but also very well-liked by the students because of his lenient approach to discipline. Although he would serve just one year before being called to France on Congregation business, his presidency made a truly lasting impression on Notre Dame. It was Dillon who supervised the construction of the second Main Building: a six-story structure that was propitiously topped by a white dome with a statue of Our Lady.

Like Alumni Hall, Dillon Hall is a collegiate Gothic building designed by Maginnis and Walsh, and it has been superbly adorned by sculpture, bas-relief, and other detail. In the Alumni-Dillon courtyard, for example, you'll notice an outdoor pulpit crowned by the Latin words *Scientia Dei* ("knowledge of God") and flanked by unicorns, the mythical animal that symbolized Christ in medieval times. Also in the courtyard is a statue of St. Jerome, the Latin scholar who translated the Bible and is often shown in the company of a lion. According to legend, St. Jerome bravely pulled a thorn from the paw of a raging lion that invaded his classroom. You'll also want to look for statues of the great theologian St. Augustine (at the southeast entrance); England's influential Cardinal John

Commodore Perry on Dillon Hall

Henry Newman (at the southwest entrance); and St. Patrick (on the south facade), who supposedly drove the snakes out of Ireland and was President Dillon's patron saint as well.

Dillon Hall's north facade shows a carving of a Viking ship inscribed with Greek letters. Chi and Rho are the traditional monogram of Christ, while Alpha and Omega signify Christ as the beginning and the end of all things. The ship is being "sailed" by St. Olaf, the heroic Norwegian king who brought Christianity to his country. Inside the hall, the altar in the chapel also holds an impressive marble statue of St. Olaf that is dedicated to the memory of Knute Rockne, a native of Norway. Rockne had lost his life only months before Dillon Hall opened in the fall of 1931, and this shrine was posthumously installed with donations from Notre Dame's students and alumni.

Among Dillon Hall's many saints, you can also find a few students. Go to the designated "Dillon Hall" entrance on South Quad, and you'll discover a bas-relief of two serious scholars. One of these young men is intently pouring over a book, while the other makes notes with a feather pen. In contrast, a weary (perhaps lazy?) student who has fallen asleep is portrayed on the hall's southwest corner. These representations of the mental side of undergraduate life are nicely balanced, however, by amusing images of its physical side. If you examine the doorway facing the South Dining Hall on Dillon's west facade, you'll discover four playful carvings of athletes. Their clothing and equipment will immediately tell you that they are a tennis player, a baseball player, a football player, and a runner.

SOUTH DINING HALL (17)

The undisputed apogee of collegiate Gothic architecture at Notre Dame, the South Dining Hall is one of the finest examples of the genre in

South Dining Hall

the United States. The fact that such an exquisite building bears such an ordinary name constitutes a devilish incongruity as well as a woeful injustice. Yes, its obvious function is to nourish the student body, but from the day its doors opened in 1927, the South Dining Hall's true feast has always been found in its form.

The hall's principal architect was no less than the estimable Ralph Adams Cram, who, as the nation's foremost Gothic Revival practitioner, had designed buildings at Princeton and West Point as well as New York City's Cathedral of St. John the Divine. The Boston-based Cram was a reactionary enthralled by the Middle Ages. He thought society should abandon mass production, the printing press, and the internal combustion engine and re-establish feudalism, walled cities, and craftsmen's guilds. In consultation with Kervick and Fagan, Cram purposely designed the dining hall to resemble a medieval guild hall that would represent "the incorporation of Western Christian culture into the modern American educational process."

The full-scale replica of the *Last Supper* that hangs in the west dining room was commissioned by Florida businessman Eugene Holton in the 1950s. Coincidentally, the original *Last Supper* had been painted on the wall of a refectory in Milan, and muralist Lumen Martin Winter traveled to Italy to study Leonardo da Vinci's strokes of genius before making his copy. The two colorful murals in the old Oak Room were done by Parisian artist Augustin Pall in the early 1940s to commemorate Notre Dame's hundredth anniversary. The one on the east wall depicts Father John Zahm exploring South America, natives at work on a rubber plantation, and Father Julius Nieuwland, who originated the formula for making synthetic rubber. Working with Father Nieuwland are two Notre Dame professors, and if you look closely, you can see President Theodore Roosevelt alongside his good friend Father Zahm. On the west wall, the mural shows Notre Dame's seminal log chapel, a traditional flag-raising ceremony on graduation day, the Golden Dome, and a set of girders that optimistically—and accurately—predicted the university's future growth.

Cram's floor plan consisted of two massive, refectory-like dining rooms connected by a two-story center structure containing the kitchen, a faculty dining room, and a public cafeteria that came to be called the Oak Room. On the building's exterior walls, reddish bricks laid in an English bond pattern provided a distinguished background for decorative elements executed in Indiana limestone. Although the dining hall had been positioned so that its best side directly faces South Quad, the entire exterior was swathed with wonderful Gothic details—a gracefully arched central porch, slender lancet windows, sharply peaked gables, oriel windows topped by battlements, and a tall lantern forming a stunning apex on the roof. On the stone arch over the east entrance, a fascinating pair of carvings depicted a football running back and an opponent eagerly waiting to tackle him. Similarly, the west entrance featured a plucky baseball pitcher and his opposing batter.

Inside the dining hall the cafeteria was rather pragmatically decorated with ceramic tiles—red ones on the floor, multicolor on the walls. The twin refectories, on the other hand, were magnificent. They had 35-foot-high ceilings spanned by hefty oak beams accented with elaborate glass-and-metal chandeliers. The walls were generously covered with oak wainscoting complemented by elegant orchestra balconies. At one end of each room stood an intricately carved limestone fireplace; at the other end was a raised platform for the rectors' and prefects' strategically placed table. Even the dining rooms' oak tables and chairs were minor works of art. They had been specially designed by Father Lawrence Broughal, C.S.C., and custom made by the Phoenix Chair Co. of Sheboygan, Wisconsin.

Given the South Dining Hall's size—each dining room held about 1,000 students—and grandiose architecture, it immediately became the benchmark for South Quad's future development. More importantly, it reinforced the Notre Dame "family" by making sure that everybody had a place at the campus table. Before the dining hall was built, the students' meals came from the "old kitchen" behind the Main Building. There, Holy Cross brothers and sisters had worked as butchers, bakers, and cooks since 1849, using the bounty of the university farms to prepare food that was then transported by wagons to the Main Building's dining rooms. The influx of students after World War I, however, made the "old kitchen" outmoded. After the Howard-Lyons-Morrissey trio ensured that all of Notre Dame's students could live on campus, the university spent nearly $2 million to provide a totally modern kitchen-dining facility where they could eat together in a civilized fashion.

From the beginning, the South Dining Hall was a success. Newspapers and magazines throughout the country carried articles applauding the quality of the building's architecture and the efficiency of its operation. Students dressed for dinner in suit coats and ties, and they marched en mass into the dining rooms, where the tables were covered with white cloths and set with china plates. Well-trained student-waiters brought in each course on silver platters, and the food was passed around family style. A clever system of electric flash signals orchestrated the serving process so precisely that the entire meal was consumed in 25 minutes. The timing was so good, bragged a Notre Dame press release, that "every student can be served ice cream without one getting a melted portion."

Alas, the gentility of these meals became a casualty of World War II. When Notre Dame was turned into a Navy training ground, the necessary evil of cafeteria lines likewise turned the South Dining Hall into a military-style mess. And as postwar America discovered TV dinners, cafeteria

It was not unusual for Holy Cross sisters and brothers to devote decades to their labors in the "old kitchen." Sister Mary Lourdes, for example, spent 40 years there and even came to be known as "Sister Coffee." She endeared herself to generations of students by slipping them forbidden treats between meals. Brother Willibrord, on the other hand, is credited with concocting the famous "Notre Dame bun." Served almost daily, the buns were apparently quite tasty, but they did not age well and hardened into objects with "the shell of a turtle and the interior of caulking compound." One student was inspired to write a poem about those "beatific buns." Another amused himself by putting an address and postage stamp on a stale Notre Dame bun and mailing it— successfully!—back home to his girlfriend.

*Annual quantities of food
consumed in Notre
Dame's dining halls:*
27,000 pounds of bacon
42,000 16-inch pizzas
71,000 heads of lettuce
*100,000 pounds of
breakfast cereal*
*166,000 pounds of
French fries*
425,000 fresh bagels
1,630,000 large eggs
*356,000 8-ounce
glasses of milk*
*900,000 8-ounce glasses
of orange juice*
1,000,000 cans of soda.

trays permanently replaced the dining hall's sit down meals. In the 1970s, the cumbersome cafeteria lines finally disappeared from the dining rooms, and students now make their selections from a central food court. Since youth must always be served, the dining hall's menus have followed the shift in student tastes from the standard steak-and-potato fare of the 1930s to today's nachos, Buffalo wings, and stir fry. When the university's food service decided to stop serving Cap'n Crunch cereal in the 1980s, the students promptly protested with demonstrations and a sit-in. Not only did the cereal reappear, but the Cap'n Crunch character also paid a visit to the campus to show his appreciation.

Remarkably, the character of the South Dining Hall has changed very little during the past seven decades. The north facade is as resplendently Gothic as ever, and the two main dining rooms have retained most of their original appointments, right down to Father Broughal's tables and chairs. In fact, the South Dining Hall did not undergo any major structural modification until 1997, when the development of West Quad put four new dormitories and 1,000 extra students at its backdoor. An architecturally compatible addition was also built on the hall's south facade. The 15,000-square-foot addition contains a retail sales area and provides an attractive approach to the dining hall for West Quad residents. Visitors will find freshly made fare at Reckers, a lounge-like restaurant featuring a wood-burning pizza oven.

Although students now come to break bread wearing sweatshirts instead of suits, the South Dining Hall still serves its original purpose as a communal gathering place. Here, the solidarity of the Notre Dame family continues to be fostered by customs large and small. Post football game buffets. Pancakes at midnight during final exams. Waffles embossed with the block N-over-D monogram. Cookies with "Beat Northwestern"

South Dining Hall detail

inscribed in icing. By taking the opportunity to eat in the South Dining Hall, you can not only experience its extraordinary architecture and atmosphere, but also observe some of these ever-evolving traditions for yourself. One of the nicest takes place on Friday evenings before home football games, when the Glee Club gives an informal concert in one of the dining rooms. The members all dine together at the raised table on the far end of the room, and just after 6 p.m., they climb on top of their chairs and break into song. The performance includes the opposing team's alma mater as well as Fighting Irish favorites such as "Hike, Notre Dame" and the "Victory March." By the way, the Glee Club conductor—in proper deference to the South Dining Hall—leads the singers with a butter knife instead of a baton.

FISHER HALL (9)

Located due west of South Dining Hall, this men's dormitory was a gift from Burtha M. "Sally" Fisher in memory of her husband, Fred, who co-founded the Fisher Body Company in Detroit. Mr. Fisher had been a member of Notre Dame's lay board of trustees, and his magnanimous widow also gave the university a revolving student loan fund and more than $1 million worth of art.

The Chicago firm of Holabird, Root and Burgee designed Fisher Hall, and when it was dedicated in 1952, its stark facade and square profiles presented quite a departure from the ambitious Gothic detailing evident on the rest of South Quad. Within a few years, however, Fisher Hall's neighbor, Pangborn Hall, was constructed in similar contemporary style. Since then, the modern architecture of these paired buildings has provided a visual counterbalance to Alumni and Dillon halls, the Gothic duo that anchors the opposite side of South Dining Hall.

Fisher Hall is easy to find when you're walking

on South Quad; just look for the concrete-and-brick building with the huge green "F" hanging on its front facade. Fisher's residents call themselves the "Green Wave," and their considerable campus fame comes from hosting the Fisher Regatta. One of An Tostal's most successful events, the regatta is a homemade boat competition held every spring on St. Mary's Lake. Various dormitories and campus organizations build their own watercraft and then attempt to sail, row, and otherwise propel their creations across the lake. No conventional rowboats, sailboats, surfboards or power engines are allowed, and some of the entries are so ingenious—a floating golf course, for example—that the race has been reported on CNN.

PANGBORN HALL (7)

A pair of lions guard the front door of Pangborn Hall, which bears the name of the two brothers who funded it, Thomas and John Pangborn of Hagerstown, Maryland. The Pangborns were not only extremely successful industrialists but also widely respected for their philanthropy and support of numerous educational, religious, scientific, and charitable endeavors. Thomas Pangborn, in fact, was lionized as one of the most outstanding Catholic layman of the twentieth century, and he received honors from three different Popes. Pius XII made him a Knight of Malta; John XXIII named him a Knight of St. Gregory the Great; and ultimately, Paul VI declared him a papal count in 1964. At the time, he was the only American ever to achieve that rank.

Pangborn lions

Count Pangborn was a member of Notre Dame's science and engineering advisory council, and when Pangborn Hall was dedicated in 1955, Pope Pius XII imparted an Apostolic Blessing on the Pangborn brothers as well as on the university. In addition to the building itself, the Pangborns donated the hall's simple but very striking chapel.

It featured green glazed brickwork, a black marble altar, and Stations of the Cross wood carvings that were imported from Italy. The stained-glass windows honored eight saints, including Pius X, who had just been canonized the previous year.

Pangborn Hall was the third and final building that Holabird, Root and Burgee designed for Notre Dame. Its completion filled the last "vacant lot" left on South Quad, and thus this dormitory became the modern period at the end of Kervick's grand Gothic statement. Originally a men's residence, Pangborn Hall was changed to a women's dormitory in the fall of 1992. The ladies promptly christened themselves "Phoxes," then cunningly titled their inaugural SYR "Twentieth Century Phox."

Rockne Memorial window

ROCKNE MEMORIAL (6)

Looking at it from the South Quad mall, you'd never guess that this beautifully proportioned brick building is an athletic facility. With its handsome arched loggia and august Gothic entrance, it looks more like a bastion of the liberal

Rockne Memorial

"If football is a good sport for the varsity player, why isn't it a good sport for the entire undergraduate body? Granted that it is, I want everybody at Notre Dame who cares to kick a football to have someplace in which to kick it."
—*Knute Rockne*

arts, and when this arresting edifice was constructed in 1938, it was actually considered not only quite large but also quite lavish for a college athletic building. This, however, was no ordinary athletic hall but a monument to Knute Rockne, the larger-than-life football coach whose incredible victories had captured the nation's imagination and made Notre Dame a household word in the 1920s. Grandeur, quite simply, was a requirement.

Coach Rockne also served as Notre Dame's athletic director, and apparently one of his ambitions was to build a campus fieldhouse that would be available to the entire student body. After his untimely death in 1931, the university decided to fulfill that goal by building a first-rate intramural facility in honor of the great coach. The memorial's placement at the far edge of South Quad would have truly pleased Rockne. Its excellent aesthetics provide a powerful focal point for the quad, but even more importantly, the building is located near the dormitories wherein lived the erstwhile undergraduates who had personally known him as "Rock." Certainly it's a real mea-

FATHER LANGE'S WEIGHT ROOM

On the third floor of the Rockne Memorial is a body-building facility dedicated to another Notre Dame legend—Bernard Herman Benedict Lange, C.S.C., the "strong-man priest" who was declared the fourth strongest man in the world in the 1920s. An opera lover with a Ph.D. in biology and chemistry, he supposedly scaled the Dome as an undergraduate and went swimming in St. Joseph's Lake even when it was choked with ice. As strong-willed as he was strong-armed, the redoubtable priest once ejected two offending Marines from the university pool by picking them both up at the same time and throwing them out of the water. Father Lange held forth in his own gymnasium, an exclusive temple of hard exercise and weight training behind the Main Building. There he spent so many years pushing boys toward muscle-bound manhood that students claimed his initials stood for "Build Healthier Bodies."

sure of the strength of Rockne's legacy that even today—several generations removed from his razzle-dazzle heyday—Notre Dame students like to call his memorial "the Rock."

Its architects were J. Maurice Carroll, class of 1919, and Chester E. Dean of Kansas City. Carroll had been a student during Rockne's first seasons as head football coach, and the memorial he helped design fosters athletics with excellent facilities—including a swimming pool; basketball, racquetball, and handball courts; and dance and aerobics rooms—as well as sophisticated symbolism. Large bas-relief figures representing various sports adorn the exterior walls, and over the entrances are the seals of the United States, Norway, France, and the U.S. military and naval academies. Norway and France were the birthplaces of Rockne and the Congregation of Holy Cross, while the United States became the land where both the coach and the order triumphed. West Point and Annapolis, of course, are two long-standing football rivals of the Fighting Irish.

At the memorial's main entrance, look for the two stone plaques that pay tribute to Robert Cavalier, the Sieur de La Salle, and Leopold Pokagon, chief of the Potawatomi Indians who lived in the South Bend area when Notre Dame was founded. La Salle was the great seventeenth-century French explorer who claimed much of North America for his king; Pokagon was the devout Catholic whose sincere faith convinced Father Badin to bring his ministry to northern Indiana. Above the front doors stands a statue of St. Christopher. According to legend, Christopher was a giant who carried the Christ Child over the river of death. The Child was carrying the weight of the world in his hands, and thus Christopher's extraordinary feat of strength makes his image just right for an athletic hall.

Although the facilities of the Rockne Memorial are not available for use by the general public,

Knute Rockne

SOUTH QUADRANGLE'S GREAT VIEWS AND SPLENDID SIGHTS
From the Rockne Memorial looking west; from O'Shaughnessy Hall looking east: These two terminal buildings enclose South Quad like a pair of Gothic bookends, and both offer a long, panoramic look at the many chapters of student life that are constantly unfolding between them.

you will want to step inside the building's foyer to view the vintage football trophies and memorabilia displayed there. Overlooking all these relics is a handsome bronze bust of Knute Rockne. Notice that the coach's nose is very shiny. That's because of one of the students' favorite pre-exam traditions: rubbing Rockne's nose for luck.

NOTRE DAME
GOLF COURSE (302)

This nine-hole course once had 18 holes, but the "back nine" were appropriated as sites for new dormitories when West Quad was developed. The course has been open to the public since it was completed in 1929. Construction of the course had been enthusiastically supported by neighbors whose homes bordered it, and as token of appreciation, Notre Dame gave them free passes to use it. Passes were even issued to the ladies of the neighborhood, who, oddly enough, could not play golf here, since pure and simple custom banned women from the course until 1970.

The golf course usually is open from mid-March through mid-November, and in winter it's used for cross-country skiing. Greens fees are very reasonable. For information about starting times, contact the Golf Pro Shop. It's located on the west side of the Rockne Memorial (6), and the telephone number is 219/631-6425. For 18 holes, try the new Warren golf course on the northeast end of campus.

SECURITY BUILDING (5)

Lots of people simply call this "the pink building." It's the last World War II-era structure left on campus, a humble, barracks-like building that the Navy put up in 1943. This was supposed to be a temporary training facility, but after the war, the building was drafted by Notre Dame's ROTC units and didn't go off duty until the Pasquerilla Center opened in 1987. Since then it's been the home of the university's Security/Police and Human Resources departments.

Notre Dame's Police Department is a private police agency fully authorized by the State of Indiana; its sworn officers not only complete state training requirements but also have the power to make arrests. They're assisted by non-sworn security officers who patrol the campus and handle emergency calls. As a rule of thumb, the officers you see in patrol cars are Notre Dame police; the ones patrolling on foot or bicycles (even in winter) are Notre Dame security.

In addition to providing law enforcement and promoting safety, Notre Dame's uniformed police and security personnel act as a round-the-clock service agency for the campus. They escort students after dark, monitor women's residence halls at night, jumpstart cars, thaw frozen locks, drive students with family emergencies to airports, and have even been known to lend a hand to panicked bridegrooms. The officers also have one of the toughest jobs on campus—manning the university's Main Gate and East Gate. Besides welcoming visitors, diplomatically determining their destination, handing out maps, giving directions, and fielding questions about the Stadium and Golden Dome, they also have the thankless task of explaining to people why they cannot drive their cars on campus.

THE EAST SIDE OF SOUTH QUAD

LAW SCHOOL (37)

Just as Alumni Hall designates the start of the residential side of South Quad, the Law School is the gateway to its academic side. Architecturally and geographically, the two buildings

Law School door

complement each other perfectly, for they share and define one of the most pivotal locations on campus: the place where Main Quad, South Quad, and Notre Dame Avenue all come together. As a result, the Law School and Alumni Hall form the university's own Bosporus and Dardanelles, a singular collegiate Gothic passageway linking the rest of the world to the life, lore, and legacy at the heart of Notre Dame.

The law building predates Alumni Hall by only a year, another Maginnis and Walsh creation replete with lancet arches, trefoil windows, and other Gothic trappings. As the school itself grew in size and statue, this impressive structure received two additions, but happily the architects—Ellerbe and Associates in the early 1970s and Ellerbe Becket in the mid-1980s—did not unduly compromise the character of its original design. Two of the Law School's most interesting features are its statues of Christ the King and Sir Thomas More. Located on the south tower, the Christ statue is a fitting counterpart to Alumni Hall's "Joe College," for taken together they represent the religious and academic aspects of Notre Dame. Sir Thomas More, of course, was the great English lawyer who was beheaded because he re-

Law School

fused to renounce his beliefs when Henry VIII broke with Rome. You'll find More's statue at the Law School's west entrance. The ceremonial robe and neck chain he is wearing indicate his importance as England's Lord Chancellor, while the book in his right hand is simply titled *Law*.

Sir Thomas More on Law School

More's assertion that he was God's servant first and the king's second emphasizes the deep Roman Catholic roots of the Notre Dame Law School. It is, in fact, the oldest Catholic law school in the United States, having been started in 1869 at the behest of the ever-aspiring Father Sorin. The first classes, held in the Main Building, yielded only a handful of graduates. But in 1883, Colonel William Hoynes, who had practiced law in Chicago, took over as the law department's first dean and began the daunting task of developing a worthy law program. Hoynes moved the school to Sorin Hall, where he lived as one of Notre Dame's legendary bachelor dons. The move was not merely a matter of convenience, for the irrepressible Hoynes had to lecture on the law several times each day because the law library lacked the materials for proper research. Fortunately, research is no longer a problem for Notre Dame's Law School. In 1973, the opening of the Kresge Law Library (largely funded by the Kresge Foundation of Troy, Michigan) and a generous collection endowment from the John P. Murphy Foundation of Cleveland, Ohio, provided the basis for what is now one of the most respected and technologically advanced law research centers in the United States.

The law library reinforces a reputation for academic excellence that had been developed under the leadership of Dean Joseph O'Meara in the 1950s and 1960s. Notre Dame's Law School currently ranks among the best in the nation, and it enjoys one of the highest percentages anywhere of graduates who pass the bar exam on their first try. In addition to its demanding, "no-nonsense" curriculum and high teaching standards, the Law

"I conceive that an engineer must be a man with a conscience in his profession. The gravest of all natural responsibilities are borne by him. He will be responsible for human safety and human lives . . . I find at Notre Dame a technical training that ranks with the best and a training in character foundation nowhere excelled."
—*John F. Cushing*

School is widely recognized for its strong emphasis on ethics, human rights, and professionalism. Ranked among the top 25 law schools in the nation, it also has been a leader in offering international study programs and joint degrees in business and engineering.

CUSHING HALL OF ENGINEERING (40) AND FITZPATRICK HALL OF ENGINEERING (39)

Engineering is one the most time-honored courses of study at Notre Dame. The first classes date back to the fall of 1873, when a fledgling civil engineering course taught by only one professor made Notre Dame the first Catholic university in the nation to offer a degree in engineering. The first graduate—a Cassius M. Proctor of Elkhart, Indiana—received his diploma in 1875, and by the turn of the century, courses in mechanical and electrical engineering had been added to the curriculum in response to the nation's expanding technological needs. The College of Engineering was organized in 1920, and during World War II, the scientific and technological training that thousands of naval officers received at Notre Dame not only significantly boosted engineering enrollments, but also prompted the postwar growth of graduate and research programs. Today, about 1,400 undergraduate and 250 graduate students are enrolled in departments of Aerospace and Mechanical Engineering, Chemical Engineering, Civil Engineering and Geological Sciences, Computer Science and Engineering, and Electrical Engineering. Notre Dame's College of Engineering is housed in Cushing and Fitzpatrick halls, but experiments are also conducted in the high tech wind tunnels and specialized laboratories of the Hessert Center for Aerospace Research (66) along St. Joseph's Drive. Opened in 1991, this world-class facility was provided by Thomas J. Hessert, a Cherry Hill, New Jersey, construction company executive and engineering advisory council member who was graduated from Notre Dame in 1928.

The opening of Cushing Hall in 1933 was a real milestone for the College of Engineering because it marked the first time that all the engineering departments were housed under one roof. Located immediately east of the Law School, the building was a gift from John F. Cushing, who had nearly dropped out of Notre Dame because he didn't have enough money for his senior year. President Morrissey, however, decided to simply forgive Cushing's tuition, which allowed him to finish his civil engineering degree and graduate with his class in 1906. Cushing eventually became president of the Great Lakes Dredge and Dock Company, and when Notre Dame needed a new engineering building, he gladly repaid Morrissey's kindness with a $300,000 donation. Designed by Kervick and Fagan in their favorite collegiate Gothic style, Cushing Hall's exterior is embellished with the names of history's great scientists and engineers as well as traditional engineering tools such as a square and compass. In the building's baronial lobby, intricate mosaics continue the engineering theme, and the gorgeous ceiling is decorated with a variety of botanical and geometric forms. If you look closely, you can spot a graceful script version of the familiar block N-D.

By the 1970s, the College of Engineering had outgrown Cushing Hall, and Fitzpatrick Hall of Engineering was built on its south side in 1979. Although Fitzpatrick is nearly twice as big as Cushing, the two co-joined buildings appear to be about the same size. The reason for this illusion is that Fitzpatrick Hall is like an iceberg: you can only see part of it. The bulk of the building is actually underground, where the two largest of its five floors hold numerous laboratories.

ALBERT ZAHM

One of the areas where the College of Engineering has played a leading research role is in systems and controls, a technology much used in the nation's space program. This high-tech journey from the shadow of the Dome to the shadow of the moon actually began back in the late 1800s with Notre Dame's first professor of mechanical engineering, Albert Zahm. A native of New Lexington, Ohio, Zahm was graduated from the university in 1883. He had been a student in its classical course, and one day in Greek class, his professor told the ancient story of Daedalus and Icarus. The fascinated Zahm "decided then and there to find a method of flight." Building numerous machines to test his theories of aerodynamics, Zahm conducted propulsion and flight experiments all over campus. He sailed model boats across the waters of the lakes, tinkered with an early wind tunnel, and even launched manned gliders from the roof of the Science (now LaFortune) Hall. When he predicted that flying machines would someday carry passengers between New York and Chicago, his classmates thought him quite eccentric, but the irrepressible Zahm continued to invent model airplanes and write papers about his research. His findings attracted widespread attention when he persuaded Octave Chanute to help him organize this country's first international aeronautical conference during the Chicago World's Fair. Soon Zahm was off to Washington, where his expertise earned him prestigious positions at Catholic University, the Navy's aeronautical laboratory, the Library of Congress, and the Smithsonian Institution. Naturally, he rubbed shoulders with other aviation pioneers, including Glenn Curtis (who helped Zahm earn his pilot's license) and the Wright Brothers (with whom he locked horns over the origins of controlled flight). Yet, Zahm never lost touch with Notre Dame. In 1925 the university awarded him the Laetare Medal for distinguished achievements, and every Christmas he rather quaintly remembered his alma mater with a donation. When his health began to fail, Zahm returned to Notre Dame, where he died in 1954 at age 92. Zahm was buried near his brother in the Community Cemetery, but his legacy lives on through the College of Engineering. In 1990, James Wetherbee, a Navy aviator who earned his aerospace engineering degree from Notre Dame in 1974, became the university's first astronaut when he piloted the space shuttle *Columbia*. On that mission, Wetherbee saluted Notre Dame's original high flyer by taking along the Laetare Medal—which shows a glider circling the Golden Dome—that 65 years before had been given to Albert Zahm.

In fact, Fitzpatrick Hall is now the College of Engineering's primary teaching, research, and computer facility, while much of Cushing Hall has been earmarked for office space.

Fitzpatrick Hall was named for another civil engineering alumnus—Edward B. Fitzpatrick, class of 1954, a New York construction company executive who was its major donor. Designed by Ellerbe Architects/Engineers/Planners of Bloomington, Minnesota, the building is more utilitarian-looking than Cushing Hall but possesses a brick and limestone exterior as well as numerous Gothic elements that make it compatible with its neighboring predecessor. Its hallways hold an interesting, museum-like display of fossils, gems, minerals, and meteorites, and you should also seek out the unusual set of stained glass windows on the second (aboveground) floor. They juxtapose representations of various engineering achievements—a missile, aqueduct, highway interchange, integrated circuit—with heavenly images that indicate divine inspiration.

THE SNITE MUSEUM OF ART (54)

This is one of the true gems of Notre Dame's campus, no aspiring diamond-in-the-rough studio, but a highly polished, multi-faceted museum

Snite Museum

with one of the largest and most sparkling collegiate collections in the nation. Although exceptional paintings and drawings by old masters are what put the Snite on the map in the world of art, the museum also has strong collections in photography, decorative arts, and nineteenth-century European, pre-Colombian, and American art. In addition, it is the home of the nation's largest and finest assemblage of works by the acclaimed Croatian sculptor, Ivan Mestrovic.

Many of the Snite's famous old masters were donated by Colonel Frederick B. Snite, the Chicago businessman who gave the university the $2 million needed to fund the museum. Art had been a highly visible part of the Notre Dame scene since the 1870s, when Father Sorin retained Luigi Gregori to paint scenes in the Main Building and Sacred Heart Church. In the 1950s, art galleries were built as part of O'Shaughnessy Hall, but Notre Dame did not have a dedicated art

"THE BOILER KID"

Maybe it was fate, or perhaps merely chance, but the Snite Museum was built just yards away from the north end zone of Notre Dame Stadium, where the donor's son—Fred Snite, Jr.—once captured the public's attention. Only a few years after graduating from Notre Dame in 1933, young Fred contracted polio while visiting China. He became paralyzed and had to rely on an iron lung, but that didn't keep the self-described "Boiler Kid" away from Fighting Irish football games. Traveling to the Stadium in a trailer that was wheeled in via the north end zone entrance ramp, Fred watched the game *backwards* with the help of a large mirror attached to his iron lung. The crowd always cheered Fred's arrival with great applause, and his spunk made him the subject of countless newsreels and editorials. The "Boiler Kid" died in 1954, but when the Snite Museum opened 26 years later, the atrium's *Madonna and Child* by Renaissance sculptor Jacopo Sansovino was dedicated in his memory.

MUST-SEES IN THE SNITE MUSEUM, A FEW PERSONAL FAVORITES OF ITS DIRECTOR, DR. DEAN PORTER:

François Boucher. *Offering of a Rose*

Victor Higgins. *New Mexico Sky*

William Glackens. *Portrait of Artist's Wife and Son*

Francesco de Mura. *Circe*

Constant Troyon. *Vue de Parc Saint Cloud*

Albert Block. *Leidi*

Olmec. *figure in serpentine*

Eskimo. *mask*

Frederick Remington. *Bronco Buster*

Phillip Pearlstein. *Two Nudes*

Egyptian. *Horus*

George Rickey. *Two Conical Segments Gyratory Gyratory II*

Edouard Steinbruck. *Nativity*

Walter Ufer. *The Battery*

Marc Chagall. *Le Grande Cirque*

Ivan Mestrovic. *Ashbaugh Madonna*

Henry Moore. *Studies for the Family*

Gustav Stickley. *chair*

William Merritt Chase. *Portrait of a Young Woman*

Master of San Miniato. *Virgin and Christ Child*

Gustave Doré. *The Madonna (with Christ Child)*

Caruelle D'Aligny. *A Landscape in Italy*

Ary Scheffer. *Princess Jeanne Elisabeth Carolyne Wittgenstein*

Gaetano Gandolfi. *The Rejection of Cain's Offering and the Sacrifice of Manoah*

Rembrandt Harmensz van Rijn. *Christ Sacrificed between Two Thieves*

building until the Snite was constructed. The opening of the museum in 1980 not only gave art a definite presence on campus but also made an obvious statement about its importance to the university. With its refined collection of more than 19,000 objects, the Snite now serves as a true teaching museum and has become a valuable educational resource for both Notre Dame students and northern Indiana. The museum's fine education department offers lively, informative tours that utilize works of art to explore topics ranging from biblical themes to how the ancient Olmec culture of Central America invented football. On request, the curators can also prepare

O'Shaughnessy Hall

Cushing Hall detail

Fitzpatrick Hall of Engineering

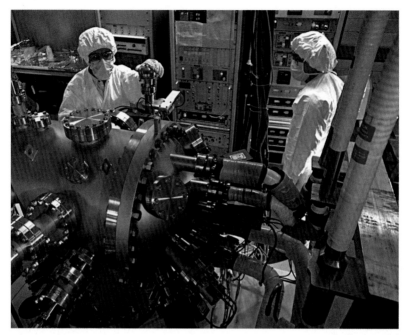

Nieuwland science lab

The Griffon "howling" at the Stadium

museum tours tailored to specific age groups, curriculums, interests, cultures, or foreign languages, and guides even provide portable stools to help keep visitors comfortable. The museum is usually open every day except Monday and major holidays; call 219/631-5466 or 219/631-7960 for information about its hours, exhibits, and tours.

You'll find the Snite Museum of Art at the southeast corner of South Quad. It's the modern-looking brick building with the lofty atrium and a formidable, 27-foot-high steel sculpture (*Griffon* by David Hayes, class of 1953) that marks its front entrance and appears to be howling at Notre Dame Stadium. The Snite sits catty-corner from the Stadium across Moose Krause Circle, and on football weekends, many people duck into the museum only to use its restrooms. That is a grievous sin, which you should not commit. It is far better to take some time to appreciate all that the galleries have to offer. Aside from works in the permanent collections by such notables as Degas, Sargent, Bierstadt, O'Keeffe and Miró, the Snite schedules dozens of important exhibits every year. In the Annenberg Auditorium, you can enjoy concerts and films, while the quiet courtyard just outside the north end of the atrium features a sculpture garden. And, you'll definitely want to view the powerful sculptures and drawings of Ivan Mestrovic on prominent display. Special exhibits are now housed in the Ivan Mestrovic Gallery, which was once the artist's studio. When the Snite was being planned in the 1970s, its architect, Notre Dame professor Ambrose Richardson, carefully incorporated that small but very special studio into the museum's design.

O'SHAUGHNESSY HALL (56)

According to the purists, O'Shaughnessy Hall is not the best of buildings for defining the end of a major quadrangle. They like to point out that its site is a bit too far west to properly balance the quad; that the main entrance is off-center and spoils a perfect line of sight with the Rockne Memorial; that the prominent tower is awkward and its clock looks somewhat silly. As for O'Shaughnessy's architecture, they delight in repeating an apocryphal story about Frank Lloyd Wright's reaction to the building—plant ivy around it and pray for rain.

Well, pay no attention to those naysayers, for their objections are quite academic. Whatever its technical flaws may be, O'Shaughnessy Hall has nobly held its own to become an indispensable part of the campus landscape as the headquarters of Notre Dame's oldest curriculum, the College of Arts and Letters. It has presided over the east side of the quad for the past half century, a solid and steadfast presence that the students affectionately call "O'Shag." The building, in fact, is rather like a dear old great uncle—a bit eccentric, perhaps, but so well-intentioned that you can't help but like it.

Certainly O'Shag's namesake, Ignatius Aloysius "I. A." O'Shaughnessy of St. Paul, Minnesota, had the best of intentions when he decided to underwrite it to the tune of $2.1 million. While walking across campus one day with President John J. Cavanaugh, O'Shaughnessy asked where the liberal arts building was located. Cavanaugh replied that Notre Dame didn't have any. On the spot O'Shaughnessy made up his mind to provide one, because as he later explained, "the heart of education lies in the liberal and fine arts." The founder and president of the Globe Oil and Refining Company, O'Shaughnessy frequently supported Catholic higher education, and his considerable philanthropy toward Notre Dame would extend all the way from funding Ivan Mestrovic's studio to leaving the university a substantial portion of his estate. A long-time

*WSND-88.9 FM,
the university's public
radio station, broadcasts
from the tower of
O'Shaughnessy Hall.
Operated by students and
community volunteers,
the station's call letters
stand for "We Serve
Notre Dame."*

member of the board of lay trustees, O'Shaughnessy was awarded Notre Dame's Laetare Medal in 1953, the same year that his liberal arts building was dedicated.

O'Shaughnessy was also the person responsible for introducing the Ellerbe architectural firm to Notre Dame, for his request that the Minnesota company design his new hall began a relationship with the university that continues to this day. Ellerbe Associates incorporated many Gothic elements into the design of O'Shaughnessy Hall, but the most successful is undoubtedly the medieval-like Great Hall that lies just inside its main entrance. There, massive oak furniture and wainscoting provide an opulent backdrop for seven spectacular art glass windows. Created by Pete Dohmen of St. Paul, Minnesota, these windows use symbols and the names of scholars to represent the seven liberal arts of antiquity—Music, Geometry, Astronomy, Arithmetic, Rhetoric, Dialectic, and Grammar. On one side of the Great Hall, a quote from Michelangelo has been carved in stone: "The True Work of Art Is But a Shadow of the Divine Perfection." On another side, an awesome Crucifix by Ivan Mestrovic hangs between a pair of arched oak doors. The doors themselves lead to the O'Shaughnessy art galleries, which are now connected to the Snite Museum of Art. Also on display in the Great Hall are the names of Notre Dame undergraduates who have distinguished themselves by winning some of the world's most prestigious academic honors. The long and impressive list begins with Notre Dame's first Rhodes Scholar, one R. D. Shea in 1923.

The whole purpose of erecting O'Shaughnessy Hall, of course, was to make sure that list continues to grow longer. Chances are that old I. A. (whose portrait in the Great Hall still casts an ever-watchful eye on things) would be pleased with the state of the liberal arts within his building, for the walls ooze so much erudition that it was used for many of the classroom scenes in the motion picture *Rudy*. Since most people will never have the privilege of attending classes in O'Shag, the next best thing is to pay a visit to Waddick's on the hall's first floor. Named for one of the liberal arts deans, Waddick's is ostensibly a sandwich shop, but its true bill of fare is food for thought. This is the place where graduate students and professors gather to converse and commune. At one table, you'll hear people chatting away in Spanish. At another, they might be talking about creative writing and character development; or interpreting St. Augustine; or discussing twentieth-century factory culture. You might go into Waddick's for coffee, but you're likely to leave with an education.

SHAHEEN-MESTROVIC MEMORIAL (307)

Ivan Mestrovic, a devout Catholic and fierce Croatian nationalist, is considered one of the twentieth-century's finest sculptors of religious subjects. He lived a life of turmoil—buffeted by the uncertain political winds of the Balkan peninsula, displaced by war, imprisoned by the Nazis, at constant loggerheads with the Communists of Yugoslavia—but his art was his constant compass. Mestrovic's recurring themes were heroic, biblical, and religious, and he created images with bold, curving forms that evoked drama, energy, dignity, and strength. After World War II, Mestrovic left Europe for the United States. He found work at Syracuse University and became a citizen, but by the 1950s, the aging Mestrovic wanted to concentrate on religious art. When then-President Hesburgh asked him to become Notre Dame's sculptor-in-residence, Mestrovic readily agreed and would spend the last years of his life in his campus studio. Notre Dame gave him a sanctuary, and although he spent only seven years (1955-62)

Christ at Jacob's well

there, the university now has so much of his art that the entire campus practically serves as one large Mestrovic gallery.

Even if you don't view any other of Mestrovic's works at Notre Dame, you must see the compelling sculptures in the Shaheen-Mestrovic Memorial at the front of O'Shaughnessy Hall. The Memorial's focal point—*Christ and the Samaritan Woman at Jacob's Well*—depicts a scene from the New Testament, and it is flanked on the south by *St. Luke the Evangelist* and on the north by *St. John the Evangelist.* Although these powerful statues are compelling in and of themselves, they are also greatly enhanced by their location: a park-like conversation area provided by Eli and Helen Shaheen of Sturgis, Michigan. The benches and landscaping in this remarkable setting have curvilinear shapes that perfectly complement Mestrovic's sweeping style, and the result is a wonderfully welcoming space where people come to rest, relax, or study. In fact, it's not unusual to see someone with their nose in a book quietly sitting beside *St. Luke* or *St. John.*

NIEUWLAND SCIENCE HALL (52) AND STEPAN CHEMISTRY HALL (16)

Completed primarily with gifts from alumni and corporate donors in 1952, Nieuwland Science Hall is located just northwest of O'Shaughnessy Hall. With more than 30 laboratories and several amphitheater-like classrooms, this sprawling brick and limestone building was intended to educate modern scientists, and architects Maginnis and Walsh executed it in a suitably functional, flat-roofed contemporary design. In the late 1980s, the hall was renovated and also gained an addition that provided space for microelectronic research, laboratories, and classrooms.

Notre Dame has been offering bachelor of science degrees since 1865, and its College of Science now has undergraduate departments in Biological Sciences, Chemistry and Biochemistry, Mathematics, Physics, and Preprofessional Studies. The College has achieved considerable recognition for its groundbreaking work in germfree and radiation research, blood chemistry and clotting, synthetic antibiotics, and mosquito genetics. It is also famous for the work of Rev. Julius Nieuwland, C.S.C., the priest-scientist who discovered the basic formula for synthetic rubber. A native of Belgium, he was raised in South Bend, received his bachelor's degree from Notre Dame in 1899, and was ordained in 1903. Only a year after his ordination, Nieuwland completed his doctorate in chemistry with a dissertation titled "Some Reactions of Acetylene." He had supposedly picked acetylene for his subject because it has a simple formula, C_2H_2, but ironically, he was to spend years of his life unraveling the compound's complexities.

Father Nieuwland personified the preoccupied inventor. A quiet, unpretentious man who smoked a pipe and was sometimes too busy to shave, he often worked all night in the laboratories of the Old Chemistry Hall on South Quad. By chance, the priest had once noticed that acetylene reacted with a mixture of copper and alkali metal chlorides to produce a foul-smelling gas. He performed countless experiments and eventually produced a new compound that he identified as divinyl acetylene. In 1925, Nieuwland, who was then chairman of Notre Dame's chemistry department, reported his findings at a symposium. His research immediately attracted the attention of the E. I. DuPont de Nemours Company, whose chemists had been searching for a synthetic rubber formula. The company signed Nieuwland on as a consultant, and by

FATHER NIEUWLAND AND BOTANY

Although chemistry was his life's work, Father Nieuwland's true love was botany. He liked nothing better than to spend hours at a time walking around campus looking for new or unusual species to add to his collection of plants, and these "botanizing" excursions took him to fields and forests all over Indiana, Michigan, and other states. With his excellent memory and scholarly temperament, Father Nieuwland acquired an encyclopedic knowledge of plants, often amazing his companions by delivering exhaustive off-the-cuff commentaries on some arcane root or blossom. He had an uncanny ability to spot an interesting leaf or flower from a car window and would insist on stopping along the roadside to investigate. Crawling through bushes and climbing trees in his cassock seemed improper to Father Nieuwland, so he found another way to retrieve plants. He started taking along a .22 caliber rifle and brought hard-to-reach specimens down to earth by shooting them off their stems. The priest became such a good marksman that he even won a shooting match arranged by some "doubting Thomas" friends. In 1909, he started the *American Midland Naturalist*, a botanical journal that is still published at Notre Dame, and by the time he died, Father Nieuwland had gathered thousands of plant specimens. His collection, which is now part of Notre Dame's noted Greene-Nieuwland Herbarium, serves as an official scientific plant repository for the State of Indiana.

1931, he had successfully used divinyl acetylene to synthesize an elastic, rubber-like material that DuPont began marketing as DuPrene and Neoprene. Although Nieuwland's research made headlines, there was not much initial demand for this new product. That changed dramatically during World War II, however, when the Japanese gained control of most of the world's rubber plantations, and the availability of synthetic rubber became enormously important to the nation and its allies. Today, the United States is the leading producer of synthetic rubber, and Father Nieuwland has quite rightly joined Alexander Graham Bell and the Wright Brothers in the National Inventors Hall of Fame.

*Father Nieuwland
in the lab*

Unfortunately, Father Nieuwland never realized the full impact of his discovery, for he died of a heart attack in 1936. While he was alive, he brought both untold prestige to Notre Dame as well as an excellent library of chemistry books that the DuPont company provided in compensation for his consulting work. When he died, Nieuwland left the royalties earned from his synthetic rubber patents to the university, and they yielded about $2 million before expiring in 1948. A portion of those royalties was used to help build Nieuwland Science Hall, a building that not only memorializes Notre Dame's most illustrious scientist, but also nurtures his abiding—and prophetic—conviction that "each new truth may become useful in the future."

Stepan Chemistry Hall was constructed adjacent to Nieuwland Hall's east wing in 1982. Designed by Ellerbe Architects/Engineers/Planners, this five-story chemical research facility is a contemporary building with its own distinctive brick and limestone facades. Its modern classrooms and up-to-the-minute laboratories replaced those in Old Chemistry Hall, the 62-year-old structure where Father Nieuwland had so intently conducted his research. Coincidentally, the new hall's primary benefactor—Alfred C. Stepan, Jr., founder of the Stepan Chemical Company and a member of the class of 1931—had known the priest and benefited from his expertise. As a senior, young Stepan wrote his thesis on "The Development of the American Chemical Industry," and his advisors were none other than Father Nieuwland and the scientist's equally esteemed colleague from DuPont, Dr. Wallace Carrothers.

RILEY HALL OF ART AND DESIGN (53)

Riley Hall doorway

Chemistry, the department that would provide one of the firmest foundations of Notre Dame's College of Science, was housed in this building from the time of its construction in 1920 until Nieuwland Science Hall opened some 30 years later. Still often referred to as Old Chemistry Hall, this is the hallowed structure where Father Nieuwland had his famous laboratory. It was apparently placed at some distance from Main Quad because of the fire hazard posed by certain chemicals, and indeed, Father Nieuwland would cause his share of smoke and explosions here while experimenting with highly flammable acetylene.

This hall was already standing when Kervick proposed the South Quad, and during the 1920s and 1930s, the parade of new structures steadily advanced from west to east and eventually enveloped it as part of the new quad. Architect Edward Tilton, who previously designed the Lemonnier Library (now Bond Hall), also gave this building a classically balanced facade, but, it is said, was forced to use brick because the university's budget was too lean for limestone. After Nieuwland Science Hall opened, Old Chemistry Hall was remodeled to provide studios and other facilities for the art department. Much of the renovation's funding came from three alumni—Allan, Gene, and William Riley—as a gift made in memory of their parents, Edna and Leo Riley.

Today, Riley Hall is a lively center of the visual arts at Notre Dame. Students of ceramics, graphic design, industrial design, painting, photography, printmaking, and sculpture all work in its studios, and many of their creations are exhibited in the building. The third floor of Riley Hall is the home of the intriguing Isis Gallery, which is definitely worth taking the time to visit. As you know, Isis was the ancient Egyptian goddess of fertility, and this small but very significant space is used to propagate the creative process by showcasing new—and often unconventional—works by emerging as well as established artists.

HURLEY HALL (41) AND HAYES-HEALY CENTER (88)

In 1930, Edward Nash Hurley informed President Charles O'Donnell that he wanted to give Notre Dame $200,000 to build a College of Foreign and Domestic Commerce. Hurley, a Chicago businessman who had chaired the United States Shipping Board during World War I, decided to make this gift because he was impressed with Notre Dame's leadership in developing a business curriculum that emphasized foreign trade. He requested that Graham, Anderson, Probst and White, the noted architects who had designed Chicago's landmark Wrigley Building, plan the structure for the university, and they produced a superb collegiate Gothic building with leaded glass windows and outstanding brick and stone facades. Among its many attributes were certain custom features designed to indicate international trade. Without a doubt, the most famous of these ornaments was the model of a ship that romantically graced Hurley Hall's front tower and inspired the business college's endearing sobriquet, "The Yacht Club."

After the business college took up residence in Hurley Hall, its focus steadily expanded to

Hurley Hall set a precedent for fund-raising at Notre Dame that continues to this day. After Edward Nash Hurley presented his $200,000 to Notre Dame, the university decided one good turn deserved another and named its new commerce building Hurley Hall. It was the university's first twentieth-century structure named for a lay patron, and the practice proved to be such an opportune way to express its appreciation that Notre Dame has been baptizing buildings with the names of benevolent donors ever since.

include management and administration. By the 1960s, the college sorely needed more space for its new master's degree program, and the remedy for its growing pains once again came from Chicago. Two of the Windy City's prominent travel industry executives—Ramona Hayes Healy and her husband, John Healy—provided much of the funding to build a two-story addition to Hurley Hall in 1968. Graham, Anderson, Probst and White were again enlisted as architects, and they innovatively joined the new Hayes-Healy Center to Hurley Hall via a fine skywalk that allows wonderful, treetop views of a landscaped courtyard between the two buildings. Their architectural encore also included executing Hayes-Healy in an innovative, contemporary interpretation of Gothic design; this styling is not only quite attractive, but also coordinates extremely well with Hurley Hall's more conventional architectural elements.

In 1995, the College of Business Administra-

Hurley Hall

BEDNAR AND KORMENDI

Except for a few works done by students, the lovely statues of religious figures that you see on the exteriors of South Quad's buildings were executed by art professors Rev. John Bednar, C.S.C., and Eugene Kormendi. Most of these statues were placed in the buildings' decorative niches during World War II, when the necessity of closing the art department prompted the professors to begin a campus-wide beautification project. A native of Cleveland, Ohio, Father Bednar received his bachelor's degree from Notre Dame in 1933, and he was one of the first people to earn a master's degree in sculpture at the Art Institute of Chicago. The internationally known Kormendi was born in Budapest, Hungary, and had studied with Rodin in France. His sculptures and monuments depicting religious, historic, and political subjects appeared throughout Europe, and he was at the height of his career when he decided to visit the United States in 1939. During his trip, war broke out in Europe, and Kormendi was unable to return to his home. He accepted Notre Dame's invitation to become its artist-in-residence, moved to South Bend, and began carving out a second successful career for himself in the United States.

tion moved into a new, worldclass complex on DeBartolo Quad. Hurley Hall and Hayes-Healy Center became the temporary quarters of the architecture school, and two years later, they were used to house administrative offices displaced by the Main Building renovation. When the business college vacated Hurley Hall, its trademark ship also departed for the new port on DeBartolo Quad. The hall's Gothic foyer, however, still contains showpieces from its heyday as a cathedral to commerce: a huge aluminum globe and richly colored murals depicting maps of major trade routes and the seven seas. In the 1930s, Mr. Hurley wanted this foyer to remind students of this nation's important role in world trade, and he had spared no expense to achieve his objective. John Warner Norton, a noted artist who had recently completed the murals in the towering new Chicago Board of Trade building, was commissioned to paint the globe and the maps, while the Rand McNally Company was consulted for the accuracy of geographic details. The globe not only revolved but also could be raised and lowered. Its mechanism came from the company that had designed the stage for the Chicago Civic Op-

REV. CHARLES O'DONNELL, C.S.C.

A poet by nature, Father O'Donnell was an unlikely builder, but he ultimately proved to be one of Notre Dame's best. O'Donnell was from Greenfield, Indiana, and entered Notre Dame at age 15. He joined its literary societies, edited the *Scholastic*, and in 1906, became editor of the first issue of the Notre Dame yearbook. After graduating with honors, O'Donnell was ordained and returned to the university, where he taught English literature and wrote thoughtful, carefully crafted verse. By all accounts, the only structures that truly interested him were sentence structures. Yet, when he was chosen to be Notre Dame's president in 1928, O'Donnell might as well have donned a hard hat as a biretta, for he constantly advanced the construction of South Quad. During his time in office, South Dining Hall, Alumni Hall, Dillon Hall, Cushing Hall of Engineering, Hurley College of Business Administration, and the Law School were all completed. In addition, he directed the first renovation of Sacred Heart Church, had the campus power plant built, and okayed the start of Notre Dame Stadium.

With his expressive soul, O'Donnell no doubt contributed some of his own keen sense of the aesthetic to South Quad's Gothic embellishments. Certainly, he augmented Notre Dame's literary life, garnering praise for his volumes of polished poetry and persuading the noted English author and Catholic apologist G. K. Chesterton to deliver a sparkling series of lectures. When the Cushing engineering building was finished, O'Donnell tastefully penned the donor's praises, and when Rockne perished in a plane crash, it was O'Donnell who found the words for a sentimental eulogy. Most significant of all, he wrote a poem, *Notre Dame, Our Mother*, whose tender phrases are now immortalized as the beloved lyrics of the university's alma mater. President O'Donnell's health seriously declined during his second term, and all through the spring of 1934, he battled to stay alive, finally passing away only hours after some 500 Notre Dame graduates had been handed their diplomas. His timing was pure poetic justice.

era. The world, of course, has changed drastically since 1932, but, happily, the foyer of Hurley Hall has not. The nations of its globe and murals remain frozen in time, a testimony both to Mr. Hurley's international vision and the generations of students he sought to inspire.

Hurley Hall globe

NORTH QUADRANGLE

North Quad is much smaller and more intimate than South Quad, but it has two very definite focal points—Haggar Hall at the north end and the Clarke Memorial Fountain at the south. Located northeast of the Dome, the North Quad is primarily residential, and four of its dormitories—Cavanaugh, Zahm, Keenan, and Stanford —are adjacent to St. Edward's Hall. A century ago, St. Edward's belonged to the "minims," and much of the North Quad now occupies the old playing fields where those grade school boys once pitched baseballs and ran races. Today, the quad's broad, grassy yard still suffices as a playground of sorts for the students who live there. You'll see them roller blading on the pathways or lobbing footballs on the open lawn. They lounge under its shade trees and of course do a bit of courting on the benches in front of the halls. Every spring the quad is also the site of Naughfest, a campuswide celebration with bands, food, and games hosted by the residents of Cavanaugh Hall.

Notre Dame's businesslike president John O'Hara initiated North Quad in the mid-1930s. Part of the area now encompassed by the quad was already occupied by two freshman and sophomore dormitories that had been hurriedly constructed during the student population explosion in the 1920s. Those makeshift wooden halls were razed to make way for well-planned permanent structures that would be sited around an entirely new quad located north of, but parallel to, the Main Quad. With the completion of North Quad's first three dormitories in the late 1930s, the university was able to house virtually the entire student body on campus. Thus, the incipi-

Since North Quad was developed on the heels of South Quad, and because the two quads flank opposite sides of the Dome, it's only natural that a competition of sorts exists between their respective residents. With the first major snow of each winter, that rivalry erupts in one of the students' favorite traditions: the North Quad vs. South Quad snowball fight.

ent quad immediately reinforced the residential experience that is a hallmark of undergraduate life at Notre Dame. North Quad's location on what was then the northeast edge of the campus also provided an effective geographic counterbalance to the South Quad halls that had blossomed southwest of the Dome only a few years earlier.

Architecturally, however, the North Quad proved to be South Quad's weak sister. Although its buildings took their collegiate Gothic cue from the splendid structures in South Quad, the style here is much more diluted and its floral ornamentation not nearly as elaborate or detailed. In fact, in the two decades from the time North Quad's first buildings were started until the last was finished in 1957, its "modified" collegiate Gothic was replaced by modern architecture. The early residence halls such as Cavanaugh and Zahm do display some Gothic elements, especially at the nicely done arched portals (which because of their flat roofs have become popular places for students to put Christmas trees during December). In contrast, Keenan and Stanford halls, which were constructed in the mid-1950s, have box-like silhouettes and a heavily horizontal orientation. Although their buff brick and limestone exteriors helped unify the two dormitories with existing campus structures, they are obviously buildings which emphasize function more than form. Indeed, Keenan and Stanford can be considered architectural turning points for Notre Dame. Since they are major campus buildings, their construction signaled the start of the university's move away from the intricacies of collegiate Gothic and toward the blandness of modern architecture.

As for North Quad per se, the transition from a simplified collegiate Gothic to modern building style was certainly a sign of the times during which the quad was conceived (the lean, sobering years of the Depression) and came to fruition (the pragmatic 1950s). It was also arguably a reflection of two different architectural firms. Boston's Maginnis and Walsh, which had a hand in the ornate South Quad, designed North Quad's earliest structures, while Ellerbe and Company of St. Paul, Minnesota, did the much more straightforward 1950s buildings.

CAVANAUGH HALL (51)

A 58-year-old custom came crashing down at Cavanaugh in 1994, when it was converted from a male to a female dormitory. Notre Dame's Board of Trustees had eliminated a long-standing cap on female undergraduate enrollment a few years before, and the university needed more space to house the increasing number of women coming to campus. At Cavanaugh, the hall that had accommodated naval officers during World War II and sustained one of Notre Dame's most enduring theater groups, long-standing traditions virtually disappeared overnight. Its rivalry with the men of neighboring Zahm Hall went by the wayside, as did its "sister dorm" relationship with the women across the quad in Breen-Phillips Hall. Given the change in gender, the male rector was replaced by a female, and Cavanaugh residents also ceased to be "Crusaders" and adopted the new nickname "Cavaliers."

Although it is now one of Notre Dame's most centrally located residence halls, Cavanaugh was the new North Quad's inaugural building when it was constructed in 1936. Maginnis and Walsh gave Cavanaugh a fair dose of collegiate Gothic with steep gabled roofs and other features that not only made it visually compatible with the existing South Quad but also set the architectural tone for the North Quad. Inside, the trappings of that styling are still evident in the Cavanaugh chapel, a rather formal Gothic chamber with dark architectural woodwork and a trio of lancet arches adorning the altar.

The hall was named in honor of the Rev.

NORTH QUAD'S GREAT VIEWS AND SPLENDID SIGHTS
Of the Golden Dome: The green space between Zahm Hall and Cavanaugh Hall provides the framework for a rare and quite remarkable view of the Dome from the east. The Dome is also beautifully visible— especially in winter— from the yard with the bike racks between Breen-Phillips and Farley halls.

Father John W. Cavanaugh

John William Cavanaugh, C.S.C., who had served as Notre Dame's president from 1905 until 1919. Described as a man who "wrote beautifully and spoke charmingly," Cavanaugh was a native of Leetonia, Ohio, and had been a professor of English at Notre Dame. He was a true hail-fellow-well-met and during his presidency became known as "Notre Dame's Ambassador," delightedly rubbing elbows with the noted literati and politicians whom he frequently invited to campus. It was said that "Cavvy" knew the name of every person at Notre

Dame, and his affable manner sweetened the strict authority with which he ran the school.

The first person to run Notre Dame free of Father Sorin's direct influence, Cavanaugh gingerly ushered Notre Dame into the twentieth century, taking small but significant steps toward turning it into a true university. He opened a new library (now Bond Hall), added the Students Army Training Corps (now ROTC) to the curriculum, started the Glee Club, and took possession of Notre Dame's first automobile (a Cadillac presented to him as a gift). Many of his flowery sermons and speeches were so eloquent that they were printed as literature, and

Cavanaugh Hall

"THE SECOND FATHER CAVANAUGH"

Although Cavanaugh Hall is named for John William Cavanaugh, nearby Cavanaugh Drive is *not*. Since the hall had commemorated Cavanaugh for 60 years, the university decided in 1996 to name a roadway for one of his successors—the "second Father Cavanaugh." He was the capable Rev. John *Joseph* Cavanaugh, C.S.C., who served as Notre Dame's president from 1946 to 1952. Although John W. and John J. were not related by blood, they were definitely connected in the broad kinship that is the Congregation of Holy Cross. John J. had once been John W.'s student secretary, and he would later serve as a pallbearer at John W.'s 1935 funeral. In fact, when John W. learned that John J. planned to put his considerable organizational talents to use in the priesthood, he reportedly advised him, "Remember, John, you're *joining* a religious community, not *founding* one . . ."

Apparently, John J. Cavanaugh took his old boss's advice to heart, for he founded no religious communities. Instead, he used his presidency to start the Notre Dame Foundation, the university's first formally organized and sustained fund-raising program. When Cavanaugh took office just after the end of World War II, he was determined to "break Notre Dame out of the monastic mentality." Cavanaugh recognized that the war veterans flooding the campus represented a challenge as well as an opportunity to transform Notre Dame into a great and modern center of learning. "Where," he pointedly inquired, "are the Catholic Salks, Oppenheimers, and Einsteins?" The answer, of course, was that he wanted them at Notre Dame.

Cavanaugh knew that achieving excellence would be expensive, and in starting the Notre Dame Foundation, he laid the financial groundwork for the university's increase in size as well as prestige during the 1950s and 1960s. He also strove to update and improve its intellectual life and academic organization. Cavanaugh introduced the Program of Liberal Studies based on the Western civilization's great books, reined in the Athletic Department, greatly enlarged the graduate school, and reorganized the administration, picking a promising young priest named Hesburgh to be its first executive vice-president. When Cavanaugh left the presidency, he took over as director of the Notre Dame Foundation. He spent the next several years finding the funding that helped his successor, President Theodore Hesburgh, construct dozens of new buildings, including Keenan and Stanford Halls on the North Quad. By the time that the Notre Dame Foundation celebrated its twenty-fifth anniversary, it had raised more than $200 million and made the university's endowment one of the largest in the nation.

A native of Owosso, Michigan, Cavanaugh had been forced to drop out of school when his father died. He learned to type and take shorthand and ended up in Detroit as a secretary to Henry Ford. When Cavanaugh discovered that the University of Notre Dame had a president with the same surname as his own, he finagled an appointment with John W. and offered to provide two years of secretarial services in exchange for a scholarship. After graduation (with honors and as his class president), Cavanaugh went to work for the Studebaker Corporation in South Bend and in only a few years became head of sales and advertising. He resigned in 1926 to join the Congregation of Holy Cross, and Studebaker's chief executive later claimed that he had encouraged Cavanaugh to do so because "otherwise, he would have had my job."

In truth, Cavanaugh was a natural leader who only took 13 years to advance from assistant student chaplain to president of Notre Dame. With his Irish warmth and wit, he not only made friends easily but also astutely used his business experience to cultivate friendships with leading educators, industrialists, and entrepreneurs. Cavanaugh solicited notables to serve as lay trustees, and he taught his administrators to network. Among the people whom Cavanaugh knew well were the Kennedys of Massachusetts. He became something of a personal chaplain to the family, and in the dark days following President Kennedy's assassination, John J. Cavanaugh went to Hyannis Port to offer comfort and support to his old friend, Joe Kennedy.

in his writing Cavanaugh fretted over the danger that "athletic sports" posed to scholarship. Ironically, his last work would be editing an autobiography of Knute Rockne, the obscure chemistry teacher he himself had hired in 1918 to coach Notre Dame's football team.

Rev. Matthew Miceli, C.S.C., class of 1947, holds the all-time longevity record as a Notre Dame rector: 30 years at Cavanaugh Hall.

ZAHM HALL (50)

The second dormitory built on the North Quad, Zahm Hall was constructed immediately north of Cavanaugh Hall in 1937. Since Maginnis and Walsh designed it to be a duplicate of Cavanaugh, Zahm Hall also has a brick exterior with limestone trim and a slate roof. Even its beautiful sunken chapel was a replica of Cavanaugh's, and to this day it is graced by high windows, golden angels floating above the altar, and rich wood columns decorated with capitals of shields and flowers.

While North Quad provides an expansive front yard for both Zahm and Cavanaugh, the rear wings of these halls also form a much smaller and more intimate "backyard" quad with St. Edward's Hall and the Main Building. The pleasant lawn between Zahm and Cavanaugh leads westward toward the Main Building, and it has been landscaped with a variety of stately evergreens. One of the tallest shelters a simple statue of *Our Lady*, whose pious presence not only bridges the two halls, but also quietly foreshadows the far more glorious Lady who stands beyond the trees atop the Golden Dome.

Zahm Hall memorializes Rev. John Augustine Zahm, C.S.C., the illustrious, Ohio-born priest-scientist whom Louis Pasteur called "the gentle scholar from across the seas." After graduating from Notre Dame in 1871, Zahm was ordained in the Congregation of Holy Cross, then returned to his alma mater to teach physics, chemistry, and natural science. His brilliant mastery of the sciences and flair as a lecturer made Zahm something of a campus legend, and he wrote numerous books on topics that ranged from acoustics to the theory of evolution's compatibility with Christianity. Zahm served as both the head of Notre Dame's science department and vice president of the university. In the late 1890s, he represented the Congregation of Holy Cross in Rome, where Pope Leo XIII awarded him a Doctor of Philosophy degree. Returning to Notre Dame in 1898, he was elected provincial superior of his order.

Zahm thought Notre Dame should be the nation's foremost Catholic university, and he was a ring leader among the late nineteenth-century progressives who wanted to transform it from a prep school into a first-rate educational institution, especially in the fields of science and technology. Zahm zealously campaigned for higher academic standards, a more advanced curriculum, greatly expanded research efforts, and up-to-date facilities. He spearheaded construction of new science and engineering buildings, acquired extensive natural history collections, expanded the library, brought steam heat to the campus, advocated private rooms in the dorms, and even had a special railroad car built just to transport students from western states between their homes and Notre Dame. In the 1880s, Zahm also made Notre Dame one of the first colleges anywhere to have electric lighting when he began installing arc lights outdoors and incandescent lamps inside several buildings.

Unfortunately for him, Zahm's ambitions were thwarted by Father Andrew Morrissey and the congregation's status quo camp. He was forced to relinquish the position of provincial in 1906, the same year that John W. Cavanaugh took office as Notre Dame's eighth president. While Cavanaugh would tread lightly toward the future, Zahm had always believed the university couldn't get there fast enough. What a wonderfully fitting coincidence it is, therefore, that Cavanaugh and Zahm halls were constructed side-by-side, the former being named for the agreeable president who kept a sentimental eye on what Notre Dame had been, and the latter for the intellectual provincial who possessed the great vision of what Notre Dame would become.

Today, Zahm Hall frequently sports a bold "Z" on its North Quad facade and has a reputation as one of the most spirited and tight-knit men's dormitories on campus. "Zahmbies," as its residents like to be called, exhibit enormous esprit de corps, and "Zahm bashing," as the act of insulting the dorm is called, is common practice among those who appreciate neither their comradeship nor social events such as Z.I.T.S. (the

When the disappointed Zahm departed Notre Dame in 1906, he took refuge at Holy Cross College in Washington, D.C., a theological institution he had helped to establish years before. Zahm spent his final years writing and traveling extensively. He developed a special interest in South America and often explored its jungles and mountains. His 1913 expedition there was led by another adventurous traveler and writer, Theodore Roosevelt. Zahm, Roosevelt once declared, is "a funny little Catholic priest, who is a friend of mine, a great Dante scholar, and with a thirst for wandering in the wilderness." But Father Zahm's final journey would be back to Notre Dame. He died in Germany in 1921 and is buried on campus in the Community Cemetery.

Cavanaugh Hall detail

Haggar Hall

Haggar Hall detail

North Dining Hall

Farley Hall

Zahm Invitational Talent Show). Zahm's budding rivalry with neighboring Keenan Hall has sparked barbs between the dorms as well as plenty of pranks. In one episode all of Zahm's shower heads disappeared. Zahmbies, however, became notorious because of Odin, the very public initiation ritual they stage on the weekend of the first home football game. The hall's freshmen dress up in bed sheet togas and then parade through the reflecting pool at Hesburgh Library.

KEENAN HALL (49) AND STANFORD HALL (48)

If Cavanaugh and Zahm halls can be considered twins, then their immediate neighbors to the north—Keenan Hall and Stanford Hall—have to be Siamese twins. Not only are these four-story dormitories architectural sister structures, but they're also joined together by a common lobby and share the same chapel. Of the two, Stanford is officially a bit older. It was dedicated in October 1957, while Keenan's dedication took place in November of the same year. Coincidentally, both were also gifts of Notre Dame graduates who would later serve as lay trustees of the university. Grattan T. Stanford, class of 1904, was an Indiana native who spent three decades as general counsel of the Sinclair Oil Corporation, and James F. Keenan, class of 1913, operated a chain of Midwest hotels from his headquarters in Fort Wayne, Indiana.

With their plain exteriors, Keenan and Stanford do little to excite the eye. They have, however, been blessed with a handsome chapel that contains one of Notre Dame's finest icons, the magnificent crucifix made by celebrated sculptor Ivan Mestrovic. Located just off the halls' connecting lobby, the Chapel of the Holy Cross has a series of exquisite stained-glass windows featuring various types of crosses. Its highlight is Mestrovic's

13-foot mahogany crucifix, which the artist-in-residence executed especially for the chapel in 1957. Originally, the crucifix hung above a companion altar made of travertine marble imported from Italy. The altar was removed in the wake of Vatican II changes, but, happily, the Mestrovic crucifix remains to immeasurably grace the chapel. In the lobby itself you can view another of Mestrovic's works, an excellent wood carving titled *Christ as Young Boy Teaching.*

When Keenan and Stanford opened, they made news for having what was then considered a real innovation: in-dorm study halls and television lounges. Keenan also had a cavernous basement, which has since evolved into the Kommons, the dormitory equivalent of a family room. It's equipped with pool tables, exercise equipment, video games, and that modern-day innovation, big screen television. On weekends, it has also been the scene of disco parties and other entertainment hosted by the hall.

An unwritten rule dictates that Keenan and Stanford residents must always enter their mutual lobby by different doors, and the men living in Keenan refer to the halls as "Keenan-Stanford" while those in Stanford prefer to say "Stanford-Keenan." But relations between these un-separate but equal dorms are generally good. They do, after all, have a lot of lobby in common, even if they are independent halls with their own rectors, identities, and nicknames: the Keenan "Knights" and Stanford "Studs." The halls also have their traditions. Keenan men have been known to streak across campus during final exam week, while the Studs get thrown in the lake on their birthdays.

The really hot North Quad competition exists between Keenan and Zahm Hall, which explains why Zahmbies are the butt of so many jokes during the annual Keenan Revue, an enormously popular winter show that is heavy on satire and light on subtlety. The Knights write and act in all of the revue's uproarious skits, and they take well-aimed potshots at everything from athletes to, of course, Zahm. As for the Studs, they stage a Mr. Stanford Contest in which the hall's hopefuls comically compete in evening wear, swimsuits, and talent competitions. The event not only lampoons beauty pageants, but also raises money for charity.

HAGGAR HALL (61)

NORTH QUAD'S GREAT VIEWS AND SPLENDID SIGHTS
Of the North Quad: From the stairwell windows inside Haggar Hall, you'll get a great view of the residence halls as well as cross-quad comings-and-goings. Also note the benches inside the doors. They bear the word "Respite," a clear indication of just what they have to offer you.

Haggar Hall is the only academic building on the North Quad. It was constructed in 1937 as a home for the biology department and named Wenninger-Kirsch Hall after the two teachers—Holy Cross Fathers Francis Wenninger and Alexander Kirsch—who were instrumental in developing the study of natural sciences at Notre Dame. In 1974 the building was renovated with funds from the Haggar Foundation of Dallas. J. M. Haggar, a Lebanese immigrant who was a trailblazer in manufacturing men's clothing, was a member of the Business College Advisory Council, and his sons were also Notre Dame alumni. The renamed hall became the new home of the psychology department, and its occupants have had their minds on science ever since.

When the hall opened, its basement housed the famous LOBUND Laboratory, a pioneering center for germfree research. Now the basement hosts the South Bend Center for Medical Education, a branch campus of the Indianapolis-based Indiana University School of Medicine. The center provides the first and second years of medical training to future physicians, and its students are accorded the same privileges and access to campus facilities as Notre Dame graduate students. In fact, they even get double report cards: one from Indiana University and one from Notre Dame.

From time to time rumors surface about bodies in the basement of Haggar Hall. While the rumors are often bizarre, be advised that they are not unfounded. Since the medical school offers a class in gross anatomy, cadavers are kept there for teaching purposes.

NORTH DINING HALL (60)

The North Dining Hall was the final building on the North Quad, and its history mirrors both the growth of the student body and the university's decision to keep the increasing numbers of undergraduates living—and consequently eating—on campus. Completed in 1957, the North Dining Hall was constructed in conjunction with Keenan and Stanford halls and, accordingly, imitated them architecturally: square and starkly modern with a buff brick exterior. It could accommodate up to 2,000 students, and all meals were efficiently dished out cafeteria style. As with Keenan and Stanford, Ivan Mestrovic once again provided a redeeming piece of art with his *Last Supper*, a fine wood relief depicting Christ and his disciples at the meal where he instituted the Eucharist.

In the fall of 1987, construction on an addition to the North Dining Hall began in conjunction with the building of Siegfried and Knott halls, two new women's dormitories on the "Mod Quad" north of the Hesburgh Library. The two-story addition on the dining hall's west side not only provided more seating, but also presented an opportunity to revamp the building's contemporary design. Ironically, architect Ellerbe Associates went back to the collegiate Gothic style that had originally inspired the North Quad in order to make the dining hall more visually consistent with older buildings on campus. The building's utilitarian look was radically altered by dressing it up with a copper-clad gable roof, clerestory windows, arches, and vaulted ceilings. Balcony as well as ground-floor seating areas were added to

Leftovers from both Notre Dame's North and South Dining halls are donated to homeless shelters and other charities in the South Bend area. It's a tradition that began in the 1800s, when the Holy Cross sisters who served as the university's cooks started giving food to the poor.

the two main dining rooms, while smaller, private rooms with granite fireplaces and wood floors also offered a traditional dining atmosphere. On the dining hall's exterior, a running series of brick piers significantly enhanced its appearance. Thus, the building that buttresses much of the student body got some well-deserved buttressing of its own.

As part of the North Dining Hall's "back to the future" update, its tired cafeteria line was replaced by a "scramble" system of scattered serving areas, which speeded the flow of students and allowed them to enjoy more made-to-order food. Today, those serving areas function as food courts that offer a variety of specialties—grill and deli items, Mexican, Oriental, traditional home-style fare, soups and stews, pasta, pizza, and desserts. On any given day some 400 different entrees are available, plus more than 20 kinds of beverages.

The dining hall is the perfect place to rub shoulders with students (even though eating there may mean elbowing your way to the ever-popular YOCREAM® machines). About 3,000 members of the Notre Dame family show up for breakfast, lunch, and dinner, so you can witness an instant cross section of the campus. You'll not only get to observe what the Irish eat (wasp-waisted women students make do with skimpy salads; brawny athletes wield trays that look like groaning boards) and what they wear (a predictably inordinate amount of Notre Dame logo apparel), but also get the all-too-rare chance to hear the irrepressible, uniquely irresistible din of youth (and well-fed youth, at that). The dining hall experience is especially nifty during special events such as the annual Circus Lunch, which features treats such as corn dogs and popcorn. And do try the Football Brunch that precedes home football games or the Candlelight Dinner buffets held after every home football game. The hearty brunches typically include a waffle bar, while the elegant buffets offer tempting entrees such as grilled trout and steamship round of beef. By the way, you'll also enjoy a variety of desserts that—no matter what the final score—will *not* include any servings of humble pie.

FARLEY HALL (59)

Located immediately south of the North Dining Hall, Farley was built in 1947. Its collegiate Gothic architecture allowed the hall to blend seamlessly with the other North Quad buildings that Maginnis and Walsh had designed during the previous decade, but Farley had a distinction all its own. It was not only one of the last dormitories on the quad, but also the first one constructed on campus after World War II in order to help meet the needs of Notre Dame's rapidly growing student body.

Farley Hall would continue to mark milestones in the university's history. At the time the dorm opened, the North Quad was dubbed "Freshman Quadrangle" because of Notre Dame's practice of housing its underclassmen on the north side of the campus. In the 1960s, however, that custom ended when the university started a new "stay-hall" policy in which students would remain in the same dormitory throughout their college careers. Farley Hall was the program's test case. Dorm life at Notre Dame changed again in the 1970s when women were admitted as undergraduates, and Farley was one of the first dormitories changed from a men's to a women's hall. The conversion took place in the fall of 1973, just one year after Notre Dame's first coeds began taking classes. As a result, Farley also became one of the first halls where alumni fathers could have the satisfaction of seeing their *daughters* living in the same room that they had once occupied.

The hall was named for one of the most beloved priests ever associated with Notre Dame, Rev. John F. Farley, C.S.C. The Paterson, New

Breen-Phillips Hall

Clarke Memorial Fountain

An Tostal sumo wrestlers on North Quad

Fire Station

Jersey, native entered Notre Dame as a student in 1897, and he soon made a name for himself as an athlete and a scholar. Though Farley weighed a mere 160 pounds, he won four letters in football, four in baseball, one in track, and captained the 1900 football team. He also graduated with honors in 1901. Six years later, Farley was ordained and would spend most of the remaining years of his life as a rector at Notre Dame.

His first assignment was Corby Hall, followed by Walsh Hall and then Sorin Hall. Farley soon made another name for himself as a strict and relentless disciplinarian with an uncanny knack for ferreting out his charges when they broke the rules. He chased them across campus on foot, and he pursued them through the streets of South Bend in the university's horse-drawn "Skive Wagon." Woe to any Notre Dame man whom Farley caught in an off-limits saloon. He also nagged slouchers into standing up straight, monitored incoming mail for hints of perfume, and once greased the walls of an underground passageway to stop students from sneaking out after bed check.

While rector of Sorin Hall, he got the nickname "King" Farley. It was a natural, given his dictatorial demeanor and Sorin Hall's rather regal architecture. Most students, though, called him "Pop" Farley. That came from his habit of calling those in his dorms "my boys." Year after year he treated them as his boys, too. Discipline aside, Farley knew them all personally and well. Whether their interests lay in athletics or the arts, he was said to never miss an activity in which one of his boys participated. Even when Farley suffered a stroke and had a leg amputated, he managed to attend campus events in his wheelchair. And when Pop died in 1939, thousands of Notre Dame students paid their respects by lining the funeral route from Sacred Heart Church all the way to the Community Cemetery.

Though Pop Farley never had the opportunity to speak of students as "my girls," the women of Farley Hall nonetheless help keep his memory alive. Every winter they hold a festival called Pop Farley Week. Activities typically include a talent show, game night, bonfire, or movie night, and its high point is a dorm dance known as—what else?—Pop Farley.

BREEN-PHILLIPS HALL (58)

Built in 1939 as a men's dormitory, Breen-Phillips was for most of its history the province of males. Its namesake benefactors were two alumni from Fort Wayne, Indiana, who also happened to be brothers-in-law—attorney William Breen, class of 1877, and banker Frank Phillips, class of 1880. When the cornerstone was laid, mementos from the two men's student days were even sealed inside it. Within a few years of the hall's opening, young naval officers training for duty in World War II were being quartered in its rooms, and Notre Dame's stalwart football coach Frank Leahy would also have an office in the hall.

William Breen was both a charter member and the first president of Notre Dame's board of lay trustees.

Now Breen-Phillips is "Banshee" territory, the residence hall of the women undergraduates whose collective nickname comes from the female spirit of Gaelic folklore. It was converted to a women's dormitory in the fall of 1973. The women of Breen-Phillips have since become known for fielding some of Notre Dame's best sports teams and have won interhall championships in soccer, basketball, and football. Every fall, just before the varsity football team's first home game, they also hold their traditional Bathrobe Breakfast by marching from Breen-Phillips to the North Dining Hall in their robes and pajamas. What, do you suppose, would the Messrs. Leahy, Breen, and Phillips have made of that?

Located on the southeast corner of the North Quad, Breen-Phillips was designed in modified collegiate Gothic style by Maginnis and Walsh. It also has a sunken chapel where comfortable floor pillows have been substituted for pews. Pope John Paul II imparted an Apostolic Blessing on Breen-Phillips Hall in 1984.

CLARKE MEMORIAL FOUNTAIN AND FIELDHOUSE MALL (301)

A survey published in a recent edition of *The Dome* revealed that 68 percent of Notre Dame's senior class had run through the waters of Clarke Memorial Fountain at least one time. Certainly an even larger percentage has gravitated here to study, socialize, and even dance in the shadow of this campus landmark. Perhaps the lure of the fountain lies in the hauntingly timeless appeal of its mammoth form, which noted New York architects Philip Johnson and John Burgee (Notre Dame class of 1956) purposely designed to mimic the mystical, monolithic monuments built in Britain during the Bronze Age. Not surprisingly, its nickname is Stonehenge.

Clarke Memorial Fountain consists of four limestone arches formed by 10-foot-long slabs that are supported by twin columns five feet square and 20 feet high. The arches each contain a fountain and rise from an underlying black granite pool that has a huge granite sphere at its center. Quarried in southern Indiana, the elephantine columns weigh 20 tons apiece and had to be trucked to Notre Dame over a designated route with permission from state officials.

Although some have denounced the fountain as a war memorial, it was actually intended as a peace monument commemorating some 500 Notre Dame alumni who died in World War II, the Korean conflict, and Vietnam. The names of those wars are carved in three of its arches, and the fourth arch bears the Latin inscription *Pro Patria et Pace*, "For Country and Peace." The granite sphere represents the earth; the water is

Clarke Memorial Fountain

symbolic of life; and the stone columns, of course, were crafted by the hand of God.

Dedicated in 1986, the fountain was underwritten by Notre Dame alumnus Thomas Shuff of Lake Forest, Illinois, and by its principal benefactor, Maude Clarke of Chicago. Mrs. Clarke's donation was made in memory of her husband John, an investment banker who once served on the business college's advisory council. Both of the Clarkes had also been Army officers in World War II.

The Fountain is the centerpiece of Fieldhouse Mall, a lovely park-like area with benches and formal gardens that graces the southern end of the quad. The mall not only serves as a crossway between the Hesburgh Library and the Main Quad, but is also a popular place for festivals, social activities, marching band rehearsals, and the innumerable snowmen that students build during the long Indiana winters. The site was created when the Old Fieldhouse was torn down in 1983, and consistent with Notre Dame's steadfast sense of tradition, there now stands a buff brick monument to that long-gone gymnasium. Look for it just west of the Clarke Memorial Fountain, and you'll discover that it contains the Old Fieldhouse's original "April 1898" cornerstone.

NORTH QUAD'S GREAT VIEWS AND SPLENDID SIGHTS
Of the Hesburgh Memorial Library: Stand just west of the Clarke Memorial Fountain and look east directly toward the Hesburgh Library behind it, and you'll see that the outline of the library actually echoes the ancient shape of "Stonehenge." The result: architectural double vision in the curious sight of a monolith standing in front of a monolith.

FIRE STATION (62)

Although the Fire Station does not face the North Quad yard, its location at the corner of Holy Cross and St. Joseph's Drives makes it a close neighbor of both Haggar Hall and the North Dining Hall. The building was constructed in 1946 to house the Notre Dame Fire Department, and, obviously, the Fire Station has remained true to that purpose. Its architect was Wendell T. Phillips of Milford, Massachusetts, an expert on ecclesiastical architecture who had been affiliated with Maginnis and Walsh for many years. As a young man, the versatile Mr. Phillips had been a talented enough baseball pitcher to attract offers from professional teams. Instead, he chose to go to Notre Dame and graduated in 1912 with both an architecture degree and a place in the Monogram Club as a star player on the varsity baseball team.

THE OLD FIELDHOUSE

Opposing teams called Notre Dame's Old Fieldhouse "The Snakepit." Adolph Rupp, the University of Kentucky's long-time basketball coach, claimed that between the deafening Irish band constantly playing behind his bench and the hundreds of priests stationed in the stands, he could not win there. For a time, some opponents wouldn't even set foot in the Fieldhouse and insisted that Notre Dame play its home games at Chicago Stadium. Little wonder. The Fieldhouse was notorious for the fanatic Notre Dame students who routinely—and raucously—packed its bleachers. By 1968, when the last varsity basketball game was played there, its clamorous crowds had cheered Irish squads to 474 wins and only 91 losses.

It was the house that Morrissey built. Actually, Notre Dame's seventh president built the Fieldhouse not once, but twice. His first Fieldhouse, built in 1898, burned to the ground the next year, and Morrissey immediately ordered a replacement. His second Fieldhouse—a castle-like structure that salvaged its predecessor's cornerstone—was said to be fireproof, and it became a campus landmark that endured for more than 80 years. In addition to basketball, the facility was used for track and field competitions, football and baseball practice, pep rallies, graduations, and untold performances and convocations. Franklin D. Roosevelt, the first incumbent president to travel to Notre Dame, paid a visit there; so did the poet William Butler Yeats and comedian Bob Hope. Even Notre Dame's renowned Collegiate Jazz Festival—which is now the longest-running one in the nation and has attracted performers such as Herbie Hancock and Quincy Jones—was launched at the Fieldhouse in 1959.

When the Joyce Center's modern athletic facilities opened in 1968, the aging Fieldhouse won a reprieve from the wrecking ball when it was turned into a studio for the art department. Fifteen years later, the building was razed, but not before its hardwood basketball floor was carved into hundreds of small pieces that would serve as souvenirs for varsity athletes who had played or practiced there. That well-used floor had been bought with Notre Dame's revenue from the 1925 Rose Bowl, the historic football game in which the famed Four Horsemen appeared together for the last time.

Fires plagued Notre Dame during much of its history, and the university initially either called on South Bend's fire fighters, or, as happened in the disastrous 1879 fire at the Main Building, relied on bucket brigades from the lakes. Following the fire that leveled the first Fieldhouse, Notre Dame formed its own fire department in 1900. The student volunteers who manned it had only hand-pulled hose carts for equipment, and their meager compensation consisted of "the use of a pair of rubber boots for the year." By the late 1930s, Notre Dame's fire department was staffed by Holy Cross brothers. They served as full-time firemen who just happened *not* to draw a paycheck. Led by Chief Borromeo Malley, Notre Dame began to modernize its fire fighting and prevention capabilities. The resourceful Brother Borromeo built the university's first fire truck—a combination pumper and hook-and-ladder—from a salvaged chassis and even started an early sprinkler system by screwing perforated nozzles into water pipes. By the time he retired in 1986, the 73-year-old brother was the oldest active fire chief in the United States.

At first, the firemen-brothers lived in Columba Hall, but their equipment was in a storage shed near the power plant. Whenever the fire alarm rang, they had to hotfoot the distance from their quarters. The Fire Station was built to hasten the brothers' response time, and architect Phillips tailored it to their particular needs. In addition to the standard firehouse kitchen and brass pole, he gave the Fire Station a chapel so that the brothers could attend mass there every morning. The Fire Station's opening also coincided with the phenomenal football teams that coach Frank Leahy fielded in the late 1940s and early 1950s. Brother Borromeo was a friend of Leahy's, and whenever the coach needed a retreat from the pressures of his high profile job, Brother Borromeo let him stay in one of the Fire Station's bedrooms. Perhaps the room's number—7 West—helped bring Leahy the luck he needed in leading the Irish to national championships in 1946, 1947, and 1949.

Notre Dame is now one of only a handful of universities with its own fire department. Although lay professionals have replaced the brothers, the Fire Station still has the chapel where mass can be celebrated and Leahy's old room is still being occupied, albeit by a firefighter instead of a coach. The department itself, however, has evolved dramatically and now boasts up-to-date fire engines as well as state-of-the-art prevention and detection systems. Since the campus has one priceless basilica, two lakes, three high rise buildings, plus more than 200 other structures ranging from a landmark stadium to historic dormitories, Notre Dame's firefighters must be multifaceted. They are trained not only to provide emergency medical services but also to perform ice and open water rescues, high angle rescue, and confined space rescue. In addition to answering about 1,000 emergency calls per year, they test and inspect 130 fire alarm systems, 5,800 fire extinguishers, and 145 fire hydrants.

BRAINS AND BRAWN
The Library-to-Stadium Quadrangle

It's said that St. Patrick used a shamrock to explain the Blessed Trinity—Father, Son, and Holy Spirit in one God—to the people of Ireland. If St. Patrick were to come to Notre Dame, he wouldn't need to go hunting for a shamrock. He'd only have to point to a trinity of buildings—the Basilica of the Sacred Heart, the Hesburgh Library, and Notre Dame Stadium—to explain the university's religious values, academic excellence, and rich athletic tradition. As Notre Dame's spiritual taproot, the Basilica belongs to Main Quad. The Library and the Stadium, however, are located directly across from each other at opposite ends of a lovely mall on the east side of campus. Their proximity is an absolutely perfect pairing, for the Library and the Stadium each stands as a symbol of that time-honored educational ideal: a sound mind and a sound body.

THEODORE M. HESBURGH LIBRARY (72)

This may look like the tallest structure on campus, but it isn't. The tallest—at 230 feet—is the spire atop the Basilica of the Sacred Heart. The Library—at 215 feet—is a full fifteen feet shorter than the spire, although it is still much taller than the Stadium (a height gap that, you must agree, provides a very graphic indication of Notre Dame's priorities). The obvious reason that the Hesburgh Library seems so big is the building's sheer bulk. It is a massive limestone-and-brick box 14 stories

BRAINS AND BRAWN GREAT VIEWS AND SPLENDID SIGHTS
From the mall:
The Stadium is on one end, and "Touchdown Jesus" is on the other—two awesome landmarks, and all you have to do is stand anywhere south of the reflecting pool.

185

Hesburgh Library

high, and its sprawling first and second floors each cover about two acres before the structure narrows into the tower that visually dominates the east side of the campus. Designed by Ellerbe Associates of Minnesota, the Library was, in fact, the largest university library building in the world when it opened in 1963. At a total cost of $12.5 million, it was also one of the most expensive, but the university raised the money to build it through numerous donations and a grant from the Ford Foundation.

Originally, it was called the Memorial Library, but when Rev. Theodore Martin Hesburgh, C.S.C., retired as the university's president in 1987, the name was quite fittingly changed to honor him. For Notre Dame, Father Hesburgh was a twentieth-century version of Father Sorin. While Sorin had made Notre Dame, it was Hesburgh who remade it into an internationally known and academically respected university. Father Hesburgh was president of Notre Dame longer than any other person (even Father Sorin), and the 35 years he so effectively spent in that office became not just an administration, but an era. He was simply the right man in the right job at the right time.

Born and raised in Syracuse, New York, Father Hesburgh was educated at Notre Dame, took his seminary training in Rome, and was ordained in 1943. He exemplified the "cuff link priest"—polished, personable, professional, and, very important in twentieth-century America, photogenic. In fact, it was a photographer who allowed Hesburgh to set the tone for his presidency. At an early press conference, he was asked to pose hiking a football, and Father Hesburgh refused. The world was thus on notice about the university's new president and his intention to transform Notre Dame's image from football factory to academic oasis. He formed a highly effective partnership with his executive vice president, Rev. Edmund P. Joyce, and together "Ted and Ned" persistently worked to develop Notre Dame into the nation's premier Catholic university. They dramatically increased the number of students and faculty members, raised the endowment from less than $10 million to about a half billion dollars, and boosted research funding from less than $1 million to $20 million.

Hesburgh's presidency was also defined by two landmark decisions that had—and continue to have—an enormous impact on Notre Dame: (1) transferring ownership and control of the university from the Congregation of Holy Cross to a

BRAINS AND BRAWN GREAT VIEWS AND SPLENDID SIGHTS
The Reflecting Pool:
It's lovely to look at, lined by relaxing benches and shady trees, and superbly positioned at the feet of "Touchdown Jesus." And if that isn't endorsement enough, the pool is also the prettiest of the many pretty spots along the marvelously landscaped mall that stretches between the Library and the Stadium.

Hesburgh Library

The Word of Life *mural closeup*

Galvin Life Science Center

Moses statue, west side of Hesburgh Library

board of trustees in 1967; and (2) admitting women as undergraduates in 1972. Father Hesburgh is still so identified with those momentous events that his effect on Notre Dame's physical plant is sometimes overlooked. He was actually the greatest builder that the university has ever known. During his years in office, not only were numerous buildings remodeled or expanded, but 40 new structures—including the Library that now bears his name and best illustrates his educational mission—were added to the campus.

"Ted's Mahal," as students dubbed the Library when it opened, has more than two million volumes, and it serves as the flagship for several specialized libraries such as architecture and engineering that are berthed in various academic buildings on campus. The Library has excellent research resources as well as premier collections in Catholic theology, medieval studies, and Dante studies. In addition to serving the mind, the building serves the human spirit with art ranging from its trademark "Touchdown Jesus" mural to exhibits on the main floor concourse. The Library is one of the busiest and most used buildings on campus. Elevators are constantly carrying people up and down the tower, and the computer banks never go empty. The Library opens early in the morning and remains open well past midnight when the university is in session. During finals week, it doesn't close at all, and on the concourse, the Campus Ministry kindly supplies bleary-eyed students with cups of coffee and hot cocoa. The students' study area on the second floor doubles as a social lounge, but do not let all of the bustle on the lower floors mislead you. The Hesburgh Library is a place of serious scholarship and study, particularly among the rarefied stacks on the upper floors of the tower. When you visit here, therefore, please defer to all those intent people you see with their noses buried in books and their eyeballs glued to computer monitors by being as quiet and unobtrusive as possible.

BRAINS AND BRAWN GREAT VIEWS AND SPLENDID SIGHTS

From the Hesburgh Library: The glass-enclosed top floor of the Library is, alas, reserved as the President's Lounge, and admittance to the meetings and social events held there is by invitation only. But do not despair too much, for almost any window you can find on the upper floors of the Library will yield an excellent view in any direction. And if you can't get football tickets, the windows on the Library's south side are a spectacularly silent way to watch the game and the crowd in the Stadium.

Since it's such an enormous repository of knowledge and information, the Library literally does have something to interest everyone, and you could consume entire days exploring its vast resources. If you spend any time at all in the Library, you'll be happy to know that the ground floor (basement) has restrooms as well as vending machines that dispense food and drink. The paragraphs below provide information about many of the Hesburgh Library's highlights. If you'd like additional details, please call the Library at 219/631-6258.

The Word of Life Mural, a. k. a. "Touchdown Jesus": In the parlance of architects, this mural is the feature that "saves" the Hesburgh Library's design from deadly monotony. It is also one of the most widely recognized images on campus, thanks to the TV network cameramen who love to scan it as a Stadium backdrop during home football games. In the finest tradition of Catholic education, the mural represents Christ as the greatest of all teachers, and its title—*The Word of Life*—comes from the Gospel of John. But its universal nickname is "Touchdown Jesus" because the mural depicts Christ with upraised arms that look uncannily like a referee's touchdown signal. Nobody intended to imply, of course, that the Son of God's message to the world should be that Notre Dame scored six points. But, from the Irish football fans' perspective the nickname could hardly be helped; after all, "Touchdown Jesus" not only can still be seen from the Stadium but also appears to be looming directly above the north goalpost.

The Word of Life is larger than life, huge, in fact. It covers the entire south facade of the Library's tower, standing 132 feet high and 65 feet wide. The head of Christ, which is the mural's single largest element, is nine feet tall, and from thumb-to-thumb, the distance between his famous "touchdown" hands is 42 feet. The gift of Mr. and Mrs. Howard Phalin of Wilmette,

Long-running campus joke about the globe-trotting Father Hesburgh: "What's the difference between God and Father Hesburgh?" "God is everywhere; Father Hesburgh is everywhere except Notre Dame."

Illinois, *The Word of Life* was designed by Claremont, California, artist Millard Sheets. It is a mosaic composed of several thousand individual pieces of 81 different kinds of stones. Stone is the earth's fundamental building material, and the types used in creating the mosaic—they include granites, syenites, marbles, serpentines, limestones—came from 16 different countries. These stones display an incredibly rich variety of colors and surface finishes, and the artist arranged them so that changes in sunlight and atmospheric conditions "play" with the stones to lend subtlety and nuance to the mural. At the base of the mural, a rectangular pool of water also constantly reflects and reinforces the complexities of the mural's design. The dominant figure in *The Word of Life* is Christ, and in it, he is surrounded by saints, scholars, and apostles. Within the landscaping at the south end of the reflecting pool, you will find a plaque that has a legend identifying the immense figures in the mural. The ones nearest Christ at the top of the mural represent the Apostles, and the sages assembled below them represent the knowledge of various eras and cultures.

"No. 1 Moses" Statue: The formidable statue of Moses that lords over the Library's west lawn was done by Joseph Turkalj, who studied with Notre Dame's eminent sculptor-in-residence, Ivan Mestrovic. It's a serious work of art that recreates the biblical account of Moses' wrath at the Israelites after receiving the Ten Commandments on Mt. Sinai. His foot is stomping their golden calf, and he points his right index finger toward heaven to signify that there is only one God. Notre Dame's students, however, have assigned their own meanings to the statue, beginning with Father Hesburgh. During his presidency, Father Hesburgh served on numerous national and international commissions and, like Father Sorin before him, traveled constantly. He took so many airplane trips that the students claimed the statue's skyward finger meant, "There goes Father

Ivan Mestrovic did the righteous-looking bust of Moses that is displayed near the circulation desk on the Library's first floor. The large abstract sculpture on the east lawn of the Library was done by Glenn Zweygartt and is titled Upheaval X.

Hesburgh." Since his retirement, the students have extended their enthusiasm for the football team from the Stadium to the statue. They now interpret Moses to be pointing out to everyone that "We're Number One."

The Christ Symbols: A handsome veneer of pinkish Oklahoma Tweed granite sheathes the exterior of the Library's entire first floor. Cut into the granite's polished surface are a series of gold-painted line drawings of symbols that represent Christ. The drawings include "The Seal of the Living God" (the cross); "The Grain of Wheat" (redemption); "The Fish of the Living" (the Greek word for fish is an acronym meaning "Jesus Christ, Son of God, Savior"); "The Sun of Justice" (light and salvation); "The Cornerstone" (Christ as part of the foundation); "The Star of Jacob" (resurrection); and "The Key of David" (Christ as the key to escaping darkness and death).

The Concourse: The large east-west passageway that runs across the Library's first floor is used for everything from book sales to exhibits to brown bag lunches. You'll want to take a few minutes to view the glass cases at either end of the concourse, for they hold attractive and interesting displays about various aspects of the university. The colorful kites that you see hanging overhead are collectively titled *Kite-Likes and Letters.* They were done by adjunct art professor Barbara Peterson and symbolize flight, aspiration, and knowledge. The gold "kite-tails" display symbols and lettering that represent the various ways in which humankind has recorded knowledge. Kite 1 shows three items used by primitive cultures to keep track of calculations, messages, and genealogy; Kite 2 has the Hebrew word for "knowledge"; Kite 3 pictorially conveys the African proverb "Apart from God, there is nothing to fear"; Kite 4 indicates the Greek letters for "wisdom"; Kite 5 bears a Latin phrase meaning "Here begins the book"; Kite 6 shows Chinese characters forming a quote from Confucius, "Knowledge has no end-

*Hesburgh Library
concourse*

"As an Irish enthusiast the aim has always been to render this cherished collection of tomes available to scholars interested in the historic past of the homeland of the Gael—a subject that receives but scant attention in the seats of learning of this day. Believing that the spiritual atmosphere of Notre Dame is most favorable to the promotion of the donor's purpose, the renowned University has been selected as the repository of my literary treasures . . . "
—excerpt of 1931 letter from Captain Francis O'Neill to Notre Dame president Charles L. O'Donnell

ing"; Kite 7 exhibits beautiful Arabic letters meaning "Knowledge is Light," and Kite 8 gives a nod to the computer age with the acronym UNLOC, which stands for <u>U</u>niversity of <u>N</u>otre Dame <u>Li</u>braries' <u>O</u>nline <u>C</u>atalog.

Must Sees: These are some of the brightest gems within the Library's vault of knowledge, and they have attracted academic fame and acclaim. The Medieval Institute has some 60,000 volumes and is a major research center on Christian civilization in the Middle Ages. The John A. Zahm Dante Collection is one of the largest and best in the world; the fifteenth-century editions here are priceless, and you'd have to go to hell and back to learn more about the *Divine Comedy*. The Frank M. Folsom Ambrosiana Microfilm and Photographic Collection boasts classical manuscripts of Milan's famed Ambrosian Library. The American Catholic archive is a comprehensive and unrivaled assemblage of materials that was begun in the late 1800s by James Edwards, Notre Dame's first librarian. The O'Neill Collection of Irish Music has more than 1,500 volumes donated in 1931 by Captain Francis O'Neill, the Irish-born general superintendent of Chicago's police department. The Joyce Sports Research Collection is a unique treasury of sports, games, and athletics; it contains

On a brisk autumn afternoon, two young men appeared at Notre Dame's public relations office. They were decked out in brand new "Fighting Irish" hats, sweatshirts, and jackets and had obviously just made a raid on the bookstore. In halting English, the young men told tour coordinator Lyn Magliola that they were from Frankfort, Germany, and had come to South Bend just to see the sights at Notre Dame. Mrs. Magliola quickly retrieved some maps and began circling the top spots on campus. When she got to *The Word of Life* mural on the Hesburgh Library, she went into great detail trying to explain it to them. The young men looked blank. Then she pulled out a picture of the mural. "Ja!" one of them immediately exclaimed, "Touchdown Jesus!"

the books and memorabilia of Walter "Red" Smith, the Pulitzer Prize-winning sportswriter who graduated from Notre Dame in 1927. The Penguin Collection holds virtually all of the popular, but literary paperbacks published between 1935 and 1965.

The Rare Book Room: Expertly staffed and wonderfully organized, this outstanding repository of Notre Dame's treasures and special collections is located at the west end of the concourse. Although oriented toward scholarly research, it is open to the public and has fascinating permanent displays. If you're looking for ancient cuneiform tablets from Babylonia, a first edition of *A Christmas Carol,* Father Hesburgh's stamp collection, Irish maps and sea charts, or a facsimile edition of the *Book of Kells,* then this is the place for you.

The Notre Dame Archives: Located on the sixth floor of the Library, the Archives are an important part of the university. Actually, it's the part that belongs to the past, for this is the storehouse of Notre Dame's history, an attic, if you will, where all manner of documents, records, manuscripts, and memorabilia are painstakingly preserved, protected, and defended against the ravages of time. If there is *anything* you'd like to know about Notre Dame, start your search here. The collections are comprehensive, and the staff is top-notch—knowledgeable, thorough, professional, and extremely helpful. But even if you're not interested in research, you should stop by the Archives anyway just to see the interesting items on exhibit and enjoy its exceptional view of the Basilica and Golden Dome.

The Thirteenth Floor: The windows here are small and narrow, but they offer a rare perspective on the everyday ebb and flow of the busy campus far below—a constantly moving, ever-changing, yet eerily silent vista. There is also a certain solitude to be experienced here among the endless stacks of books. You will not, however, be totally alone on the thirteenth floor, for it also holds the

Ralph McInerny, the Professor of Medieval Studies who directs the Jacques Maritain Center in the Hesburgh Library, is not only an authority on St. Thomas Aquinas but also a popular mystery writer. Under the pen name of Monica Quill, he writes about the adventures of the unlikely detective, Sister Mary Teresa. But McInerny's best-known series is the Father Dowling mysteries, which were the basis of a television series. One of McInerny's latest novels— On This Rockne—*is set at Notre Dame.*

One of the Rad Lab's first pieces of sophisticated equipment was an oval-shaped electron accelerator that was painted brown and decorated with white stripes, "stitching," and "laces" to look like a giant football. It was even autographed by Notre Dame coaches and players such as Dan Devine and Joe Theismann.

offices of "Ted and Ned," the now-retired, but always active Fathers Hesburgh and Joyce.

RADIATION RESEARCH BUILDING (71)

Scientists who work in the "Rad Lab" call it the BMOC: Big Mirror on Campus. As you approach the Rad Lab by walking southwest from the Library, you'll readily see why, because all of the windows in this very contemporary concrete building are covered with a highly reflective mylar film. Designed by the Chicago firm of Skidmore, Owings and Merrill, the Rad Lab was built by the U.S. Atomic Energy Commission in the early 1960s, and it is operated by the university under an agreement with the U.S. Department of Energy. The radiation chemistry research that is conducted here began with the Manhattan Project during World War II, when the electron accelerator in Notre Dame's physics department was used to study the effect that radiation has on matter. The Rad Lab is now

Decio Hall

considered the nation's foremost radiation chemistry laboratory. It has one of the world's highest concentrations of researchers in that field, and many of its specialized facilities are the finest to be found anywhere.

DECIO FACULTY HALL (83)

This office building for Arts and Letters professors occupies a most apropos location: the foreground of Christ the Teacher as depicted in the Library mural. The hall's innovative staggered design advantageously allows every office to have a window, and although a modern structure, its buff-colored bricks and distinctive gables help to make it architecturally compatible with the collegiate Gothic buildings on nearby South Quad. Dedicated in 1984, the building was designed by Ellerbe Associates of Bloomington, Minnesota, and its benefactor was Arthur J. Decio, president of Skyline Corporation, a manufactured housing and recreation vehicle company in Elkhart, Indiana.

COMPUTING CENTER AND MATHEMATICS BUILDING (74)

Located just southeast of the Library, this contemporary, flat-roofed building opened in 1962 and was another product of Minnesota's Ellerbe Associates. It was specifically designed to be the home of a UNIVAC 1107 Computer that used solid state technology, took up half the building, and served as Notre Dame's official introduction to the computer age. By 1990s standards, the UNIVAC was a dinosaur, and it became extinct long ago. Notre Dame, however, continues to be a leader among colleges and universities in using computer technology as an education and communications tool. The campus is now riddled with state-of-the-art computers and computer clusters; DeBartolo Hall has been hailed as a world-class

For information about almost every facet of Notre Dame, you can access the university's home page via the Internet at www.nd.edu.

showcase for bringing technology into the classroom; and the university even has a campuswide, fiber-based network that provides access to information, e-mail, and research resources.

Notre Dame's Office of Information Technology is headquartered in this building, and one of its pioneering projects is RESNET, which links the university's computer network to every dormitory room. The idea is to have "one connection per pillow" so that students can not only maximize their use of computers but also be prepared for the digital environment of the future. As mission control for computers, the Office of Information Technology also ensures that students have the right technology for their courses. The office consults with academic departments to find out what kinds of hardware and software students will need, and then works with students to put together computer systems tailored to their curriculum. The Computing Center even contains a computer store; it sells equipment and programs and provides repair service for students, faculty, and staff members.

GALVIN LIFE SCIENCE CENTER/FREIMANN LIFE SCIENCE CENTER (84)

As you may have surmised from their names, biology is the science that is under the microscope in these adjacent research centers. The Galvin Center is the home of the Vector Biology Laboratory, which is renowned for its groundbreaking research in using genetics to control mosquitoes and other insects, and its biologists and microbiologists have also earned international recognition for their investigations of parasites. The Freimann Center conducts biomedical research, and its animal studies have life-saving potential for human beings. Museum-like natural history exhibits are frequently displayed at the Galvin Center, and it has an excellent biology library. The center also houses a very large—about 265,000 specimens—and important collection of plants, the Greene-Nieuwland Herbarium. Now an official plant repository for the State of Indiana, the herbarium is based on the extensive collections personally acquired by botanists Edward L. Greene and Rev. Julius Nieuwland, C.S.C.

The Galvin and Freimann Centers are both contemporary brick buildings attractively designed by Ellerbe Associates. Dedicated in 1972, the Paul V. Galvin Life Science Center memorializes the founder of the Motorola Corporation and was funded primarily through a gift from his family. The Frank M. Freimann Life Science Center was added in the 1980s. It honors the former chairman of the Magnavox Corporation and was underwritten by the Freimann Charitable Trust of Fort Wayne, Indiana.

The first Notre Dame alumnus to win the Nobel Prize was Dr. Eric F. Wieschaus, a molecular biologist who earned his bachelor's degree in biology in 1969.

REYNIERS LIFE BUILDING (68)

A research complex located north of Douglas Road, the Reyniers building houses the biology department's world-renowned affiliate, the LOBUND (Laboratory of Bacteriology at the University of Notre Dame) Laboratory. Germfree research in sterile environments was virtually invented at LOBUND, which was founded and directed by Notre Dame professor James Reyniers, a Mishawaka, Indiana, native and member of the class of 1930.

HANK FAMILY HALL OF ENVIRONMENTAL AND HEALTH SCIENCE (86)

This building was funded with a gift from Bernard J. "Jerry" Hank and his wife, Joyce McMahon Hank, of Moline, Illinois. A Notre

Coach Frank Leahy statue

Football game

Marching Band

Football postgame activity

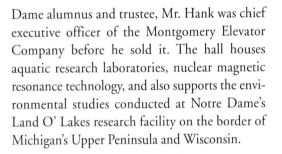

Dame alumnus and trustee, Mr. Hank was chief executive officer of the Montgomery Elevator Company before he sold it. The hall houses aquatic research laboratories, nuclear magnetic resonance technology, and also supports the environmental studies conducted at Notre Dame's Land O' Lakes research facility on the border of Michigan's Upper Peninsula and Wisconsin.

NOTRE DAME STADIUM (73)

Coach Lou Holtz once said that the sight of his gold-helmeted players gathered under the goalpost before a game always gave him chills. Him and every other Fighting Irish fan in the Stadium. Chills—and thrills—are the essence of the Stadium. This is not merely a football field. It is an *experience*, a uniquely Notre Dame synthesis of sport, tradition, pride, loyalty, and belief. Even when the Stadium is empty, even when the gates are locked and the stands are silent, even when all you can see of it are the outside walls and the gold letters that say "University of Notre Dame," you cannot help but sense the lure—and the lore—of this place. It is haunted by a thousand ghosts of glorious seasons past: the Four Horsemen riding into immortality on the words of Grantland Rice; the multi-talented George Gipp and "Jumpin' Joe" Savoldi; Joe Montana, a field general in a green jersey; Raghib "The Rocket" Ismail flying toward the end zone; and, of course, Knute Rockne, pioneer of the forward pass, master of the locker room speech, brilliant motivator, relentless innovator, and though gone from the gridiron since 1930, still the most victorious coach (winning an amazing .881 of his games) in college football history.

People frequently make the mistake of calling this "Knute Rockne Stadium." The correct name is Notre Dame Stadium and has been ever since Rockne himself nipped the efforts of the fans and

The first game in Notre Dame Stadium was played on October 4, 1930, against Southern Methodist University. The Irish won, 20-14. The Stadium's dedication game came a week later, and Notre Dame prevailed again to defeat Navy, 26-2.

sportswriters who pushed to have his name put on it. There is no mistake, however, that the Stadium will always be "The House that Rockne Built." It was Rockne's phenomenal coaching success and flair for publicity during the 1920s that captured banner headlines as well as a legion of fervent Fighting Irish fans. Probably more than any other individual, Rockne helped make college football a national spectator sport, and in the process, he also made Notre Dame a household word. The Norwegian-born coach with the cockeyed grin and rumpled suits was an unlikely patriarch, but he founded a football dynasty at Notre Dame and his legacy is incomparable. Just as the nation associates the names Rockefeller with wealth and Kennedy with politics, Rockne means college football. And Coach Rockne's one and only home was Notre Dame.

Notre Dame Stadium as you see it today is not quite the stadium that Rockne knew. It is an expanded and updated version, the most concrete evidence of Notre Dame football's continuing appeal and of how well Rockne's successors have fulfilled their individual destinies as Fighting Irish coaches. The "original" Notre Dame Stadium opened in 1930. It replaced the university's old

"I don't want anybody going out there to die for dear old Notre Dame. Hell, I want you fighting to stay alive."
—Knute Rockne

Stadium

Stadium-north entrance

football facility, Cartier Field, which had been made obsolete by Rockne's dazzling wins and the mounting clamor for tickets to the games. Rockne wanted a showplace worthy of his team's stature as a major football power, and the splendid new art deco-looking Stadium fit the bill perfectly. Considered one of the premiere facilities of its day, Notre Dame Stadium became an instant American landmark and the unofficial capital of big-time college football.

Although fate allowed Rockne only one season in Notre Dame Stadium (he perished in a plane crash in the spring of 1931), he was very much the mastermind of the Stadium's character. As he traveled around the country, Rockne made a point of inspecting stadiums. The one that the Osborn Engineering Company from Cleveland, Ohio, had designed for the University of Michigan caught his eye, and the Osborn company—which also created New York's Yankee Stadium—was hired to build a scaled-down version for Notre Dame. Rockne insisted that the Stadium be used only for football; made sure that every seat had a great sight line; and minimized the distance between the fans and the playing field. He helped to lay out the parking and traffic pattern around the Stadium, and as a finishing touch, Rockne also had the emerald Cartier Field sod on which his teams had had such luck transplanted to Notre Dame Stadium.

For more than 60 memorable years, the original Notre Dame Stadium admirably served the Irish faithful. But by the early 1990s the Stadium was starting to show its age, every home game was a sell-out, and the unmet demand for tickets was greater than ever. Wisely deciding not to tamper with tradition, the university opted to modify the bowl-shaped Stadium rather than tear it down and build a new one. The Ellerbe Becket architectural firm in Kansas City devised an ingenious and attractive plan to erect an outer brick wall around the Stadium. The wall supports an entirely new upper deck that increased the seating capacity from 59,075 to 80,225 yet left much of the original structure in tact. The $53 million expansion took about two years and was largely financed by issuing fixed-rate bonds. Throughout the construction, Notre Dame's Office of Information Technologies kept a camera aimed at the Stadium so that fans of the Irish—and the Internet—were able to watch its progress on the World Wide Web.

*The Four Horsemen
The most celebrated backfield in the history of college football consisted of Harry Stuhldreher, Elmer Layden, Jim Crowley, and Don Miller. With great speed and timing, they demolished opponents during the 1922-1924 seasons and ultimately took Notre Dame to the 1925 Rose Bowl, where they ran over Stanford, 27-10. After Notre Dame handily defeated Army on October 18, 1924, the players' performance was compared to the Four Horsemen of the Apocalypse by New York writer Grantland Rice. His column began with a now-famous lead, "Outlined against a blue-gray October sky, the Four Horsemen rode again. In dramatic lore, they are known as Famine, Pestilence, Destruction, and Death. These are only aliases. Their real names are Stuhldreher, Miller, Crowley, and Layden . . ."*

The remodeled Stadium debuted on September 6, 1997, for the re-dedication game against Georgia Tech. Although the Irish won the game 17-14, the real excitement of the day came from the Stadium itself, which, as the cliché goes, is bigger and better. It has, to be sure, been modernized. There are new goalposts and scoreboards; a fancy, four-level press box; entry gates designed to look like the gridiron; and open, elevated concourses that provide panoramic views of the campus. But the most remarkable aspect of the Stadium is the seamless way that the new has blended with the old so that its sense of intimacy and tradition has not been trampled. "Touchdown Jesus" still lords above the crowd, and players still have the famous "PLAY LIKE A CHAMPION TODAY" sign to touch for good luck. The familiar brigade of yellow-jacketed ushers patrols the stands; the playing field remains

THE "FIGHTING IRISH"

Nobody knows exactly how Notre Dame's football team came to be called the "Fighting Irish." Maybe it was Father Corby's famous blessing on the Irish Brigade. Or Irish freedom fighter Eamon De Valera's visit to Notre Dame in 1919. Or maybe it was rooted in the university's historically large number of Irish-Catholic students, priests, and faculty. There's no doubt, however, about how "Fighting Irish" won out over sobriquets such as "Papists" and "Ramblers." It was popularized in the late 1920s by Francis Wallace from Bellaire, Ohio, a member of the class of 1923. Wallace was a *New York Daily News* sportswriter who habitually used "Fighting Irish" when writing about Notre Dame football in his columns. The columns were widely distributed by the wire services, and Notre Dame President Matthew Walsh (whose own father came from County Cork) also gave his blessing to the "spirit" of the nickname. With the acceptance of "Fighting Irish" as a nickname, Notre Dame also acquired the Irish terrier as a mascot. The first was Tipperary Terence, who was followed by a string of dogs called Clashmore Mike. The dogs lasted until the 1960s, when they were replaced by a green-suited, acrobatic, invariably red-headed Leprechaun.

natural, not synthetic grass; the end zone retains its diagonal stripes; and, best of all, no garish neon lights, no commercial advertising signs, and no private luxury boxes sully either the scoreboard or the atmosphere.

Notre Dame Stadium continues to be a single purpose facility, and in spite of the great crowds that fill it with expectation and color on autumn afternoons, it is also the least often used structure at the university. The expansion certainly gave the Stadium a higher profile on campus, but it is by no means a megastadium clumsily looming on the skyline or dominating the university. Unlike the Dome, the Basilica spire, or the Hesburgh Library you won't be able to spot the Stadium as you're driving into South Bend. And once you're on campus, its location won't be immediately obvious. You'll probably have to ask someone for directions, but when you do find the Stadium, you'll quickly realize that it represents just one thread in the complex fabric of the university. The "mystique" of

the Stadium does not spring solely from football. It is about *heritage*, and the countless small ceremonies that are performed as part of each game—the blessing given the players before they leave the tunnel; the announcer reading the Preamble to the Constitution, the students linking arms and swaying during the "Alma Mater," the Band performing its pre-game rendition of "Hike Notre Dame"; the Leprechaun doing back flips across the field while old grads creak toward their seats—outlast every coach, every player, every win-loss record. Like the venerable old bricks that are still visible on the original walls and will forever fix the Stadium in 1930, these rituals are the ties that bind each generation of Domers, the stuff of legend in their own right, and as cherished as any family heirloom. And that is really something to cheer about.

ALUMNI SENIOR CLUB (91)

This small building south of the Stadium is precisely what its name implies—a place for alumni and members of the senior class (who are on the verge of alumnihood) to socialize. Also known as "Senior Bar," it was built in 1982 by the Chapple Co. and is often used for dances and post-game celebrations.

BRAINS AND BRAWN GREAT VIEWS AND SPLENDID SIGHTS

From the Stadium: One of the greatest dividends of the Stadium expansion has to be the superlative views of the campus from the upper concourse. Because the concourse circumnavigates the Stadium, you'll get a full, 360° look at the university that encompasses familiar landmarks as well as rooftops and treetops that you've never seen before. And on a football Saturday, there's no better place to watch the crowd and the Marching Band coming into the Stadium. The choice view of

"Touchdown Jesus" from the Stadium stands is a campus favorite and standard fare for picture postcards. You can also get a slightly different ground-level perspective on "Touchdown Jesus" from the graceful new entry plaza that was added on the north end of the Stadium during its expansion. Not only is the decorative oval in this well-designed plaza reminiscent of a football, but the shape of its half walls also mimics the curvature of Jesus' upraised arms.

MOD QUAD
The Northeast Quadrangle

The very word "Mod" conjures up images of the 1960s, when the country was shooting for the moon and the entire culture seemed a little lost in space. Since this quad was born in that era, it's no surprise that its first two buildings—Flanner and Grace towers—stand as quite telling signs of their time. All of Mod Quad's buildings were designed by Minnesota's Ellerbe Associates or Ellerbe Becket architects. At its south end the quad is shadowed by the most towering building on campus, the Hesburgh Library. On its north end the quad is bordered by the geodesic Stepan Center, which many people say reminds them of a flying saucer. In truth, Mod Quad isn't even a quad in the strict sense of the word, for it has no defining axis or no broad expanse of space to showcase buildings. It's actually more of a cluster, with multiple sets of structures separated by narrow—but quite handsomely landscaped—corridors and courtyards.

Before Mod Quad was built, however, the site was occupied by another cluster of buildings called "Vetville," and they also were very much a sign of their time, the postwar 1940s. When hundreds of World War II veterans took advantage of the revolutionary GI Bill and enrolled at Notre Dame, the university was faced with a real problem. Many of the vets were married, and Notre Dame had no housing to accommodate couples, let alone couples trying to live on very small incomes. Father Theodore Hesburgh, the young Holy Cross priest who was serving as the vets' chaplain, found 39 surplus barracks that had been used to house Japanese prisoners of war in

MOD QUAD'S
GREAT VIEWS AND
SPLENDID SIGHTS
From the middle ground:
Mod Quad's small colony
of dormitories is divided
by a narrow corridor of
grass and greenery that
affords a fine southward
view of the Hesburgh
Library and a northern
exposure toward the
Stepan Center. In
addition, the passageway
between Pasquerilla West
and Siegfried halls will
lead your eye westward
toward the Golden Dome.

Missouri. The barracks were shipped to Notre Dame, where each one was converted into three small apartments for the men and their wives. The walls were thin and the furnishings minimal, but the rent was rock bottom. It didn't take long, of course, for the couples to become parents, and the "fertile valley" of barracks made baby carriages a common sight on campus for the first time in Notre Dame history. These young families quickly turned Vetville into a close-knit community. They held town meetings, elected their own mayor, published the newsy "Vet Gazette," and held Saturday night dances in yet another revamped surplus building.

Vetville existed until the early 1960s, when University Village (4), an apartment complex specifically designed for married students, was built north of Douglas Road. The old barracks were demolished to allow for the construction of the Hesburgh Library, and shortly after that, Mod Quad was started on the vacant land. By that time, many of Vetville's first babies were ready to attend Notre Dame themselves and would soon be living in the modern dorms that sprouted on the "fertile valley" their parents had known so well. Today, a plaque between Knott and Siegfried halls commemorates the trials—and the blessings—of life in Vetville.

FLANNER HALL (89) AND GRACE HALL (90)

This pair of office buildings was constructed in 1969 as Notre Dame's first—and only—high-rise dormitories, and they were funded though the generosity of two individuals. Chicago's Helen Kellogg, whose second husband was president of the famous cereal company, donated Flanner Hall in memory of her deceased son, Thomas Flanner III. Grace Hall was the gift of a

Notre Dame trustee, J. Peter Grace of New York. It was named in honor of his father, Joseph P. Grace, an international businessman who had been a close friend of Father John O'Hara, the university's president in the 1930s.

From the beginning, these twin, 11-story towers were an anomaly among Notre Dame's small-scale dormitories. With 20-20 hindsight, it now seems totally incongruous to have put highrise residence halls on open prairie land, but at the time, modular, nondescript dormitories like these were popping up on campuses across the country. Though many universities saved their construction budgets, they unfortunately also sacrificed their sense of style. When Flanner and Grace opened at Notre Dame, the hotel-like halls were highly coveted by undergraduates. Together, the two dorms housed 1,000 men, and they were known on campus as the Flanner "Gamecocks" (who were a major power in interhall sports) and the Grace "Lightning" (whose tower boasted a huge number "1" that was lighted whenever Notre Dame had a top-ranked football team).

By the 1990s, however, it was obvious that the times were passing these dormitories by. Although their rooms offer some extraordinary views of Notre Dame, the two towers were the visual "sore thumbs" of the campus and did not relate well to the university's more traditional buildings. Even more important, the elevators and segmented rooms in Flanner and Grace did not foster the broad personal and social relationships or general sense of dorm unity that have always been one of the most valued aspects of residence hall life at Notre Dame. In the late 1990s the university once again joined the national trend in education and converted its highrise dormitories to better uses. Grace Hall was remodeled into an administrative office building, while Flanner Hall was earmarked for academic offices.

PASQUERILLA HALL WEST (76) AND PASQUERILLA HALL EAST (64)

Pasquerilla West and Pasquerilla East were built, respectively, in 1980 and 1981, as the result of a gift from commercial real estate developer Frank J. Pasquerilla, the president of Johnston, Pennsylvania-based Crown America Corporation. These L-shaped, side-by-side dormitories were Notre Dame's first residence halls built specifically for women undergraduates. When Pasquerilla West opened, one of its apartments was occupied by Rev. Robert Griffin, C.S.C., the University Chaplain and the first Notre Dame priest ever to live in a women's dormitory. His dog, Darby O'Gill, also moved into Pasquerilla West, which, as Father Griffin astutely observed, also made Darby the first cocker spaniel in the university's history to live in a women's dorm.

The residents of both Pasquerilla West (a.k.a. "PW") and Pasquerilla East (a.k.a. "PE") are now formidable competitors in interhall sports, especially football. The women living in PW are nicknamed the "Purple Weasels," and every fall, their lively Queen Week includes events such as talent shows and obstacle courses. The "Pyros" of PE invite faculty and staff members to participate in dorm activities through their much-admired hall fellows program. They also sponsor Pyromania, a week of spirited fun and games that usually starts with a bonfire.

"I was a bit reluctant to have something named after me in my lifetime, but I looked around campus and thought there were too many halls with Irish names on them."
—*Frank J. Pasquerilla*

KNOTT HALL (65) AND SIEGFRIED HALL (209)

Another matched pair of L-shaped dormitories, Knott Hall and Siegfried Hall, both opened in August of 1988 as residence halls for women. In addition to study lounges and computer rooms, they featured coordinating, wood-paneled chapels adorned by works of art. Knott Hall's chapel held a wood relief crucifixion scene carved by Rev. Anthony Lauck, C.S.C., professor emeritus of art, while the Siegfried chapel had a 500-year-old madonna and child on loan from Notre Dame's Snite Museum.

Marion Burk Knott Hall was the first Notre Dame dormitory named for a woman; it was funded by her husband, Henry J. Knott, head of the Arundel Corporation, a construction and land development company in Baltimore, Maryland. Siegfried Hall was the joint gift of a father and son from Tulsa, Oklahoma—insurance and banking executive Robert M. Siegfried, class of 1937, and

NOTRE DAME'S OTHER C.S.C., THE CENTER FOR SOCIAL CONCERNS (70)

This small, flat-roofed structure just west of Mod Quad was built in 1955. Designed by the Notre Dame architecture team of Frank Montana and Robert Schultz, it originally served as the studios of the university television station, WNDU. Today, it's still being used for broadcasting, but instead of images, the Center for Social Concerns is transmitting a call to service. A commitment to social service and volunteerism is one of the Notre Dame community's strongest traditions, and it goes all the way back to the university's religious roots as a Holy Cross mission. Since 1983 the Center for Social Concerns has been coordinating Notre Dame's dozens of on-campus volunteer groups as well as the national and international service projects and social action programs in which Notre Dame students, faculty, and staff members participate. It also operates as an educational facility for seminars, workshops, and courses in social justice and concerns. Currently, around 80 percent of Notre Dame's students participate in some kind of community service activity—including tutoring the illiterate, volunteering in homeless shelters, visiting nursing homes, and working with disadvantaged children—during their college careers. In addition, about 10 percent of each graduating class spend at least one year in social service programs such as the Peace Corps after receiving their diplomas. To find out more about its humanitarian mission, you can contact the Center for Social Concerns at 219/631-5293.

Raymond H. Siegfried II, class of 1965 and chairman of Nordam, Inc., an aerospace company. The Knott women, who called themselves "Angels," were renowned for their dances and social activities, but Siegfried's "Slammers" specialized in sports and service projects. In 1997, however, the ladies vacated these halls for even newer dormitories on West Quad. They were replaced by the men who had been ousted from Flanner Hall when it stopped serving as a dormitory. These days, Knott's men are known as "Juggerknotts" and Siegfried's have adopted the old Notre Dame football team nickname, "Ramblers."

STEPAN CENTER (69)

This is Notre Dame's *other* dome, the geodesic one that weighs 27 tons, sits atop a circular wall of bricks, and is made of aluminum anodized with—what else?—gold. Dedicated in 1962, the Stepan Center was one of the first geodesic structures ever built in the United States, and its distinctive dome was specially designed by the Kaiser Aluminum Company. The center's wide-open interior space makes it ideal for activities such as convocations, conventions, and concerts, while students use the adjacent Stepan Fields for playing basketball, volleyball, rugby, football, and other sports. Stepan Center was named for its benefactors, Alfred and Mary Louise Stepan of Winnetka, Illinois. A university trustee, Mr. Stepan was the founder of the Stepan Chemical Company.

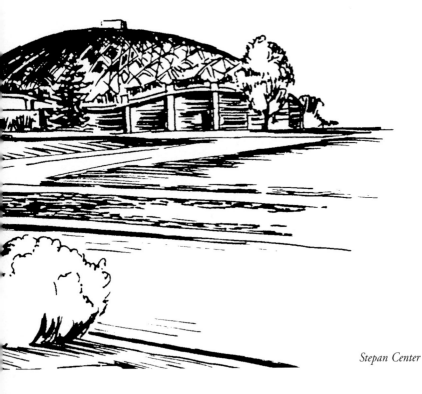

Stepan Center

DEBARTOLO
QUADRANGLE

In ambiance and architecture the DeBartolo Quad is the most modern on campus and stands in direct contrast to the stately, tradition-bound Main Quad where the university long ago set down its roots. Big contemporary buildings and state-of-the-art, computer-equipped classrooms are the stamp of this academic quad, which was underwritten by Edward J. DeBartolo, Sr., in 1989. DeBartolo, a leading real estate and shopping mall developer from Youngstown, Ohio, was a member of the class of 1932, and the $33 million that he bestowed upon his alma mater was the largest individual gift in Notre Dame history.

Considered the university's new "front door," DeBartolo Quad occupies the area once known as Notre Dame's "front yard"—an expansive field between Notre Dame Avenue and the Stadium formerly used as a football game parking lot. The openness of the site and bareness of its incipient landscaping have caused an unavoidable void between the large-scale buildings, which still await the softening effect of mature arbor and ivy. This starkness was temporarily—and quite creatively—eased in the mid-1990s, however, by the Public Sculpture Project exhibiting more than two dozen contemporary works among the buildings. DeBartolo Quad's main axis runs north to south, with the pergola of Sesquicentennial Common gracefully punctuating its northern point. Its intended southern terminus is the Marie P. DeBartolo Center for the Performing Arts, a memorial to Mr. DeBartolo's wife, planned for the now vacant area opposite Sesquicentennial Common and adjacent to Angela Boulevard. The

Business Administration

quad's buildings are the handiwork of either Ellerbe Becket Architects, Minneapolis, or University of Notre Dame architecture professors Frank Montana and Robert Schultz.

SESQUICENTENNIAL COMMON (299)

A series of airy arches forms a vine-covered canopy above bubbling fountains to provide one of Notre Dame's most delightful gathering spots. Linger a while in the seating area here, and you'll undoubtedly encounter students and others from the university community beckoned by the beauty of this pergola. Built in 1992 to celebrate Notre Dame's 150th anniversary, the Sesquicentennial Common not only signals the entrance to DeBartolo Quad, but also visually links it with the rest of the campus. The Common's pointed arches echo the tried and true Gothic architecture of adjoining South Quad, while its flowers and formal plantings offer a fine transition between the fully grown flora of older campus areas and the aspiring saplings of DeBartolo Quad. If you stand at either end of the pergola and look through the arches, you'll also discover that they "frame" a unique view looking both eastward toward the Stadium and westward toward *Our Lady of the University*, the well-known Virgin Mary statue standing opposite the Main Building at the end of Notre Dame Avenue.

DEBARTOLO HALL (150)

When it opened in the fall of 1992, Edward J. DeBartolo Hall was hailed as "the world's most technologically advanced classroom building." That's quite a claim, but then, DeBartolo Hall is quite a facility. With a $22-million price tag, it's one of the most expensive buildings ever constructed at Notre Dame, and with almost four acres

Sesquicentennial Common

under its roof, also one of the largest. Its groundbreaking heralded a new quad that advanced the direction of campus growth irrevocably southward, and its completion practically doubled the number of classrooms at Notre Dame. But most importantly, DeBartolo Hall was quite literally a concrete turning point for the university, for it marked Notre Dame's technological transition from chalkboard to motherboard. The building boasts highly sophisticated computer and audiovisual equipment whose use is controlled by "Media-on-Call," an innovative

DeBartolo Hall

delivery system that utilizes a master computer and fiber optic network. By merely pushing a button or two, professors can bring television and satellite transmissions, laser discs, videocassettes, electronic still photos, slides, and other instructional media directly into their classrooms.

Given DeBartolo Hall's high-tech capabilities and the fact that its namesake/benefactor earned his Notre Dame degree in Civil Engineering, you might expect that its 84 classrooms, seminar rooms, lecture halls, and auditoriums would be earmarked for science and engineering courses. Not so. DeBartolo Hall is a general academic building available for use by all departments and colleges, and classes taught there have included math, theology, and literature. The architecture of this brick, limestone, and slate structure, however, is totally compatible with the contemporary teaching tools that it harbors. Designed by Ellerbe Becket, DeBartolo Hall consists of five connected pavilions characterized by large windows and high-pitched gable roofs. The steep roofs are a Gothic element, but say some detractors, they only serve to make the boxy pavilions look like milk cartons. Yet no matter how modern its appearance or operation, DeBartolo Hall—in keeping with everything else at Notre Dame—is still touched by faith. Crucifixes hang on the walls of its electronic classrooms, and just inside the building's main entrance (at the middle pavilion facing west toward the interior of DeBartolo Quad) stands a striking statue of the Virgin Mary. It's the original version of *Our Lady of the University*, carved by Rev. Anthony Lauck in the 1950s.

COLLEGE OF BUSINESS
ADMINISTRATION (152)

This building is a first cousin to DeBartolo Hall. It's located just south of DeBartolo Hall, is about the same size, had a comparable cost, and is made of the same structural materials. It also

OUR LADY OF THE UNIVERSITY *AND*
REV. ANTHONY LAUCK, C.S.C.

He enjoys a national reputation as a sculptor and has been called the father of Notre Dame's art movement. Yet, the man who carefully nurtured the university's art collection says the title of "Father" that means the most to him comes from his priesthood. Born in Indianapolis, Lauck attended the Herron School of Art there before earning his bachelor's degree at Notre Dame. He was ordained in 1946 and spent more than two decades teaching art. In the early 1950s Lauck became director of Notre Dame's first art gallery in O'Shaughnessy Hall, and his expeditions to galleries and museums far and wide helped to build not only the university's collections but also recognition for the arts at Notre Dame. Respected as a highly skilled sculptor with a deceptively simple style, Lauck specialized in works with religious themes, many of which are now displayed on campus. Ironically, his most visible effort— the bronze *Our Lady of the University* located in the circular cul-de-sac at the end of Notre Dame Avenue—is a copy. Lauck carved his original *Our Lady* statue from limestone in the mid-1950s at the request of then Notre Dame President Theodore Hesburgh. For years it stood vigil in the circle, until a hapless motorist accidentally toppled the landmark statue. After being repaired, *Our Lady* found safe haven in DeBartolo Hall, and the copy took her place at the prominent, but precarious, post at Notre Dame Avenue.

boasts a similarly stunning array of up-to-the-minute teaching aids, including a library database accessible from all of the classrooms and a groundbreaking audiovisual conferencing capability that services MBA students in distant locations. With their respective bags of technological goodies, DeBartolo and Business Administration are arguably two of the most advanced academic buildings in the nation. Both buildings had the same architect, but Ellerbe Becket blessed the College of Business Administration's modern design with certain elements—a stair tower and battlement-like projections, for example—that make it a bit more compatible with the Gothic architecture that prevails on much of the Notre Dame campus. And while DeBartolo Hall consists of five pavilions, the Business Administration building is a complex of four wings that house all graduate and as well as many undergraduate classes. Think of it as a giant capital H. Each leg of the H corresponds to a wing consisting of business classrooms or offices. The crossbar joining the wings is

College of Business Administration

a three-story high atrium flanked by an auditorium on one side and by the stair tower on the other. Dedicated in 1995, the building cost a hefty $25 million. Thus, its wings and auditorium have been named for their benefactors, five businessmen who, appropriately enough, also happen to be Notre Dame alumni or trustees—Terrence J. McGlinn of Wyomissing, Pennsylvania (northwest wing); Donald P. Kelly of Chicago (northeast wing); Vincent J. Naimoli of Tampa (southeast wing); Raymond H. Siegfried of Tulsa (southwest); and John W. Jordan of Chicago (auditorium).

The College of Business Administration dates back to 1913, when six students registered for Notre Dame's

In 1996, U.S. News and World Report ranked Notre Dame's undergraduate business program among the top 25 in the nation.

first course in commerce. Today, it has some 2,000 students and is second only to the university's College of Arts and Letters in enrollment. The college offers concentrations in accountancy, finance and business economics, management, and marketing, and it is widely esteemed as a leader in both business ethics and international business. Undoubtedly, the emphasis on ethics stems in large part from the university's Catholic character and educational tradition of imparting values, but moral issues have become such a strong thread throughout the business curriculum's fabric that a few years ago, *Business Week* magazine declared, "Instead of sending insider traders and other white-collar criminals to prison, maybe the government should make them earn an MBA from Notre Dame."

The college's international bent, on the other hand, can be traced directly to Rev. John Francis O'Hara, C.S.C., the indefatigable priest from Peru, Indiana, whose worldly vision was inspired by his experiences as the son of a diplomat living in South America. Colorful, charismatic, and ambitious, he made a name for himself as Notre Dame's prefect of religion, publishing the *Religious Bulletin* that dispensed commonsense advice and urged students to turn the campus into the "City of the Blessed Sacrament" by taking daily communion. His penchant for business also made it the home of the nation's first four-year degree in foreign commerce in 1917, and by 1921 he'd drummed up the funding and faculty to establish a full-fledged business college at the university. O'Hara became the first dean of the new "College of Foreign and Domestic Commerce," only to progress to President of Notre Dame in the 1930s and eventually Cardinal Archbishop of Philadelphia.

When Notre Dame's first business building—Hurley Hall—was constructed on the South Quad in 1932, the college's interest in glo-

"The primary function of commerce is service to mankind. Business has a code of ethics based very largely on divine principles. When this code is followed, commerce can and does advance civilization. When it is overlooked by selfish interests, individual or national, every sort of injustice, from petty thievery to world war, may result."
—Rev. John F. O'Hara, C.S.C.

bal commerce was allegorized by a model of the classic international trade vessel, a three-masted clipper. Conspicuously mounted above the hall's main entrance, the ship soon lent the business college a nickname that lasted for decades: "The Yacht Club."

That splendid copper clipper is now the focal point of the pleasant courtyard formed by the Naimoli and Siegfried wings on the College of Business Administration's south side. With a nod to tradition, the ship was moved from Hurley Hall and placed atop a wave-like pedestal in the courtyard, so that it—like the business college—continues to "sail" on. Many features of this new building were, in fact, designed to symbolize the business college's focus on scholarship, ethics, and international interests. In the northwest corner of the courtyard, you can't miss the imposing exterior of the stair tower, which for obvious reasons has been dubbed "The Silo." The concrete at its base has concentric bands suggesting lines of longitude and latitude as well as wave-shaped areas representing the "journey" of business across the seven seas. Inside the building, the tower holds a magnificent circular staircase. The tower's floor is patterned to look like a mariner's compass, while its ceiling holds a skylight signifying the unlimited prospects of the future.

If you go into the College of Business Administration through the main entrance on its west side (facing the DeBartolo Quad's interior), you'll be delighted to find a vintage New York Stock Exchange trading post displayed on the first floor lobby. Trading Post No. 6 was donated by Thomas A. Coleman, class of 1956, who is a member of the New York Stock Exchange, and it's equipped with an interesting video disk that explains its history and tells about the stock market. Besides being a very apt addition to the business college, this trading post sometimes serves as a storefront where students sell T-shirts, mugs, and

Business College clipper

"I'll hear your confession anytime, night or day. You can't tell me anything I haven't heard before."
—*Rev. John F. O'Hara, C.S.C., in the* Religious Bulletin

other novelties. You can also observe young entrepreneurs in action at Salud, the student-run
snack bar on the building's lower level. It's the af-
ter-hours complement to the neighboring business college café, the Common Stock Sandwich
Company.

THEODORE M. HESBURGH CENTER
FOR INTERNATIONAL STUDIES (156)

The Hesburgh Center's formal opening in
mid-September 1991 was momentous for two
reasons: (1) the ceremonies were the first event of
Notre Dame's Sesquicentennial Year celebrations;
and (2) it was the first building to encroach on
the broad field that had been prime tailgate party
territory but would soon be absorbed into
DeBartolo Quad. Too bad for the football fans,
but Notre Dame couldn't have picked a better
spot to put the focus on international studies.

Situated on the southwest corner of
DeBartolo Quad, the Hesburgh Center is directly
across from the College of Business Administration. It fronts on Notre Dame Avenue, however,
and therein lies the most significant aspect of its
location: the Center is one of the first buildings
on the university's main entrance. Notre Dame
Avenue was designed by Father Edward Sorin
himself as an impressive approach to the school
that he and a handful of other Holy Cross members painstakingly started in the Indiana hinter-
land. As Notre Dame grew, not only did its
campus advance southward along Notre Dame
Avenue, but its interests also advanced across the
globe in ways that ranged from manning far-flung
Holy Cross missions to scholars and students recruited from foreign nations. The positioning of
the Hesburgh Center at the campus edge, therefore, is a fitting indicator of both the Center's international purpose and Notre Dame's long reach
into the world at large.

The Center, of course, is named for Rev. Theodore Hesburgh, C.S.C., the Notre Dame president emeritus whose hallmark has been involvement in global issues such as peace and human rights. He also has a strong interest in nuclear disarmament that is shared by Joan Kroc, the widow of Ray Kroc, who founded the McDonald's restaurant chain. Mrs. Kroc provided Notre Dame with $12 million that not only built the Hesburgh Center but also funded one of its two occupants, the Joan B. Kroc Institute for International Peace Studies. The other occupant is the Helen Kellogg Institute for International Studies, which is underwritten by an endowment from the John L. and Helen Kellogg Foundation of Chicago. While the Kroc Institute concentrates on the relationship between peace, justice, and human rights, the Kellogg Institute examines issues such as democratization and development, especially in regard to Latin America. Thanks to fine conference facilities and an international scholars program, the Hesburgh Center hosts visitors from around the world. Greenfields, the

Hesburgh Center

Sesquicentennial Common in summer and winter

Hesburgh Center

University Club

A DeBartolo Hall classroom

on-site restaurant open for breakfast and lunch, also makes it a popular work week destination for Notre Dame staff and faculty members.

Yet another Ellerbe Becket creation, the Hesburgh Center consists of three units with distinct functions—academic and administrative; conference and dining; residential—that surround a beautifully landscaped central courtyard. Although it displays a brick and slate roof exterior consistent with the DeBartolo Quad's other contemporary buildings, the Center's architecture mimics the cloistered quality of monastery buildings traditionally constructed to enclose an unroofed, open space. Accordingly, the Hesburgh Center features an impressive Great Hall with Gothic style lancet windows accented by art glass. And as a gentle reminder of the Hesburgh Center's ultimate purpose, the building's dedication plaque recalls Christ's words from the Sermon on the Mount: "Blessed are the peacemakers, for they shall be called children of God."

UNIVERSITY CLUB (78)

Located immediately north of the Hesburgh Center along Notre Dame Avenue, this private facility serves as a social center and informal forum for members of the University Club of Notre Dame. The organization draws its core membership from the alumni, faculty, and staff of the University of Notre Dame, Saint Mary's College, and Holy Cross College. Opened in 1968, the contemporary brick structure was the gift of Florida philanthropist Robert H. Gore, whom President Franklin Roosevelt appointed Governor of Puerto Rico in the 1930s. Gore was a proverbial self-made man who overcame the poverty of his youth to build an international business empire based on publishing and insurance. He not only spent many years on the Advisory Council of Notre Dame's business college, but also sent six sons to be educated at the university.

Along with the building, Notre Dame received Gore's collection of more than 100 steins. The unusual trove included valuable Villeroy & Boch porcelains from Germany as well as elaborately detailed tankards that supposedly had belonged to notables such as Martin Luther and Napoleon Bonaparte. Gore highly prized the collection, and rather than risk shipping one particularly precious three-foot-tall stein to Notre Dame, he reportedly enlisted university executive vice-president Edmund Joyce to personally transport the item on a commercial airline flight. Since the steins required an appropriate setting, architects Montana and Schultz gave the University Club's interior a rathskeller atmosphere with a vaulted ceiling and stout brick arches accented by a massive corbeled brick fireplace. Special glass cases were also designed to showcase the steins, which the University Club proudly keeps on display.

MCKENNA HALL (CENTER FOR CONTINUING EDUCATION) (81)

A first-rate conference facility, the Center for Continuing Education extends Notre Dame's educational mission by annually hosting hundreds of programs for academic, business, and professional associations. Seminar rooms have multimedia capabilities, and like a mini-United Nations, the auditorium offers instant translations. Its staff provides "one stop shopping" service to conference organizers by handling every meeting detail from registration to refreshments, and there is even an underground concourse that connects the Center to the Morris Inn.

Situated north of the University Club, the Center was designed by Montana and Schultz

DEBARTOLO QUAD'S GREAT VIEWS AND SPLENDID SIGHTS

From Our Lady of the University *looking north and south: This statue in the circle at the end of Notre Dame Avenue occupies one of the more scenic sites on campus. To the south it offers a fine perspective of tree-lined Notre Dame Avenue, which leads from the university to the world at large. To the north it provides a direct line of sight that encompasses the Sorin and Sacred Heart statues and culminates in the Golden Dome. This vista is especially effective in late fall and winter, when the trees on Main Quad cooperate with sightseers and shutterbugs by conveniently losing their leaves.*

and built in 1965 with funding furnished by a grant from the W. K. Kellogg Foundation of Battle Creek, Michigan. The foundation is the philanthropic legacy of Will Keith Kellogg, the cornflake manufacturer who literally put his signature on breakfast cereal boxes across America. The building was named McKenna Hall in 1998 to recognize the leadership and benefactions of alumnus Andrew J. McKenna of Chicago, chairman of the University's Board of Trustees. As soon as you enter the building, you'll notice one of the Center's nicest touches—the display of flags that rings the lobby's perimeter to represent each country where Notre Dame students are studying abroad.

POST OFFICE (24)

You wouldn't think that something as prosaic as a United States Post Office would have much significance for a university. Certainly there is nothing about the appearance of the Notre Dame Post Office to indicate otherwise. It's a rather ordinary looking, one-story structure with a functional, contemporary design by Montana and Schultz. Yet when this building opened in 1967, it became the fourth in a series of post offices that truly have helped put Notre Dame on the map.

Father Sorin had boldly conceived a "university" in 1842, but as the middle of the nineteenth century approached, Notre Dame was still very much a fledgling institution. Coping with the struggles of fiscal as well as physical survival, Sorin shrewdly pursued having the U.S. government start a post office at Notre Dame. His reasons were many and eminently practical. A post office would not only ease Notre Dame's communications with the world beyond the campus, but even more importantly, the school's placement on a postal route would result in the government's having to keep the roads leading to it in good condition. A post office also meant free publicity for Sorin's aspiring, but still quite unknown, university. The words "Notre Dame" would be printed on all government maps, and a Notre Dame postmark would spread the school's name far and wide. Sorin's request for a post office was at first turned down, but with help from prayer and Henry Clay, he eventually succeeded. The reason for the unlikely connection between a young priest from France and an elder statesman from Kentucky seems to have been lost to history, but Clay apparently wielded his considerable in-

Notre Dame Avenue

fluence in Washington to secure a post office for the obscure school on the Indiana frontier. In 1851 President Millard Fillmore made it official and appointed Father Sorin Notre Dame's first postmaster. At about the same time (and by very fortunate coincidence), the good Father also managed to have himself appointed Inspector of Public Roads.

Notre Dame got its first post office building in 1856, a small, but stylish brick structure with bracketed eaves characteristic of the Italianate architecture that had become extremely popular before the Civil War. It was located at what was then the doorstep of the university—a site at the end of Notre Dame Avenue, just east of the statue of Father Sorin that today graces the interior of the Main Quadrangle. Although Notre Dame Avenue now ends in the circle that embraces *Our Lady of the University*, that was not the street's first campus terminus. Father Sorin had originally stopped Notre Dame Avenue farther to the north nearer to the present Main Building. As the campus expanded over the years, however, Notre Dame Avenue literally lost ground to the university. It became progressively shorter, and its end point receded southward accordingly.

The locations of Notre Dame's successive postal buildings have followed the course of Notre Dame Avenue. A second, significantly larger post office, for example, was constructed in 1914 on the same site as the first post office. But within 20 years Notre Dame outgrew it, and that yellow brick building was annexed to the old chemistry hall. The university's third post office was designed to coordinate with the Gothic style buildings that were popping up on Notre Dame's new South Quad during the 1930s, and it had a new location that reflected the campus's advance to the south. It was on the west side of Notre Dame Avenue, immediately south of Walsh Hall and facing toward the interior of the South Quad.

POSTMARK: NOTRE DAME

Father Sorin wanted a post office at Notre Dame because he thought that "the sight of the mail coach sweeping up to the door each day will add dignity and attract attention to the university." As it turned out, the post office, as well as the nation's post office department and postal service, brought attention to his beloved school in ways that he could hardly imagine.

Consider, for example, the dedication of the campus's third post office in 1934. Notre Dame by then was no longer a backwater university. It had acquired a national reputation, thanks to the success of both Knute Rockne's football teams and of graduates who were assuming leadership roles throughout the land. To prove the point, the press widely reported the building's dedication, which featured two alumni. They were Ambrose O'Connell, executive assistant to the U.S. Postmaster General, and Frank Walker, a Democratic Party official described as President Roosevelt's "right-hand man." Mr. Walker purchased the new facility's first stamp and affixed it to the first letter, a thank you message for the President, which Mr. O'Connell promptly mailed.

Notre Dame also had the honor of being associated with U.S. postage stamps and a commemorative postal card. In 1893 *Return of Columbus and Reception at Court* was reproduced on a 10-cent stamp commemorating the 400th anniversary of Christopher Columbus's discovery of the New World. The painting is one in the series of murals by Luigi Gregori that hangs in the Main Building. Nearly a century later, in 1988, Notre Dame's legendary football coach Knute Rockne became the first athletic coach ever featured on a U.S. postage stamp. Rockne's 22-cent stamp was dedicated at Notre Dame by then-President Ronald Reagan, who had portrayed football player George Gipp in the film *Knute Rockne—All American.* And in 1991 the U.S. Postal Service recognized Notre Dame's 150th birthday by issuing a commemorative postal card featuring the Main Building and its Golden Dome accompanied by the words, "Notre Dame / Sesquicentennial / 1842-1992." The 19-cent card was part of the postal service's Historic Preservation Series highlighting landmark buildings. In 1998, the Post Office issued a stamp commemorating The Four Horsemen.

Today that building serves as the Knights of Columbus Council Hall, but for years it handled large volumes of mail, especially during World War II when Notre Dame was a major training center for Navy officers. In the 1960s Notre Dame's burgeoning student body made the third post office obsolete, and the present postal building was constructed along the east side of Notre Dame Avenue at what was then the southern border of the campus.

Father Sorin remained the university's postmaster until his death in 1893, a remarkable 42-year tenure during which he served under 11 U.S. presidents. The position then went to another former Notre Dame president, Father William Corby, and after that to yet a third president, Father Andrew Morrissey in 1898. Morrissey was postmaster until 1915, when the Holy Cross brothers took on the task of supervising the post office. For most of its history, in fact, the university's postal operation was staffed primarily by brothers who passed the required civil service tests and donated their salaries to their order. Notre Dame's post office continued to have a "Brother Postmaster" at the helm until its first lay postmaster was appointed in 1980, thereby ending a 129-year-old tradition of Holy Cross management that stretched all the way back to Father Sorin.

WEST QUADRANGLE

This is Notre Dame's most recently developed quad. It includes a quartet of smart new dormitories and the Eck Center, an exceptional facility containing the large campus bookstore and a first-rate visitors' center where you'll be warmly—and informatively—welcomed to the university. The center, in fact, should be your first stop at Notre Dame. Not only is it the perfect place to acquaint yourself with the university, but there is also convenient parking adjacent to the building. You'll find it along Notre Dame Avenue just north of the Main Gate (205).

West Quad was created in the mid-1990s on land that had previously been part of the Notre Dame Golf Course, and it occupies the southwest corner of the campus immediately north of Holy Cross Drive and west of Notre Dame Avenue. Obviously, logic as well as geography dictated West Quad's name. It is a well-known fact, however, that Notre Dame's students have an unusual aptitude for tongue-in-cheek nicknames. Thus, they've dubbed it "Coca-Cola® Quad," because one of its first dormitories was funded by the soft drink company's retired president and chief operating officer. It is also called "Golf Quad" and, because of the Irish names of its halls, "Auld Sod Quad."

Construction of West Quad touched off a lengthy chain reaction of moves at Notre Dame. The first male residents in its new dorms were transplanted from Grace Hall, which was turned into an office building. The first female residents were transplanted from Knott and Siegfried halls, which were then converted into dormitories for the men of Flanner Hall, which also became an office building. As you might expect, the moving process took a few years. But when the dust (and students) finally settled in the fall of 1997, West Quad had about 1,000 undergraduates living in four separate but very equal brick dormitories exhibiting virtually the same architecture, materials, and color schemes.

These balanced and uniform halls—two for men and two for women—were all designed by Ellerbe Becket of Minneapolis, and each consists of two wings joined at a central lobby. Although the dormitories are definitely contemporary buildings, they do display features such as gabled roofs and corner towers that echo the more elaborate architectural elements seen on Notre Dame's classic collegiate Gothic buildings. The undergraduates who live in West Quad are just beginning to create the customs and spin the stories that in time will give character and nuance to their individual dormitories. Meanwhile, they are luxuriating in the many up-to-date amenities that these bright and well-appointed dorms have to offer.

ECK CENTER (520)

A campus that is replete with beautiful and historic structures deserves an outstanding building at its doorstep, and in 1998, the university got exactly what it deserves with the completion of the Eck Center along Notre Dame Avenue. This impressive Gothic Revival-style building was designed by S/L/A/M Collaborative, an architectural firm in Glastonbury, Connecticut, and it provides a splendid introduction to the famous collegiate Gothic buildings that distinguish South Quad. The Center was made possible by a $10-million gift from Frank Eck of Columbus, Ohio. A member of the class of 1944 as well as the College of Engineering Advisory Council, Mr. Eck is the chairman and chief executive officer of Advanced Drainage Systems, Inc.

The Eck Center is the perfect place for you to get acquainted with Notre Dame. This two-building complex not only includes the headquarters of the Notre Dame Alumni Association and a visitors' center, but also is the new home of the Hammes Notre Dame Bookstore. The visitors' center has an excellent reception area to welcome you, and you can also pick up maps of the university and get information about campus tours there. Always well-organized and enjoyable, the guided walking tours last about an hour and are typically conducted by students. Many of the people who visit Notre Dame make a beeline for the Hammes Notre Dame Bookstore, which offers an incredible assortment of logo merchandise, apparel, and souvenirs. It also has books, a lot of books, in fact, for this is the flagship operation of the Follett college bookstore chain. Actually, the two-story bookstore occupies the lion's share of the Eck Center's space, and although its primary purpose is to stock academic titles, you'll also find a worthy selection of general interest books there.

THE MORRIS INN (21)

The inn is the university's hotel, a very traditional establishment with a fireplace and library in the lobby and an excellent dining room that has two notable features—huge windows looking out on West Quad and murals of the campus painted by Mario Innocinitti of Florence, Italy. Notre Dame, of course, is often visited by prominent people, and the inn's roster of famous guests includes Presidents Eisenhower, Kennedy, Nixon, Carter, Ford, Reagan, and Bush; astronaut Neil Armstrong; film director Otto Preminger; writers Norman Mailer, Tennessee Williams, Flannery O'Connor, James Michener, and Arthur Miller; and entertainers Bob Hope, Perry Como, Red Skelton, Liberace, Helen Hayes, and Irene

Notre Dame's Alumni Association is one of the oldest and most successful in the nation. It was established in 1868, and its first president was Rev. Neal Gillespie, C.S.C., of Lancaster, Ohio, who was the university's first graduate (in 1849). At the time Notre Dame had only a few hundred alumni. Today the Alumni Association has some 98,000 members and more than 230 clubs around the world. Its myriad—and far-reaching—programs include alumni recognition awards, tours and travel, reunions, continuing education, fund-raising, and community service projects.

Dunne. Needless to say, if you stay at the Morris Inn, you'll be in very good company. For information about reservations, call 219/631-2000.

The Morris Inn is practically a Notre Dame heirloom. A fixture on campus since 1952, it has acquired a certain "old shoe" familiarity for many graduates, who remember it fondly from their student days and now like to stay there whenever they visit Notre Dame. One alumnus, in fact, even declared that his daughter should be admitted to Notre Dame just because she was conceived in the Morris Inn during the weekend of a home football game against Michigan State. The inn has played host to countless events, large and small, in the lives of the Notre Dame "family," and one of the best indications of how strong those family ties are can be found on a bulletin board in the lobby's vestibule. There, alumni who are visiting Notre Dame post their business cards, jotting down their year of graduation and a local phone number just in case an old classmate or professor also happens to be on campus.

Actually, the Morris Inn itself was the gift of an alumnus, Ernest M. Morris, a South Bend businessman, civic leader, and philanthropist. He presented Notre Dame's president, Father John J. Cavanaugh, with a $1-million check to build the inn, which Chicago's Holabird, Root and Burgee designed in "tastefully blended" collegiate Gothic and modern architecture. Mr. Morris's generosity made headlines in the early 1950s because of a widely circulated story written by *another* Notre Dame graduate, syndicated newspaper columnist J. P. McEvoy. According to McEvoy, Morris was an orphaned and nearly penniless young man when he drove a horse and buggy to Notre Dame and asked President John W. Cavanaugh if he could somehow go to college there. Apparently, "the first" Father Cavanaugh helped Morris so much financially that he was able to graduate from the Law School in 1906. Morris later be-

"I've had a warm spot in my heart for Notre Dame ever since I was a law student. I never got over a Catholic school doing what it did for a poor Protestant boy, and I've had it in my heart for several years to do something substantial for the university."
—Ernest M. Morris

came extremely successful in finance and banking, and he repaid Notre Dame's kindness by giving his "thanks a million" check to "the second"
Father Cavanaugh. Mr. Morris's family, by the
way, still maintains an active interest in the university, and his daughter, Ernestine M. Raclin,
serves on the Board of Trustees.

*Displays in the Morris
Inn's concourse honor
major benefactors of
Notre Dame, which has
the eighteenth largest
endowment among
American colleges and
universities and one of the
highest rates of alumni
giving.*

WELSH FAMILY HALL (512)

Opened in the fall of 1997, this is the home
of some 265 women who call themselves the
"Welsh Whirlwind." Its construction was funded
by a gift from Robert and Kathleen Welsh of
Valparaiso, Indiana, who also supplied the dorm's
inaugural residents with special Welsh Hall hats,
T-shirts, and chocolates. Mr. Welsh, a member of
the class of 1959 and Notre Dame trustee, is
president of Welsh, Inc., which operates convenience stores and restaurants. Mrs. Welsh and
their four daughters were all graduated from Saint
Mary's College.

Welsh Family Hall

MARILYN M. KEOUGH HALL (510)

Almost as soon as the foundation was dug for this dormitory, Notre Dame's undergraduate men began saying that things really do go better with Coke®. The hall's benefactor was veteran Coca-Cola® executive and university trustee Donald Keough of Atlanta, and it was named in honor of his wife, Marilyn. Mr. and Mrs. Keough are the parents of five Notre Dame graduates, and they had previously endowed the university's Institute for Irish Studies and the Keough-Notre Dame Study Center, Dublin, Ireland. The dormitory was dedicated in 1996, and an apropos Irish proverb—"People live in one another's shelter"—is displayed in its lobby. Keough Hall's residents are known as the Kangaroos.

O'NEILL FAMILY HALL (511)

Dedicated in September 1996, this was not only the first men's dormitory on West Quad, but also the first one built at Notre Dame since Flanner and Grace towers in 1969. Although O'Neill's residents are nicknamed the "Angry Mob," the hall memorializes a Notre Dame team player, Joseph O'Neill, Jr., a member of the class of 1937 who earned two football monograms as a punter and left-end. A native of Philadelphia, he started O'Neill Properties, Ltd., a highly successful oil and investments company based in Midland, Texas. Funding for the hall was provided primarily by his son, Joseph O'Neill III, class of 1967, and his daughter and son-in-law, Helen and Charles Schwab.

O'Neill Hall

During the dedication festivities, the O'Neill family posed for a photograph with the hall staff and the entire Angry Mob. Everyone in the picture received a souvenir copy of the photo, and since then, a ceremonial group shot has become customary for every dorm opening on West Quad.

MCGLINN HALL (513)

A women's dormitory, McGlinn Hall was underwritten by Terrence and Barbara McGlinn of Wyomissing, Pennsylvania, whose four children are all Notre Dame graduates. Mr. McGlinn, a member of the class of 1962 and a university trustee, is the founder and chairman of McGlinn Capital Management, Inc., an investment company. As part of the hall's grand opening in September 1997, the McGlinn family hosted a picnic for all of the residents, who are known as the "Shamrocks."

WEST QUADRANGLE'S GREAT VIEWS AND SPLENDID SIGHTS

From Notre Dame Avenue: Since the early days of the university, Notre Dame Avenue has been more than just a street. It's a revelation—the grand gateway that focuses everyone's sight and psyche on the Main Building and its incomparable Golden Dome. Stand anywhere along Notre Dame Avenue and look northward toward that shining vision; you will not be disappointed by what you see.

From the dormitories: The garden-like terraces on the south side of the dormitories offer a fine perspective on the architecture of the Eck Center as well as the quad's pretty grove of maples.

CEDAR GROVE CEMETERY

Located immediately south of the Main Gate (205), this fascinating graveyard actually pre-dates the university. It's believed that the missionary priest Stephen Badin set the ground aside as a burial place in the 1830s, and after the Congregation of Holy Cross acquired the property in the 1840s, it became a graveyard for Catholic settlers and Native Americans. For several decades, in fact, the university had a very successful undertaking business

continued

operated by Brother Francis Xavier Patois, the versatile campus carpenter whose sideline was building coffins. Today, Cedar Grove is used to bury Notre Dame's "civilians," namely, people affiliated with the university who are not members of the Congregation of Holy Cross, as well as others who choose it for their final resting place.

Most of the trees for which this cemetery was named disappeared long ago, but many of the old monuments and headstones remain in remarkably good condition. Near the entrance gate on Notre Dame Avenue, for example, you'll see the tall granite monument of pioneer Alexis Coquillard, whose family befriended Father Sorin. Also interred here are the French fur trader Pierre Navarre; Joe Boland, the football player turned broadcaster who started the "Irish Network" in the 1950s; and Edward "Moose" Krause, Notre Dame's beloved basketball coach and athletic director. Contrary to popular belief, Knute Rockne is *not* buried in this cemetery; the famous coach's grave site is off-campus in Highland Cemetery on Portage Avenue. However, the Notre Dame Band Director who was Rockne's contemporary—and some say his musical counterpart—was laid to rest in Cedar Grove. He was music professor Joseph Casasanta, who wrote the melodies for some of Notre Dame's "greatest hits," including "Notre Dame, Our Mother" (the Alma Mater), "Hike, Notre Dame," "On Down the Line," and "When the Irish Backs Go Marching By."

Cedar Grove Cemetery

THE EAST END
Notre Dame's Fields of Dreams

The campus east of Juniper Road is the haven of athletics at Notre Dame, the part of the university devoted primarily to places where young people can run, march, throw, row, swing, swim, skate, hit, jump, and pump. Sports is the university's strongest and most pervasive student subculture. More than 75 percent of the undergraduates lettered in at least one sport in high school, and at Notre Dame about 80 percent of them participate in some form of organized athletics, whether at the varsity, interhall, or club levels. Notre Dame's athletic tradition, although richly enhanced by varsity football (which its many fans claim has produced the world's most famous coach, fight song, and stadium), actually goes back to the earliest days of the university when dirt and grass playing fields were set aside for games and intramural sports. The first varsity sport, in fact, was baseball, which reigned supreme until 1913, when it was dethroned by college football's first passing duo, Knute Rockne and Gus Dorais. Today, Notre Dame offers more than 25 different varsity sports for men as well as women, and most of these programs—including men's and women's basketball; women's soccer and volleyball; men's and women's fencing; men's cross country; men's and women's tennis; men's lacrosse; and, of course, football—have brought national titles or recognition to the university. In addition, the university's Office of Recreational Sports (RecSports), an umbrella program aimed at non-varsity athletes, operates about 10 club sports, 60 intramural sport competitions, and some 40 recreational and fitness activities ranging from gymnastics to table tennis.

While varsity football has always laid claim to historic Notre Dame Stadium, the fields and facilities on this side of Juniper Road were constructed by and large to break new ground—and ultimately new champions—in other varsity and intramural sports. Much of this vast athletic plant was designed by Ellerbe Associates of Minnesota and constructed within the last 20 years. Because Notre Dame is a residential campus and it has such a high proportion of athletic undergraduates, these facilities seldom, if ever, go unused, and they're especially busy in the late afternoon after classes are finished. The granddaddy of the East End is the 30-year-old Joyce Center, which was originally intended to accommodate all of the university's non-football sports. But when women undergraduates were admitted to Notre Dame in the 1970s, the Joyce Center was no longer adequate. The women added a whole new dimension to sports at Notre Dame, and new facilities were needed so that they could train and compete successfully at every level. That, coupled with the nationwide explosion of interest in all kinds of fitness and athletics, spawned a sports building boom on the East End that continues to this day.

THE EDMUND P. JOYCE CENTER AND ROLFS AQUATIC CENTER (79)

You cannot miss the Joyce Center. It's the huge, double-domed building directly across from Notre Dame Stadium. Like the Stadium, the Joyce Center is a low-rise "background" building used for athletics. Unlike the Stadium, it's used constantly and, in fact, is one of the few buildings on campus designed to serve the public as well as the university. Since a significant amount of the $8.6 million needed to build the Joyce Center was raised in South Bend, the university made it a dual-use athletic and convention facility that would be available as a civic resource for cultural and community events. The center has hosted Bill Cosby, Barry Manilow, Bob Barker, the Lipizzaner stallions, the Ringling Brothers circus, home shows, a motor coach convention, an evangelistic camp meeting, gatherings of Jehovah's Witnesses, and countless other speakers, groups, and performers. It's also the scene of campus events such as pep rallies, freshman orientation, graduation exercises, and, of course, sports.

Notre Dame's "double bubble" is fittingly named for Rev. Edmund P. Joyce, C.S.C., a member of the class of 1937 who served as the university's executive vice president during the Hesburgh years. A certified public accountant from Spartanburg, South Carolina, Father Joyce acted as President Hesburgh's "right-hand man." He took charge of the university's finances and athletic programs as well as the extensive campus construction that took place from the 1950s through the 1980s. One of his prime projects was the massive Joyce Center, which opened in 1968 and holds play and practice facilities for a wide variety of varsity, intramural, and club sports. It covers 10.5 acres and consists of two domes joined by a two-story concourse. The north "fieldhouse" dome is a multi-use athletic center

The original name of the Joyce Center was the Joyce Athletic and Convocation Center, or JACC for short. But soon after it opened, varsity basketball player Austin Carr set scoring records and led the team to so many victories that the students called it "Austin Carr Coliseum."

Joyce Center

with an ice rink, weight room, and Tartan track. It's the home of Notre Dame's ice hockey team and is also open for public skating. The south "arena" dome can be utilized as either a basketball court or an auditorium seating up to 11,000 people; the men's and women's basketball teams and the women's volleyball team play here. The Joyce Center also has several auxiliary gymnasiums and other spaces for fencing, boxing, handball, squash, and exercise. Between the domes, the concourse houses varsity coaches' offices, lockers, meeting rooms, ticket and sports information offices, and the Sports Heritage Hall.

Located on the second floor of the concourse, the Sports Heritage Hall is a combination museum and hall of fame filled with a first-rate collection of photographs, trophies, and other memorabilia that goes back to the dawn of Notre Dame athletics. Notre Dame's version of a varsity letter is the monogram N-over-D, and this spacious, beautifully appointed hall was presented to the university in 1988 by the members of the Notre Dame National Monogram Club. The names of every monogram winner are displayed decade-by-decade along the periphery of the ceiling, and the chronological display cases trace the history of varsity sports at Notre Dame. As you'll soon discover while you browse at the exhibits, the Sports Heritage Hall emphasizes team accomplishments rather than individual efforts. That's why you won't find Notre Dame's seven Heisman Trophy winners featured together. You'll have to search for them among all the other varsity athletes. Allow yourself plenty of time when you visit the hall so that you can fully enjoy and appreciate all of the unique and interesting items on display. One of the first things you'll see, for example, is an 1892 letter; it was written to Walter Camp by a novice Notre Dame coach who wanted advice on how to develop a good football team. In another nearby case there is a yellowed newspaper

The Fighting Irish have had more Heisman Trophy winners than any other university. Here are the magnificent Notre Dame seven named the nation's outstanding college football players:
Angelo Bertelli, 1943
John Lujack, 1947
Leon Hart, 1949
John Lattner, 1953
Paul Hornung, 1956
John Huarte, 1964
Tim Brown, 1987

article about an early University of Michigan win over Notre Dame. The numerous photos, which constitute a veritable family album of Irish athletes, include the knickers-clad 1930 golf team, the 1936 national champion basketball team, and the first varsity swim team.

Although the Sports Heritage Hall is free, the two Varsity Shops inside the Joyce Center are, unfortunately, not. The shops, which specialize in "authentic Notre Dame sportswear" are for the real connoisseur of Irish athletics, and they stock everything from baby booties decorated with shamrocks to monogram-laden cashmere sweaters. You'll find one of the shops on the concourse adjacent to the Sports Heritage Hall; the other is in the fieldhouse dome near the ice rink.

In 1985, Rolfs Aquatic Center was added to the east side of the Joyce Center. It features a 50-meter swimming pool with moveable bulkheads that allow several activities to occur at the same time. The facility is used by the men's and women's varsity swim teams as well as the Notre Dame Water Polo Club, and you can enter its spectator gallery directly from the Joyce Center. It was the gift of two brothers, Thomas Rolfs, class of 1944, and Robert Rolfs, class of 1950, whose family business is the Amity Leather Products Company in West Bend, Wisconsin.

When the Irish basketball team upset top-ranked San Francisco on March 5, 1977, NBC-TV gave the MVP award to Notre Dame's students. The unprecedented award was made because of their thundering support of the team.

ROLFS SPORTS
RECREATION CENTER (75)

Another gift from Thomas and Robert Rolfs, this building opened in 1998 and is located just north of the Joyce Center. It was designed by Architecture Design Group of South Bend specifically to serve the fitness and recreational sports needs of amateur and non-varsity athletes. It includes a 5,000-square-foot workout room and multipurpose courts that are used not only for basketball and volleyball but also for

Marching Band

Pasquerilla Center, Band Building, Loftus Sports Center

Rolfs Aquatic Center

Baseball, Eck Stadium

Volleyball, Joyce Center

dance, aerobics, indoor soccer, floor hockey, and in-line skating.

CARTIER FIELD AND MOOSE KRAUSE STADIUM (303)

Notre Dame's original Cartier Field was located on the mall in front of today's Hesburgh Library. Around 1900, Warren Cartier, an alumnus who owned a lumber mill in Michigan, built a grandstand there, and for years Cartier Field was the site of Notre Dame's football and baseball games and track and field events. When Notre Dame Stadium opened in 1930, Cartier Field was relocated to its present location east of the Joyce Center.

In the 1980s Moose Krause Stadium was built on Cartier Field. With a "fast" Mondo track, 5,000 bleacher seats, and its own press box, the stadium is used for track meets and lacrosse matches. It honors the memory of Edward "Moose" Krause, class of 1934, the Chicagoan who was a gentlemanly fixture on Notre Dame's athletic scene for more than 50 years. A three-time All-American basketball player as an undergraduate, Krause later became Notre Dame's head basketball coach and longtime athletic director.

ECK TENNIS PAVILION (208) AND COURTNEY TENNIS CENTER (304)

This award-winning building ranks as one of the premiere indoor collegiate tennis facilities in the nation. Designed by Borger Jones Leedy architects of Elkhart, Indiana, the 35,000-square-foot pavilion has six courts and a glass-walled observation deck where spectators can keep an eye on the balls and the players. Although the pavilion is used primarily for recreational tennis, the men's and women's varsity teams also play here, and the facility has hosted NCAA championship tournaments. It also was a gift from businessman Frank Eck and his wife, Bryce.

East of the pavilion is Courtney Tennis Center, an extensive outdoor complex of 20-plus courts built in the late 1960s. Its benefactor was Jeremiah Courtney of Washington, D.C., a seasoned tennis player whose sons attended Notre Dame.

The softball diamond and soccer fields that you see south of Eck Tennis Pavilion are known, respectively, as Ivy Field and Alumni Field (110). Both facilities have press boxes and are used by the varsity teams.

FRANK ECK STADIUM AND JAKE KLINE FIELD (204)

This deluxe, 3,000-seat baseball facility was designed by Cole Associates in South Bend and opened in 1994. It features a covered hitting cage and powerful, high-wattage lights with innovative shrouds that focus lighting on the diamond and away from nearby neighborhoods. The stadium was the gift of alumnus Frank Eck, a Columbus, Ohio-based manufacturer of corrugated plastic drainage pipe. Its grass playing field was named in honor of Clarence "Jake" Kline, the dedicated coach who headed Notre Dame's baseball program from 1934 to 1975.

LOFTUS SPORTS CENTER, HAGGAR FITNESS COMPLEX, AND MEYO FIELD (309)

This huge indoor sports facility melds so neatly into an old grove of oak trees that it's difficult to realize just how big the Loftus Center actually is. How big is it? Well, the outside dimensions are 614 by 210 feet. But the really telling number is 100 yards, because the buildings holds an AstroTurf® football field complete with end zones and a surrounding Olympic-quality, six-lane Mondo track (Meyo Field). And, the Center even has room left over for a comprehensive weight and exercise training facility that is considered one of the best in the nation (Haggar Fitness Complex).

Notre Dame's varsity football team practices on Meyo Field whenever the weather is severe or it has a road game scheduled on an artificial playing field. The players also use the Haggar Fitness Complex (where all of the barbells are embellished with an ND monogram) for conditioning. Loftus Center, however, does much more than keep the football team fit and comfortable. This all-sports athletic and recreational facility can also handle soccer, lacrosse, baseball, softball, and even golf. Unlike indoor sports centers at many other universities, the Loftus Center is *not* restricted to varsity athletes. It's used by the entire Notre Dame community—students, staff, faculty, alumni, and retirees.

Designed by Ellerbe Becket of Minneapolis, the Center was the gift of John Loftus, a varsity basketball player in the 1940s who heads JRL Investments real estate development in St. Charles, Illinois. Members of the Edmund R. Haggar family, which operates the Haggar Apparel Company in Dallas, Texas, provided the Haggar Fitness Complex. Meyo Field was funded by Raymond D. Meyo, a 1964 alumnus who heads

Irish Guard

the Telxon computer manufacturing company in Akron, Ohio.

BAND BUILDING (210)

Many people think that the high, curving roof of this contemporary-style building looks like a band shell. What could possibly be more appropriate for the home of the collegiate marching band that has been in continuous existence longer than any other in the United States? The University of Notre Dame Marching Band—the famous "Band of the Fighting Irish" that entertains during every halftime—dates back to at least 1845 and was yet another creation of Notre Dame's eminently resourceful founder, Father Edward Sorin, who supposedly played a pretty fair clarinet himself. A Music Hall with an auditorium for band concerts was actually one of the first structures built at Notre Dame, and the present, Ellerbe Becket-designed Band Building was constructed in 1990 to replace an aging rehearsal hall near Main Quad that the Marching Band had simply outgrown.

Although Notre Dame has several bands (including concert and jazz bands, woodwind and brass ensembles, and the "varsity" bands that play at pep rallies and basketball games), the Band Building is definitely tuned to the Marching Band. Not only does the Marching Band get to practice in the main rehearsal hall beneath that prominently curved roof, but the building's lobby is also lined with cases featuring mementos and miscellaneous tokens of esteem—a Paul Revere silver bowl from the mayor of Boston; an alligator from Orlando, Florida; the Keys to the City of Lebanon, Pennsylvania—that have been presented to it. And, you certainly can't miss the 1976 citation from the National Music Council declaring the Marching Band a "Landmark of American Music."

The 300 or so members of the Marching Band are an elite group on campus. Since any student enrolled at the university or at neighboring Saint Mary's and Holy Cross colleges is eligible for the Band, the pool of potential Band members is huge, and hopeful musicians go through several days of intense auditions to earn the privilege of marching at innumerable halftime shows, bowl games, university functions, and parades (especially on St. Patrick's Day). Because the university doesn't require music majors to join the Band, all of its members are volunteers. They run the gamut of academic majors, and surprisingly, only a small percentage of them are products of the music department.

Ever since the Marching Band played at Notre Dame's first varsity football game in 1887, it has been the team's anything-but-silent partner. Not once in the ensuing 100-plus years has the Band missed performing at a home game, and it became one of the first college bands in the nation to use "picture formations" when its members started spelling out "Irish" and "ND" on the football field. The Marching Band has been playing Notre Dame's "Victory March" since the early 1900s, when the Shea brothers wrote the rousing tune that's now called "the greatest of all college fight songs." Band members, in fact, keep a running tally of how often they play the "Victory March," and the current count is about 4,000 times per year.

Notre Dame football is arguably the most tradition-laden athletic endeavor in the country, and as one of the team's adjunct institutions, the Marching Band has developed a related set of its own weighty traditions. On the night before a football game, for example, the saxophone section goes off-campus to visit Knute Rockne's grave. They play a little music, do some praying, and if Notre Dame is facing a tough opponent, will try to ensure the luck of the Irish by picking some grass off of Rockne's grave and scattering it in the

Stadium the next day. Very early on game day morning the entire Band gets together for their "Captain Crunch Breakfast" of cereal and juice. Then shortly before 8 a.m., they gather their instruments and march around campus playing the "Victory March" to wake up the rest of the student body. Around noon the Marching Band gives a concert on the steps of the Main Building and then parades toward the Stadium with an exuberant crowd of Notre Dame fans following behind.

In the 1940s, Director H. Lee Hope wanted to add a unique but dignified element to the Marching Band and created a precision marching unit of stalwart young men called the Irish Guard. His successor, Robert F. O'Brien, designed a distinctive plaid kilt for the Guardsmen to wear and also wrote a lively victory clog called "Damsha Bua" for them to perform every time Notre Dame wins a game. The Irish Guard is now an integral part of both the Band and the pageantry of every Notre Dame football game. The Guardsmen lead the Marching Band from its Main Building concert to the Stadium; raise the flag while "American the Beautiful" and "The Star Spangled Banner" are played; join in the half-time show; and whenever Notre Dame scores a touchdown, dance a jig. Ten Guardsmen are selected every year on the basis of their marching ability, demeanor (they have to remain as stoic and stone-faced as the guards outside Buckingham Palace), and their height (they have to be at least six-feet, two-inches tall). Their resplendent uniform includes the plaid kilt, a red jacket, and a black bearskin shako that extends their full height to at least eight feet. With their towering persona and resolute steps, the Guardsmen are a formidable sight as they precede the Band. Officially, their purpose is to protect the Band from any interference; in reality, they're part of the show. Besides, it's against Indiana state law for anybody to obstruct the progress of the University of Notre Dame Marching Band.

The plaid used in the Irish Guard's kilts is a trademarked and copyrighted pattern called "Notre Dame Plaid." The colors in the plaid signify the following:

Green—for the Fighting Irish

Gold and Blue—for the University of Notre Dame colors

Red—for the Church and the Congregation of Holy Cross

Black—to outline the design.

During football season, the Marching Band and Irish Guard practice for about an hour and a half every weekday, and you can watch them as they perfect their halftime performances. They typically use the southwest corner of the Joyce Center parking lot, which is located at the corner of Juniper and Edison roads. It should be easy for you to find because of the observation tower that the Band's leaders use. On Monday, Tuesday, and Friday, practices begin at 4:30 p.m. On Wednesday and Thursday, they start at 6:30 p.m.

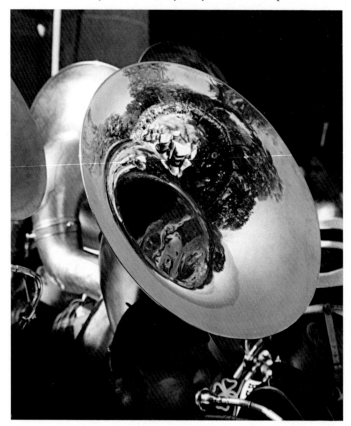

PASQUERILLA CENTER (211)

Notre Dame is one of only a handful of universities in the country to have Reserve Officer Training (ROTC) programs for all three of the U.S. armed services—Navy, Air Force, and Army. The military tradition at Notre Dame is a long and proud one that extends from the battlefields of the Civil War to the sands of the Gulf War, and it encompasses the service and sacrifice of thousands of Holy Cross priests and nuns, faculty members, students, and alumni. On this campus where service is so highly valued, service to the nation continues to be one of the strongest—and perhaps most often taken for granted—expressions of the illustrious ideal emblazoned over a doorway to the Basilica: "God, Country, Notre Dame." More than 5 percent of all Notre Dame undergraduates participate in ROTC programs, and the university frequently leads the nation in the number of students who merit ROTC scholarships. Since the early 1970s the university has also produced more regular Naval officers than any other educational institution except the U.S. Naval Academy. All three of the ROTC units at Notre Dame have been cited as the best in the nation, and their instruction emphasizes leadership development, discipline, and high academic standards.

ROTC was firmly established at Notre Dame during World War II, when nearly 12,000 officer trainees "occupied" the campus. After the war, Air Force and then Army ROTC units were added, and the building now used by Security and Human Resources sufficed as the programs' headquarters until the Pasquerilla Center opened in 1990. Ellerbe Becket was the architect of this modern, slate-roofed building, which was the gift of Frank Pasquerilla, a university trustee and shopping mall developer from Johnstown, Pennsylvania. At the time, the 50,000-square foot Pasquerilla Center was the largest privately funded ROTC facility that had ever been built.

The flagstaff array on the south side of the Pasquerilla Center displays the United States flag as well as the colors that represent the Army, Navy, Marine, and Air Forces officers trained at Notre Dame. Every morning and evening ROTC students conduct flag raising and lowering ceremonies here. Inside the Center, display cases in the second-floor lobby contain excellent exhibits that synthesize the university's long and close relationship with the military. Numerous photographs show how the Navy virtually took over the campus during World War II, and there are uniforms and models of ships and aircraft on display. You'll also find out about the two Notre Dame presidents who were military chaplains; about Mother Angela, whom General Sherman put in charge of the Union Army hospitals; and about Heartley "Hunk" Anderson, a Rockne-era lineman who went to drill practice in the morning and football practice in the afternoon.

WARREN GOLF COURSE (405)

After the construction of West Quad gobbled up the back nine holes of the old golf course, Notre Dame almost immediately went to work on creating this new par-71, 18-hole course. PGA golfer Ben Crenshaw and his design partner Bill Coore of Austin, Texas, are the masterminds behind the layout of the course, which is located on a 260-acre site at the northeast corner of Juniper and Douglas roads. Its $7-million cost was underwritten by William Warren, class of 1956, who is a businessman from Tulsa, Oklahoma.

ALONG BULLA ROAD

This part of the East End caters to Notre Dame's graduate students. Its housing complex includes the Charles A. Fischer Graduate Residences (FG1-14, FG15-33, FG 35) and the O'Hara-Grace Graduate Apartments (97). Wilson Commons (98) is a social center, and the Early Childhood Development Center (100) provides day care for children of Notre Dame students, faculty, and staff members.

GLOSSARY
A Guide to the Notre Dame Vocabulary

An Tostal—the students' annual spring celebration featuring assorted fun and games, which have included eating contests, sack races, volleyball tournaments, scavenger hunts, and concerts. An Tostal is a Gaelic word meaning "to gather" or "to pageant," and the Notre Dame event is modeled after an Irish celebration.

Arkie—slang for an architecture major

Bengal Bouts—a campus tradition since 1931, this annual student boxing tournament raises money for the Holy Cross Missions in Bangladesh, which was once the Bengal province of India.

Blue-Gold Game—the intra-squad varsity football scrimmage played in the spring

The 'Brare—slang for the Theodore M. Hesburgh Library

Claddagh ring—a piece of jewelry that originated in Ireland and is very popular at Notre Dame; the design consists of two hands (signifying friendship) holding a heart (for love) with a crown on top (for loyalty).

Coca-Cola® Quad—slang for West Quad, a.k.a. Golf Quad

C.S.C.—letters that signify the *Congregatio a Sancta Cruce*, which is Latin for the Congregation of Holy Cross

Dogbook—an annual publication featuring photos and names of the entire freshman class; it's widely consulted by students before every SYR.

Damsha Bua—the Victory Clog performed by the Irish Guard at football games

The Dome—the gilded hemisphere featuring a large statue of the Virgin Mary that tops the Main Building; a.k.a. the Golden Dome

The Dome—Notre Dame's yearbook, which takes its name from the Dome (see above)

Domer—a graduate of the University of Notre Dame

Double Domer—a person who has earned two degrees at Notre Dame, typically an undergraduate as well as a graduate degree

The Eck—slang for Frank Eck Stadium, a baseball facility

Father Ted—the Rev. Theodore M. Hesburgh, C.S.C., president emeritus of Notre Dame

God Quad—slang for Main Quad

Golden Dome—a.k.a. The Dome (see above)

Golf Quad—slang for West Quad, a.k.a. Coca-Cola® Quad

Graffiti Dance—the traditional freshman mixer during which Notre Dame's newest students write their names and campus phone numbers on each other's shirts

HTH—a "hometown honey," a boyfriend or girlfriend from a student's home

The Huddle—the popular food court in LaFortune Student Center

JACC—abbreviation for the Joyce Center

JPW—Junior Parents Weekend; an annual fete honoring the parents of third-year students. It brings thousands of proud moms and dads to campus.

Laetare Medal (pronounced Lay-tah-ray)—Notre Dame's highest honor, this award is presented annually to an outstanding American Catholic. The recipient's name is always announced on Laetare Sunday, the fourth Sunday in Lent.

Lou—Louis Leo Holtz, former Notre Dame football coach who led the Fighting Irish to the 1988 national championship

Loft—used by students as both a noun and a verb, this word indicates the highly creative methods dorm residents use to elevate or stack their beds in order to create more floor space.

Lyons Beach—the grassy area between Lyons Hall and St. Mary's Lake

Monk—Notre Dame President Edward Malloy; the nickname goes back to Malloy's childhood and was derived not from his piety, but from his playmate, "Bunk."

Mod Quad—the area of campus around Flanner and Grace Halls

Monk Hoops—pickup basketball games led by Notre Dame President "Monk" Malloy

Observer—the student newspaper, which is published Monday through Friday during the school year and distributed throughout the campus

O'Shag—slang for O'Shaughnessy Hall

Parietals—residence hall visitation hours; members of the opposite sex must leave dorms by midnight on weekdays and 2:00 a.m. on weekends.

Provincial—the priest who heads the Indiana Province of the Congregation of Holy Cross.

PE— Pasquerilla East, a women's residence hall

PW— Pasquerilla West, a women's residence hall

Rad Lab—slang for the Radiation Research Building

RecSports—non-varsity sports programs and events

The Rock—slang for the Rockne Memorial, the South Quad athletic building named in honor of Knute Rockne

Scholastic—Notre Dame's oldest student publication, this magazine first appeared in 1867. Its articles focus on campus life.

Subway Alumni—the zealous football fans who are not Notre Dame graduates but follow the team religiously

The Shirt—a T-shirt specially designed for each football season and the preferred student attire at home games. This extremely popular garment is one of Notre Dame's newest traditions, having debuted in Kelly green at the first home contest (Notre Dame vs. Michigan) in 1990. A student-operated enterprise, sales of The Shirt raise thousands of dollars for various charities, scholarships, and campus events.

Stonehenge—slang for North Quad's Clarke Memorial Fountain

SYR—dances sponsored by each dorm during the academic year. The letters stand for "Screw-Your-Roommate," an obvious reference to the blind dates that roommates traditionally arrange for each other. The events are such a campus tradition that an SYR dress code has evolved: black dress for women; blue blazers and khaki trousers for men.

Ted and Ned—nicknames of the president and executive vice president of Notre Dame for more than three decades, Father Theodore M. Hesburgh and Father Edmund P. Joyce

This Week—Notre Dame's calendar of events. Published by the Public Relations and Information office, it's widely distributed on campus.

Triple Domer—a person who has earned three degrees at Notre Dame, typically one undergraduate and two graduate degrees

Two-to-Sevens—off-campus parties that start after parietals and end with the sunrise

YOCREAM®—the rich-tasting frozen yogurt that has to be *the* favorite dessert of Notre Dame students. It's served primarily in the dining halls, but as the frequent sight of cone-carrying students attests, YOCREAM® is consumed all across campus.

SELECTED BIBLIOGRAPHY

"'Alumni Hall' Is the Name of New Dormitory." *Notre Dame Alumnus*, Apr. 1931.

Andrews, Wayne. *Architecture, Ambition, and Americans: A Social History of American Architecture*. New York: The Free Press, 1978.

Apone, Carl. "Notre Dame's $7-Million Man." *Pittsburgh Press*, Nov. 23, 1980.

Baraban, Regina S. "A Theatrical Revival on Campus." *Food Management*, May 1989.

Beal, Mary Pat Dowling, ed. *Grotto Stories: From the Heart of Notre Dame*. Published by MarySunshine Books, in cooperation with the Notre Dame Alumni Association, 1996.

Belleranti, Shirley W. "Artist 'in full spirit of Leonardo' re-creates *Last Supper*." *South Bend Tribune*, May 31, 1987.

Brown, Dennis K. "Alive and Well." *Notre Dame Magazine* 24, 4 (Winter, 1993-94).

Brown, Patricia Leigh. "Architecture's New Classicists: A Young Bunch of Old Fogies." *New York Times*, Feb. 9, 1995.

Byersmith, Ronald, and Dick Mellett. "Beautification Project Progresses." *Scholastic*, Aug. 18, 1944.

"City Shocked by Death of W. J. Burke; Funeral Monday." *Portsmouth* (Ohio) *Daily Times*, July 28, 1928.

Cohen, Ed, and Steve Myers. "The Halls Divided." *Notre Dame Magazine* 25, 2 (Summer, 1996).

Conklin, Richard W. "Grand Old Church Resounds with Magnificent New Voice." *South Bend Tribune*, Apr. 2, 1978.

Costin, Sister M. Georgia, C.S.C. *Priceless Spirit: A History of the Sisters of the Holy Cross, 1841-1893*. Notre Dame: University of Notre Dame Press, 1994.

Coyne, Kevin. *Domers: A Year at Notre Dame*. New York: Viking Penguin, 1995.

Davis, Keith F. *George N. Barnard, Photographer of Sherman's Campaign*. Kansas City, Mo.: Hallmark Cards, 1990.

"Dr. Tom Dooley, Jungle Doctor of Laos, Dies in New York Hospital of Cancer at 34." *Philadelphia Evening Bulletin*, Jan. 19, 1961.

Fagan, Christopher B. "A $2 Million Dollar Discovery." *Notre Dame Magazine* 20, 2 (Summer, 1991).

Fallon, Nancy. "The Town-Gown Waltz." *Notre Dame Magazine* 23, 4 (Winter, 1994-95).

Findsen, Owen. "Vision of the Father, Schickel's Art Sets Tone for Family Affair." *Cincinnati Enquirer*, Apr. 16, 1995.

Fischer, Edward. "Hooked on a Feeling." *Notre Dame Magazine* 18, 2 (Summer, 1989).

———. *Notre Dame Remembered: An Autobiography.* Notre Dame: University of Notre Dame Press, 1987.

"Four Generations of Notre Dame Coquillards." *Notre Dame Alumnus* 16, 5 (Mar.-Apr. 1938).

Foy, Felician A., O.F.M., and Rose M. Avato. *Our Sunday Visitor's 1996 Catholic Almanac.* Huntington, Ind.: Our Sunday Visitor, 1996.

Francis, Ronald M. "Entertainers Extraordinary." *Notre Dame*, Winter, 1956.

Freddoso, David "Hesburgh Recalls Vetville." *Observer*, Dec. 5, 1996.

"Funeral Parlors to Leave Notre Dame." *South Bend Times*, Nov. 4, 1911.

"Golf Course under Construction at Notre Dame." *Notre Dame Scholastic*, June 2, 1928.

Griffin, Rev. Robert. "An Apartment for Darby." *Observer*, Sept. 4, 1981.

Grimm, Herbert L., Paul L. Roy, and George Rose. *Human Interest Stories of the Three Days' Battles at Gettysburg.* Gettysburg, Pa.: Tem, 1983.

Gruenke, Bernard E., Jr. "Notre Dame's Sacred Heart Chapel." *Professional Stained Glass*, Oct., 1989.

"Guide to the Best Business Schools." *Business Week*, issue 3131 (Oct. 30, 1989).

Harp, Bill. "Ravages of Fire Erased from Notre Dame Landmark." *Elkhart Truth*, Aug. 29, 1981.

Haugh, David. "The Shrine in the Concourse." *Notre Dame Magazine* 23, 3 (Autumn, 1994).

Hellenthal, Barbara J., Thomas J. Schlereth, and Robert P. McIntosh. *Trees, Shrubs, and Vines on the University of Notre Dame Campus.* Notre Dame: University of Notre Dame Press, 1993.

Hesburgh, Theodore M. *God, Country, Notre Dame.* New York: Doubleday, 1990.

"History, Tradition and the New Dining Hall." *Notre Dame Alumnus* VI, 3 (Nov. 1927).

Honour, Hugh, and John Fleming. *The Visual Arts: A History.* Englewood Cliffs, N.J.: Prentice-Hall, 1984.

Hope, Arthur J., C.S.C. *Notre Dame One Hundred Years.* Notre Dame: University Press, 1943.

Hughes, Marilyn. "Vetville, Hard Times on Campus Not Forgotten by Those Who Lived in Complex." *South Bend Tribune*, Oct. 27, 1996.

Jorgensen, Melanie, and Mike Moses. "King of the Boys." *Scholastic*, Feb. 20, 1976.

Kelly, Ben. "Notre Dame's Midwife." *Notre Dame Magazine* 21, 1 (Spring, 1992).

Kervick, Francis. "The New Dining Hall Architecturally." *Notre Dame Alumnus* VI, 3 (Nov. 1927).

Klimek, Anne. *The Zahms' Legacy: A History of Engineering at Notre Dame, 1873-1993*. Notre Dame: University of Notre Dame College of Engineering, 1993.

Lawson, James R. "North America's First Carillon." *Bulletin of the Guild of Carillonneurs in North America,* Jan. 1986.

Liebeler, Dolores. "Women Win Way to N.D. Golf Course." *South Bend Tribune*, Apr. 28, 1970.

Lutkus, Gerald. "Notre Dame's Morris Inn, Grateful Protestant's Gift." *South Bend Tribune*, Nov. 9, 1975.

Maier, Frank. "A Man of Letters." *Notre Dame Magazine* 18, 3 (Autumn, 1989).

Madison, James H. *Indiana through Tradition and Change: A History of the Hoosier State and Its People, 1920-1945*. Indianapolis: Indiana Historical Society, 1982.

Malloy, Edward A. *Notre Dame: The Unfolding Vision*. New York: Newcomen Society of the U.S., 1994.

Marszalek, John F. "Call to Arms." *Notre Dame Magazine* 21, 3 (Autumn, 1992).

———. "The Faithful Scholar." *Notre Dame Magazine* 26, 2 (Summer, 1997).

———. "The Inventor of Total Warfare." *Notre Dame Magazine* 18, 2 (Summer, 1989).

———. "Who Was Stephen Badin?" *Notre Dame Magazine* 23, 2 (Summer, 1994).

McEvoy, J. P. "Notre Dame Got Million From Presbyterian Grad." *Elmira* (N.Y.) *Sunday Telegram*, June 4, 1950.

McIntosh, Robert P. "A Long Look Back." *Notre Dame Magazine* 23, 4 (Winter, 1994-95).

Meagher, James P. "The Heart of the Campus." *Notre Dame* 9, 4 (Winter, 1956).

Monczunski, John "A Classical Solution." *Notre Dame Magazine* 25, 2 (Summer, 1996).

———. "The Big Leagues." *Notre Dame Magazine* 21, 1 (Spring, 1992).

Moore, Dennis. "Big Time Bucks." *Notre Dame Magazine* 23, 3 (Autumn, 1994).

Mueller, Thomas J., and Charlotte A. Ames, eds. *Commitment, Compassion, Consecration: Inspirational Quotes of Theodore M. Hesburgh, C.S.C.* Huntington, Ind.: Our Sunday Visitor Publishing Division, 1989.

Murphy, James E. "The Oldest Carillon in North America." *Notre Dame* 9, 4 (Winter, 1956).

"Nieuwland Science Hall Dedicated." *Chemical and Engineering News* 31, 45 (Nov. 9, 1953).

Noll, Mark A., et alia, eds. *Eerdman's Handbook to Christianity in America.* Grand Rapids, Mich.: Eerdman's, 1983.

Norris, Eileen. "Which Way Does the Dome Lean?" *Notre Dame Magazine* 25, 3 (Autumn, 1996).

Notre Dame, A Sense of Place. Photography by William Strode. Intro. by Michael Garvey. Prospect, Ky.: Harmony House, 1988, in cooperation with University of Notre Dame Press.

Notre Dame Magazine, Sesquicentennial Edition 20, 2 (Summer, 1991).

"Notre Dame's President Dies, Rev. Fr. O'Donnell Sick for More Than Year." *South Bend Tribune,* June 4, 1934.

"Obituary, Death of Rev. Father Lemonnier." *New York Freeman's Journal,* Nov. 21, 1874.

"150 Years of Notre Dame" (Special Section). *Observer,* Jan. 31, 1992.

O'Rourke, James S., IV, ed. *Reflections in the Dome, Sixty Years of Life at Notre Dame.* Notre Dame: privately published, 1996.

O'Sullivan, James C. "Role of Timothy E. Howard in History of South Bend." *South Bend Tribune,* Sept. 21, 1975.

O'Toole, William. "Curious Bits of Architecture Adorn Walls of Notre Dame's Magnificent Structures." *South Bend News Times,* Oct. 10, 1937.

Peralta, Elizabeth. "Lessons in War and Morality." *Notre Dame Magazine* 18, 1 (Spring, 1989).

Poppeliers, John C., S. Allen Chamber, Jr., and Nancy B. Schwartz. *What Style Is It? A Guide to American Architecture.* Washington, D.C.: Preservation Press, 1983.

Pothorn, Herbert. *Architectural Styles: An Historical Guide to World Design.* New York: Facts on File, 1979.

Powers, John J. "The Charm President." *Notre Dame Magazine* 21, 1 (Spring, 1992).

Price, Tom. "Devotion to Mary Marks Notre Dame's Heritage." *Elkhart Truth,* Nov. 14, 1992.

Rappoport, Ken. *Wake Up the Echoes, Notre Dame Football.* Huntsville, Ala.: Strode, 1984.

Reedy, Jerry. "A Priest Forever." *Notre Dame Magazine* 22, 2 (Summer, 1993).

Reid, Joseph. *The Book of Buildings.* New York: Rand McNally, 1980.

Rifkind, Carole. *A Field Guide to American Architecture.* New York: New American Library, 1980.

Roemer, The Honorable Timothy J. "Notre Dame's 150th Anniversary." (Special Order in the House of Representatives), *Congressional Record* 137, 166 (Nov. 12, 1991).

Rubin, Jeffrey. "Traditional Church Architecture for the 21st Century." *Latin Mass,* May-June, 1994.

Sandoval, Annette. *The Directory of Saints: A Precise Guide to Patron Saints.* New York: Dutton, 1996.

Schaal, Carol. "Nothing Ventured, Nothing Gained." *Notre Dame Magazine* 21, 2 (Summer, 1992).

Schlereth, Thomas J. *A Dome of Learning: The University of Notre Dame's Main Building.* Notre Dame: University of Notre Dame Alumni Association, 1991.

————. *A Spire of Faith: The University of Notre Dame's Sacred Heart Church.* Notre Dame: University of Notre Dame Alumni Association, 1991.

————. *The University of Notre Dame: A Portrait of Its History and Campus.* Notre Dame: University of Notre Dame Press, 1976.

————. "A Man of Many Parts." *Notre Dame Magazine* 14, 1 (Spring, 1985).

Schmuhl, Robert. *The University of Notre Dame: A Contemporary Portrait.* Notre Dame: University of Notre Dame Press, 1986.

Schoor, Gene. *100 Years of Notre Dame Football.* New York: William Morrow, 1987.

Sieber, Gary. "A Marvelous Racket." *Notre Dame Magazine* 24, 2 (Summer, 1995).

Singular, Stephen. *Notre Dame's Greatest Coaches.* New York: Simon and Schuster, 1993.

Sorin, Edward, C.S.C. *The Chronicles of Notre Dame du Lac.* Trans. by John M. Toohey, C.S.C., ed. James T. Connelly, C.S.C. Notre Dame: University of Notre Dame Press, 1992.

Sperber, Murray. *Shake Down the Thunder: The Creation of Notre Dame Football.* New York: Henry Holt, 1993.

Spring, Denise. "The Radiation Research Lab: A Look Inside" *Notre Dame Science Quarterly* 20, 4 (May, 1982).

Stritch, Thomas. *My Notre Dame: Memories and Reflections of Sixty Years.* Notre Dame: University of Notre Dame Press, 1991.

Stuhldreher, Harry A. *Knute Rockne, Man Builder.* Philadelphia: Macrae-Smith, 1931.

Swintz, Jessie Gobin. "Voice of the Bell." *Indianapolis Star Magazine*, Oct. 31, 1954.

Taylor, Robert M. Jr., and Connie A. McBirney. *Peopling Indiana: The Ethnic Experience.* Indianapolis: Indiana Historical Society, 1989.

Taylor, Robert M., Jr., et alia. *Indiana: A New Historical Guide.* Indianapolis: Indiana Historical Society, 1989.

Teaford, Jon C. *Cities of the Heartland: The Rise and Fall of the Industrial Midwest.* Bloomington: Indiana University Press, 1993.

Temple, Kerry. *O'Hara's Heirs: Business Education at Notre Dame, 1921-1991.* Notre Dame: University of Notre Dame College of Business Administration, 1992.

———. "Old Sorin Window Returns to Rebuilt St. Edward's Hall." *South Bend Tribune*, Aug. 16, 1981.

———. "The Day Notre Dame Burned." *South Bend Tribune*, Apr. 22, 1979.

Truitt, Jill. "An Attachment of Love and Devotion." *Observer*, Jan. 27, 1975.

"University of Notre Dame in Flames." *South Bend Tribune*, Apr. 23, 1879.

Wallace, Francis. *Notre Dame: Its People and Its Legends.* New York: David McKay, 1969.

Wallace, Howard A. "Notre Dame Indiana Post Office." *S.P.A. Journal* (Society of Philatelic Americans) 40, 6 (Feb., 1978).

Ward, Leo R. "Notre Dame's Corby Hall—Misfit and Maverick." *South Bend Tribune*, Nov. 23, 1975.

———. "Sacred Heart Church . . . More Notre Dame Than the Stadium?" *South Bend Tribune*, May 19, 1974.

Whitaker, Frederic. "Millard Sheets, the Story of a Giant." *American Artist*, Dec. 1964.

Willy, John. "University of Notre Dame Dining Halls." *Hotel Monthly* 36, 419 (Feb. 1928).

Winkler, Erhard M. "Stone Mosaic." *Earth Science*, Mar.-Apr. 1966.

———. "Word of Life Stone Mural Dominates Notre Dame Library." *Stone Magazine*, Oct. 1967.

PUBLICATIONS PRODUCED AT
THE UNIVERSITY OF NOTRE DAME

The Dome, 1982. University of Notre Dame yearbook, vol. 73.

The Dome, 1992. University of Notre Dame yearbook, vol. 83.

The Dome, 1994. University of Notre Dame yearbook, vol. 85.

The Dome, 1995. University of Notre Dame yearbook, vol. 86.

Federowicz, Brother John. "Forces Affecting the Development of Libraries at the University of Notre Dame, 1843-1968." Master's thesis, Kent State University, 1968.

Final Report, Colloquy for the Year 2000. Report submitted by President Edward A. Malloy, C.S.C., to the Trustees of the University of Notre Dame, May 7, 1993.

Inquiry, Belief, Community, 1842-1992.

McCandless, Kenneth William. "The Endangered Domain: A Review and Analysis of Campus Planning and Design at the University of Notre Dame." Master's thesis, University of Notre Dame, 1974.

Notre Dame, a Tradition in Athletics since 1887.

125th Anniversary, University of Notre Dame, 1842-1967.

Selected Works from the Snite Museum of Art. Dean A. Porter, director. Photography, Steve Moriarty, Steve Toepp. Notre Dame, Ind.: Snite Museum of Art, University of Notre Dame, 1987.

The University of Notre Dame Friends and Alumni Collect: A Sesquicentennial Celebration. June 7-Sept. 20, 1992, Snite Museum of Art.

INDEX

The numbers in boldface indicate drawings or photographs.

DAMAINE VONADA is the author of numerous books and travel publications. Her byline also appears frequently in magazines and newspapers. She resides in Ohio.

ROBERT F. RINGEL is the staff architect with Facilities Engineering at the University of Notre Dame. His artwork and photography have been featured in several exhibitions and books, and he is a direct descendant of explorer Louis Joliet, who visited the mission on St. Mary's Lake in 1673.

The author and publisher are grateful for the use of photographs and sketches throughout the book and on the cover. All sketches are by Robert F. Ringel. All photographs inside the guidebook are by Robert F. Ringel, except for the following: pages 141 (top, photo by Tony Kelly), 175 (top), 201 (top), 231 (bottom), and 253 (middle and bottom—bottom photo by Gary Mills) are courtesy of University of Notre Dame Publications and Graphic Services; pages 36 (top), 44, 45, 108, 129, 149, and 159 are courtesy of the University of Notre Dame Archives; pages 140 (top right) and 253 (top) are courtesy of Damaine Vonada.

Cover: photographs (the Grotto, weeping student on Howard Hall, Hesburgh Library mural, Father Sorin statue, and squirrel) and sketch (Main Building) are by Robert F. Ringel. All other photographs courtesy of University of Notre Dame Publications and Graphic Services, including DeBartolo classroom and Lyons Hall by Gary Mills, and Nieuwland science lab by Tony Kelly.

All photographs and sketches are used by permission and all rights are reserved.